Turkey & Erdogan
GAMECHANGER

TRUMP CARD

Erbil Gunasti

Post Hill
PRESS

A POST HILL PRESS BOOK
ISBN: 978-1-64293-459-5
ISBN (eBook): 978-1-64293-460-1

GameChanger:
Trump Card: Turkey & Erdogan
© 2020 by Erbil Gunasti
All Rights Reserved

Cover design by Radoslav Iliev

Post Hill Press
New York • Nashville
posthillpress.com

Published in the United States of America

For Ismail, Sevim, and Serpil

CONTENTS

PREFACE

I came to realize that it is time to write this book now, though I have been qualified to do it for years. The timing is now.

1. Hotly contested 2016 presidential elections in the US brought Donald J. Trump to power. He is an unconventional nationalist, and the hope of conservative, evangelist, blue-collar America.
2. In Turkey, President Recep Tayyip Erdoğan is in power. He has won successive elections for the past two decades, albeit with slim margins and with support of mostly pious people living in the margins and in the countryside.

Two headstrong presidents, leading two powerful countries. One is a superpower. The other is a militarily and economically fast-growing regional power. They have been staunch allies since the 1950s, against a common communist enemy that is no more. Now, they are looking for ways to reconnect but are distracted by the complex times we live in.

This book intends to bridge the gap between two leaders at a time when American people need to understand what Turkey is and who Erdoğan is, so that what was wasted in the 20th century does not repeat itself at the expense of prosperity in the United States of America that we all love and for the good of the rest of the world as well.

* * *

My qualifications for this book are numerous. I know a lot about the US and Turkey, both academically speaking and in practice. I have resided in both countries for a long time. I am citizen of both. I have tasted the feeling of being in my homeland time and again. I understand better what is in print, broadcast, gossip, or spirited debate since I am fluent in both English and Turkish. I have also been a part of the media and of Hollywood for decades now. I am ingrained in both cultures and a fan of the Celtics, Red Sox, and Besiktas. I have travelled all of the forty-eight states in the continental US and have visited all corners of Turkey many times over to realize how varied people live in each locale and how varied their interests are from food to music.

History, philosophy, literature, and political science are my forte, as part of my formal studies in the States. I have also worked for president Erdoğan when he was prime minister between 2002 and 2007. And I decided to work for president Trump. I will have joined his administration by the time this book is published. So, I have all the more reason to write this book because I know both leaders up close and personal. I have had opportunities to converse with them and with the First Ladies, too. My partner Daphne is a well-known TV personality, and she is also close to both Erdoğan and Trump. One would never guess how close one could be, as one of her other friends Hillary Clinton once put it, "people usually have six degrees of separation, Daphne has none…"

Yet, I have one other but very important reason why I believe it is time that I write this book now, and I will tell my story *my way.*

* * *

I did not want to write it with empirical data or with quotes from many opinionated people with well-earned reputations on the topics at hand. I wanted to rely on the thousand or so books that I read when I earned my BA and MA, attending great American institutions like Boston University, the University of Miami, and New York University. I also wanted to include what affected me up to my teenage years when I attended schools in Europe, including the French Catholic boarding school in Istanbul that exposed me to both the clash and the alliance of civilizations, while becoming fluent in French as well.

So, I write this book mainly with American audience in mind.

Turkey & Erdoğan are two important topics. Their path to the future is sure to affect Americans directly. Billions of people from many countries are familiar with the country and its leader, what they stand for, and what they bring to the table together. But Americans do not. I have known it all along and for a long time since I began my studies at American universities with mostly liberal academia dictating the rules. But neither the time nor the conditions were right to rise-up. Until now. Here is how I met my audience.

* * *

I have explained many aspects of Turkey & Erdoğan to many Americans since 2015. First in California, when I ran for mayor in Palm Springs. I noticed that Americans had no clue about Turkey, the region, and its leader whatsoever. To my further astonishment, they also knew very little or practically nothing about Israel. Of all people, even some of the elected officials I had to relate to, the fact that they did not know much about Israel was a testimony to how much they would know about the Turks, Arabs, Iranians and other countries in the region and the cultures there. The inconsistencies of US foreign policy objectives were atrocious and to the detriment of Western hegemony throughout the 20th century.

* * *

The same problem, trying to explain the region and the culture of Turkey to the American people, became even more exacerbating when I arrived Washington DC. on December 31, 2016 from California. My partner, Daphne Barak, and I were recommended to stay at the Trump International Hotel in Washington, and where we would sojourn regularly for the next two years whenever we were in town. There I started to meet more people, ranging from ordinary folks, to bureaucrats, to elected officials on the Hill. I first thought that Washingtonians would be much more informed than Southern Californians. I was wrong. It was the same old story. Turkey & Erdoğan, the Middle East and anywhere beyond like Europe, Russia, Central Asia, Africa, China, no place was spared the general ignorance I encountered. Other than a few exceptions, most were ill-informed at best, as if they were a perfect constituency that only cared about pocketbook issues but cared nothing at all for the foreign policy objectives of the US. It was painfully so true.

I easily concluded that the problem was with the US media. Their job was to inform the citizens by reporting the news. It was obvious to most of us by now that some of them had stopped doing that altogether in the past two decades. Not that quite a few of them were doing a great job until then! The excuse all along was to ask the question back: whose fault is it if the citizens do not care about the foreign news in the first place? The answer is obvious. Nowadays, with "echo chambers," mainstream news media has lost it altogether. Like my partner Daphne says, "it's like being in a submarine" and until there is an "emergency," like Donald J. Trump winning the presidential elections in 2016, the media submarine does not surface to meet the realities.

In the 1990s, the media was on a different boat.

* * *

For more than two decades until 2007, including the fifteen straight years when I was working for eight consecutive prime ministers of Turkey, based at the UN, I read anything and everything about Turkey, the region and beyond that, that was published in the US.

My job was to cover religiously *The Wall Street Journal, The New York Times, The New York Post, The New York Daily News* and *Newsday*, every day, including weekend editions; plus weekly and monthly periodicals like *Time Magazine, Newsweek, USA News and World Report, Forbes*, and *Fortune* without missing a single issue, and then some more, like *The Economist, National Geographic, Political*

Science Quarterly, Foreign Policy, National Review, and *Foreign Affairs,* and report back what was relevant.

Practically none of them published anything I would like, that would not to make me cringe, or that someone back home would not get angry about or get turned off against the US. The American media was then simply toeing the line towards some centers of power and interests in Washington or the Wall Street or Hollywood, and rightly so. They were living in a capitalist society.

From the cozy and privileged perch that I was in then, I understood all too well the role of the US media but also the frustration of the elite to whom I was reporting. With a barrage of attacks and insults coming their way, they felt they were being treated beyond decency every time something was printed or reported. From the vocabulary used in the articles to statements, narratives, analogies, topics, and subjects, nothing was right. Everything was another hammer bashing and betraying the alliance of two countries that were supposed to have been in a common defense of values and livelihoods against the USSR and the Warsaw Pact under the umbrella of NATO.

* * *

When Donald J. Trump came down the stairs and announced that he was running for president and declared that he would "Make America Great Again," I understood well that it was time to right the ship. It was time to communicate about the Trump revolution back to Turkey and to Erdoğan, in particular, who I worked for last, until 2007. Somebody had to tell them clearly what was about to change in the US and with US foreign policy objectives that had not been going right since the beginning of the 20th century in the region, especially when the so-called "Globalists" were in power since the end of Cold War in the early 1990s.

Yet, by now, since I was all for "Americans First," having become a naturalized citizen in 2012 and run for mayor as soon as I was eligible for an elective office in 2015, I had a newly gained vigor. Having learned, lived, and enjoyed my life, I had a great deal of experience under my belt. I had received my BA and MA from University of Miami and New York University, respectively, studying political science, philosophy, and international regimes. I have lived in as varied places as South Boston and Brookline in Massachusetts and in Rhode Island; Great Neck in Long Island, Manhattan East and The Upper Eastside in New York, Coral Gables in Miami and in Beverly Hills and Palm Springs in California. And, I have travelled the world many times over. I was privileged, and I had a tremendous edge. Plus, I was in the company of my partner Daphne, "Private Benjamin," or "The Scooper" as they call her in her domain among the elite of the US network television world. She had been making top ratings for the likes of *ABC 20/20, NBC Dateline,* and

CBS 48 Hours regularly, in prime time, for decades. In short, I knew a lot about America and Americans, and it was time to give back to them First, making right with "America First."

Simply put, it was time to come out of the closet and to say that I am the only one who can deliver personal account about Turkey & Erdoğan to my fellow American patriots, making it as immediately relevant and personal to them as it is for me.

Erbil Gunasti

CHAPTER I

INTRODUCTION

IMAGINE!

The US, as the sole Christian and Western power, down to third slot from top, squeezed out by China and India, the number one and two economies in the world, and challenged by two upcoming Muslim countries, Indonesia and Turkey, from the other end.

All the while Germany, UK and France are struggling to hold on to the bottom of the barrel in the top ten list being of no help to the US during this onslaught.

No, it is not a horror movie. It is about to become reality. And as early as within a decade!

Unless Donald J. Trump...

The West Has to Wake Up Before the Nightmare Turns into a Calamity

The world population was 1.6 billion when the US embarked on route to becoming the biggest power in the world in the early 1900s. A full century later, the world population today stands at 7.6 billion, having increased by six billion people in only one hundred years. But what is remarkable is that, in the next thirty years, it will have increased by another two billion and will become 9.5 billion in total.

A mass of humanity from the south and from the east will migrate west with ever-increasing numbers. The "poor and huddled" masses from Asia and Africa will come with Western Europe and the European Union on their minds. They will come in hordes both legally and illegally—mostly over the natural land bridge that Turkey is. This fast and uncontrollable demographic growth and westward movement will be a nightmare singly and formidably for Western civilization.

Even by the most conservative estimates, the migration of only 5 percent of this mass of humanity to Western Europe will lead to an approximately 20 percent increase in the population in Europe. That 5 percent amounts to 100 million more

Africans and Asians. Perhaps as many as 90 percent will be Muslims. Christian Europe will change radically and forever.

The end results of the steady migration of Muslims are already apparent in Europe. London, for the first time in history, elected a Muslim mayor in May 2016. Paris is another one of the mostly liberal cities in Europe with heavy concentration of immigrant Muslims from African countries. Who could tell if Berlin, Brussels, Amsterdam, Stockholm—where African and Asian demographics are increasing rapidly—will not eventually support Muslim candidates for the highest offices and for the most prestigious posts as what happened in London?

Change is here for the Western Europe and there is no point of return or realistic chance to reverse it. More liberal estimates predict that within three decades Muslims will be a bigger population than Christian white Europeans on the continent.

Yet, this migrating mass of humanity from east to west is not the only problem of Europe or of the US.

Seven of the top twenty Western economies in the world, within a decade or so, are projected to be replaced with seven fast-rising Muslim economies. Among the seven, two of them are even projected to make it to the top five as the biggest economies in the world. Basically, when the US is projected to regress to third biggest economy in the world, it will be in the company of Indonesia and Turkey in the fourth and fifth slots, respectively.

As JFK famously said, when economy is in bad shape nothing will be right. Fast-rising eastern economic powers will, over time, naturally acquire a formidable military might as well. They, in totality, will present further regression of the Western powers on economic, military and cultural grounds.

This book is not about the nightmare that is about to fall upon Western civilization in the next thirty years. Nor it is about the avalanche of migration of non-Christian and non-white masses towards West. Rather, this book is about a way out of this situation before Westerners wake to a nightmare turned calamity.

The Theme of This Book Is: "How to Save the Western Civilization"

This book is about the modern Republic of Turkey, founded by Gazi Mustafa Kemal Ataturk in 1923 and its last and current president Recep Tayyip Erdoğan. This book is about the country, its people and the leaders who will save Western civilization in Europe from the destructive effects of eventual and natural demographic forces.

This book is about the economic, military, and demographic realties that are too big for Western Europe to deal with alone. Western powers will have to work with the leading Muslim leaders, but most importantly with President Recep Tayyip Erdoğan of Turkey. He has a massive following around the world. He will not only be instrumental for Europe's survival but also for its prosperity.

This book points out the facts and simply argues that working with Turkey and the Erdoğan regime is the only way out for Europe. If Turkey and the Erdoğan regime are ignored, it will be the end of Western civilization in Europe as we know it.

Then the question comes home, to us, here in these United States of America, the last bastion of the Western civilization. By then, Turkey will either turn to the East and ally with China and Russia and others or it will remain neutral and leave most of the Muslims to pose a constant and ever-growing, potent threat for the West.

Finally, this book also talks about Western methods and strategies concerning the rest of the world in the 20th century. Unless, these methods are discarded in the 21st century, calamities will fall upon Europe as early as the 2040s—a decade before Muslims are predicted to become the majority population in the world. For example, in 2015, 1 million Syrians walked through the Middle East all the way to European Union and the world watched them as if it were a reality TV show. Turkey prevented the next potential wave of migrants in the millions two years later, single-handedly.

* * *

The Chicago Tribune once reported: "Turks could be our best allies." A commentator for the Soviet TASS news agency then, icily, addressed American troops: "This time, it was the Turks who saved you!" The reference was to the Korean war. When American and British armed forces were withdrawing, Turks, out of ammunition, put on their bayonets and 717 gave their lives in order to save their American brethren. President Dwight D. Eisenhower summarized the tragedy best after Turkish brigade saved the 2nd Division of the US forces from the complete annihilation in Korea, "No doubt the strongest and most reliable protector of European civilization is the Turkish Army."

Today's Turkey and Erdoğan are no different. Turkish Army and the Turkish people, living in secular Turkey and under Islamist regime of Erdoğan, are again ready to save Western civilization in Europe not only for white Christians but also for the good of the planet. This book makes this point clearly.

This book solidly, historically, and factually explains that Turkey and the Erdoğan regimes are "game changers" for the future of Western civilization in Europe. The West must keep Turkey and the Turks as an integral part of *Western* civilization. Without Turkey and Turks, Christian Europe will be no more. Having Turkey involved is the only way to save Western civilization.

But there is one caveat: Erdoğan and Trump must work together for that to come about.

Turkey Can Save the Western Civilization if Erdoğan and Trump Work Together

The good news is that presidents Recep Tayyip Erdoğan of Turkey and Donald J. Trump of the US are on the same page. What is missing from the equation is the US Congress. Even then, having Trump on board with Erdoğan means the US is halfway there with Turkey.

Turkey and the US acting together is vitally important because Turkey in the 21st century will not put up anymore with the "nation building" methods and strategies of the Western powers. Unfortunately, "globalist" Westerners are still living in the 20th century, despite losing hegemony over the Middle East and Africa since the turn of the millennium.

The realities of the 21st century is different. The West has to wake up and smell the roses. First of all, Turkey unlike in the past century, is no longer subservient to the West. It is independent. Two, economically, militarily, and spiritually, it is a dominant regional power. Third, there is a big mass of Muslims in the billions already viewing President Erdoğan of Turkey as the leader of the Muslim ummah (community).

Considering that within thirty years, there will be more Muslims in the world than Christians for the first time ever, Erdoğan's leadership becomes more important to note. Muslims were 19 percent of the world population at the beginning of the 19th century when the Christianity was at 33 percent. A century and a half later, in 2050, the Muslims will be 35 percent, Christianity will be thirty-four.

This demographic reality alone requires that two strong leaders have to lead these two mass majorities. Erdoğan as the leader of the Muslim ummah and Trump leading the sole superpower in the world, will be in a position to sway these two big masses on earth in the right direction and in a coordinated way.

Trump and Erdoğan Acting Together Will Have Beneficial Ripple Effects

When Trump and Erdoğan work together, Turkey will continue its role in the Western alliance. During the Cold War Turkey was the southern flank of NATO, a bulwark against the Soviet Union, blocking its only warm water outlet single-handedly. Since the turn of the millennium, Turkey has assumed three roles that are vitally important to the Western powers. Each one will not be able to stem an existential threat if it is not implemented wholeheartedly.

Turkey and the Erdoğan regime started to play these roles only after they thought Western leaders would change their hearts and minds, move with times, leave what is past in the past and accept the present. When Turkey realized that they had not done so, it started to act alone and for its own interests. That is how more migrants ended up in Europe in 2015 and again how Turkey was able to stem the flow of migrants two years later—alone.

This demonstrated that Turkey, even with the best of intentions to protect Western civilization in Europe, will not be fully effective without help. Unless Donald J. Trump can sway Western hearts and minds for their own good and pursue a common good in a coordinated fashion on equal grounds and without imposition, the task will remain too big for anyone to accomplish alone. Simply put, there will not be any steady and dependable beneficial ripple effects for anyone in the West. Until then, no one can expect Turkey and Turks to commit their lives like they did in Korea for the sake of Western civilization.

* * *

Equally important, the betrayals, backstabbing, brashness, and crazy behavior of Democrat presidents from JFK to Lyndon Johnson and then from Jimmy Carter to Barack Obama show how the task at hand for Donald J. Trump is a difficult one. Yet, for the US, acting genuinely with Recep Tayyip Erdoğan is the only hope to keep Turkey on board. The Erdoğan regime, in sync with the Trump administration, would do wonders for Europe and for the world at large and Christian white Western Europeans would be the immediate beneficiaries.

The roles Turkey plays depend on these realities:

1. Turkey will continue to remain the only natural land bridge that brings prosperity to Europe as: a) the main energy supply corridor from east to west but also, b) the main route for the Belt and Road Initiative of China, connecting supplies from Beijing to London in fifteen railroad days. Both are essential for the prosperity of Western European powers. If Europe goes, the US, then remains the only isolated bastion of Western civilization. Nothing good would come from such scenario.

2. Turkey will continue to be the gate keeper of Europe in the next century. Byzantine existed for a thousand until the Turks came to Anatolia through Manzikert when they defeated the Byzantines for the first time in 1071.

3. Three, Turkey will continue to act as a pressure valve from the Middle East to Africa to Asia—where more than two billion Muslims live—so that when the US turns its attention to bigger problems like the Eastern powerhouses: China, Russia, and India. Turkey in the lead, the world will need to deal with these nations with Muslim majority and large Muslim populations, that make up one third of the world, in order to re-establish a balance of power between the East and the West. Otherwise, Muslims will either side with the East against the West (and tilt the balance of power against the West) or continue to be the soft belly of the West and undermine its position against the East.

The Trump Revolution Is a Good Sign that the US Can Now Work with Turkey

Neither the Bush 43 nor the Obama administrations had good relationships with Turkey. Their globalist compatriots in Europe were also on the same boat with their Atlantic partners regarding Turkey during the same period.

As a result, Turkey drifted away more and more from the West and soon all but declared its economic and military independence. After that, it started to dominate the Middle East. Nowadays, it is expanding its influence all over Africa and even further beyond, reaching out to Latin America.

Turkey simply stopped working with the West about a decade ago, which is very detrimental to the West. In truth, Turkey had actually started on its path towards independence in the mid-1970s, yet no one in the West noticed until it was too late. Most did not even realize it until after the 2016 presidential elections in the US.

It was President Donald J. Trump that first realized, alone, on December 2018 that it was time to work with Turkey and Erdoğan. It was a big surprise for everybody because no one had advised him in that direction. At least no one knew if he embarked on his own without any weight behind him. As usual, they were wrong again. Trump knew and had always understood, long before anyone else, history, character, conditions and realities of the region.

He was right about North Korea, Iran, Russia, China, Israel, and Saudi Arabia. He was also right about Turkey. He knew he had to work with Turkey and Erdoğan on equal grounds as the long-time staunch allies two countries have been all along. Taking a cue from the Korean and Cyprus wars, the botched coup d'état against Erdogan, Turkey's formidable leverages over Iraq and military incursions to northern Syria, it was time to move and start working with Turkey and the regime in power instead of working against it.

* * *

In a sense, he was ready to make his mark in history, to turn the tables and start anew in the new century. For Turkey, that means 2020, the second term of the Trump presidency! Considering how the Trump revolution needs time to take root within the US federal bureaucracy, it is only reasonable to argue that President Trump will only really begin to implement his policies with Turkey after the 2020 presidential elections.

No one knows who will become the 46th president of the United States, but what Trump has so far accomplished has already made a big dent in history. His administration has opened eyes to new directions, new policies, new priorities, new goals, new heights, and to a new style that must be implemented for the US to remain the sole superpower in the world.

Trump has also discovered that the US needs new friends and allies, now that the Western European powers no longer can be counted on as much as they were in the past century. On that note, Erdoğan and Turkey, the "Gamechanger" makes an important case. One, Trump and Erdoğan are both pious, nationalist, "homeland first" leaders looking for free and fair trade or, as Erdoğan puts it, a "win-win" in trade relationships. Two, they are both headstrong, tough, street-smart, loyal leaders dedicated to their causes and principles.

What, if Anything, Does Turkey and Erdoğan—the "Gamechanger"—Have to Do with Everyday Americans?

One, it talks about a divine intervention. Two, it puts forward the stakes involving the future of the only superpower in the world. Finally, it makes a strong case about the pocketbook and security issues for everyday Americans.

First, this a divine intervention: a message Americans must heed.

Eerily, President Donald J. Trump and President Recep Tayyip Erdoğan have many things in common. Their hometowns New York City and Kasimpasa, a neighborhood of Istanbul, have similar characteristics: "If you can make it there, you can make it anywhere."

What are the chances that Trump and Erdoğan would have such similar characteristics, personalities, devotions, patriotic beliefs against the betrayers of their countries, plus stubbornness to purse agendas despite "take-down" attempts against their rule?

The similarities are uncanny. As if these examples are not enough, they also come from very different cultures, religions, historical, spiritual, sociological, and philosophical backgrounds. They also have different belief systems and had totally different experiences in life before assuming their respective posts.

There could be no other two leaders that could be on such opposing ends of the spectrum of human experience, yet they could not be more alike. How ironic is that? Two total strangers who seem almost identical. Who can say it that this not a divine intervention: a match made in heaven to bring them together for the good of billions on earth!

Isn't this odd couple coming together, to do good, nothing other than the will of God?

Second, this is the only way to save the only superpower in the world—by saving the US dollar, the Navy, and Hollywood.

The US has become the superpower that it still is today simply because it built the most powerful Navy in the world. Then, it brought the dollar into prominence as the de facto currency of the world. Finally, Hollywood played its role and promoted American brands—from cars to cigarettes, from chewing gums to colas, basically yet effectively, marketed *The American Dream*, to everyone on the planet.

Today, when and if Trump and Erdoğan come to work together, the ever-weakening US dollar will still remain the currency of the world. The Chinese economy is soon to become twice the size of the US economy. The Yuan will surely rise up and challenge the dollar in the world for supremacy, but Muslims under the Erdoğan leadership are more likely to select the Dollar over Yuan. What currency will rule the world will make a big difference. The dominance of the Dollar around the world brought a prosperity that the American people are still enjoying today even in meager times. With the Yuan in prominence, economic conditions in the US are sure to get even worse.

The US Navy will also benefit tremendously from the close relationship between two countries. Today, the US Sixth Fleet, that roams the Mediterranean Sea, face numerous challenges that it never faced in the 20th century. Russia and China recently held joint exercises in these waters for the first time ever. Currently, of the unprecedented 200 surface warships that are present in this semi-closed sea, 90 percent of them, including half that belong to the Western European powers, are in contention with the US Navy even though they are supposed to be in the same alliance under NATO. The European Union started to build its own navy under PETCO. To many its main adversary is a NATO that is under US leadership, rather than any of the Eastern powers.

* * *

But more importantly, in 2019, Turkey under the Erdoğan regime recently laid claim to a significant portion of the eastern Mediterranean, Aegean and Black seas with a 103-piece naval exercise that lasted almost a week. It was a massive undertaking and it was impressive. Turkey called it "Mavi Vatan," meaning an exclusive zone for the security and integrity of the modern Republic of Turkey. Turkey repeated another naval exercise two months later in May, with an even bigger version of the same in all three sees simultaneously, now with more than 150 warships.

Currently, Turkey is poised to become the regime that rules in these waters, that also contains a seabed which is the future of the world and where the next main energy source of the world lies.

Simply put, having a gutsy and visionary leader like Erdoğan, and a powerful and a resourceful Turkish state, acting in common interest with President Trump, the US Navy will instantaneously tilt the balance of power on behalf of the US. As a result, the American flag will fly high, American brands will sell more, and American tourist and businessmen will have the security to enjoy their lives abroad and conduct their business fairly while their homeland will be more secure.

Even Hollywood may see benefits as a ripple effect from these good relations. American movies can again embellish the glories of the US Armed Forces and the good life America enjoys with the help of mighty dollar and with a renewed energy.

Finally, this involves Bottom Line Issues for the Americans

With Turkey and Erdoğan on board with the Trump Administration, Americans can once again witness American power sailing across the open seas—formidably an against the rising new economic giants of China and India or their old nemesis Russia or the current wave of terrorists.

Without Turkey and Erdoğan in the Western alliance, they will certainly see their wealth, prosperity and happiness disappear much faster, on a path of no return for the better.

In specific, without Turkey and Erdoğan, the US will surely sink in further into the number three slot in the world. Soon after a deeper economic regression, the military will start to feel more of a strain as well. After that, the dollar will degenerate to a second-class currency, if not challenged by even more than that. Hollywood, that has been in decay for the past few decades, will lose it value and power even more against its competitors like India, China and Turkey to name a few.

With the Dollar's regression, inflation will become a constant and uncontrollable problem.

With US Navy not dominating the open seas at will, American business interests will lose their protection. The homeland will be under bigger much more varied attacks, starting with terrorists.

When economy is in constant struggle, the divisions within society will increase.

The "good life" America that America experienced throughout the 20th century will leave no traces.

The good life from other corners of the world will overshadow the life in the United States. Unfortunately, it will take place like an avalanche. More and more countries around the world will continue to build better and bigger of everything. Technology and innovation will have other centers around the world, rather than in the US.

Worse than that, migration from overseas will eventually reach American borders in mass.

By then, with Europe having lost itself to incoming hordes of Africans and Asians, Muslims will be in charge in more places than any American can imagine today.

And, as a result, Western values as we know them now will go through an irreversible transformation, accordingly, forever.

How could reading *GameChanger* change all that?

First of all, no one has ever touched on these taboos until now.

Second, it is about time to confront the realities in the world once and for all, but openly and realistically.

Thirdly, maybe more importantly, this book is written by a newly naturalized American who was educated in the fine universities in the United States, who is worried about his own future in his newfound country that looks more and more on the verge of losing the virtues of good life, prosperity, and ingenuity.

After all, this author knows it best from his own personal experiences. There was chaos in Europe in the 1970s when he set his course to emigrate to the US. If, God forbid, there is chaos in America due to economic decline and the loss of international power, he wonders, then where do you go from here?

America is the last bastion of the Western civilization and it must be protected for the sake of not only Americans but for the world at large and for the good of the planet.

GameChanger is, in a sense, a warning for the end of our world as we know it.

It is written to help you to protect yourself and your future.

CHAPTER TWO

TURKEY

Turkey is a republic, founded in 1923, by Gazi Mustafa Kemal Ataturk.

It is the 17th state that the Turks have founded throughout their glorious history. Some of these states even passed in magnitude the British or Roman Empires at their height. But this one promises to become one of the most celebrated.

Turkey is projected to become more powerful than most major powers of the past century. Within a decade, it is expected to reach parity with UK, France, and Germany.

Turkey already has a fast-growing economy and formidable military prowess. It is now a dominant regional power and holds additional cards to play. Similar cards made the US the superpower it is today.

I. The Modern Republic of Turkey

Modern Turkey sits on one-of-a-kind pillars of strength. It has a unique geo-strategic location, a vicious warrior-race and a god-fearing religion to rely on. They provide insurmountable advantages and leverages to the state.

Turkey went through growing pains to achieve the status it has now. Wars, coup d'états, anarchy, bullying, and betrayal were valuable lessons in its history. None of these was strong enough to bring down Turkey's resiliency. A century later, it looks forward to a promising second century.

1. What does the Turkish republic have?

One Tangible and Four Intangibles
Location, location, location.
Turkey's location is its only tangible pillar.
It is a geo-strategic country, situated between Europe, Asia and Africa.
It is the most travelled land-bridge for the millions of refugees heading West.

The Turkic race is one of the intangibles.

It traces its line back to Atilla the Hun, Tamerlane, and even touches Genghis Kahn.

The Muslim religion is another intangible.

It is the last vestige of the Caliphate that was abolished by Ataturk.

Another pillar is that it is heir to a most successful and enduring socio-political revolution that turned a Muslim state into a capitalist-country.

The last pillar is that it has a future not only with the West, but also with the other six Turkic states and all other Muslims too.

A. Geo-strategic Country

Turkey is a geo-strategic country like no other. But it is also a country that has a vital energy supplier and a self-appointed "refuge migration regulator" roles, "Saving Western Civilization."

a— Geological Realities

Land-bridge
Turkey is at the crossroads of the East and the West. It is the only land-bridge that brings together Asia, Europe, and Africa. China and European states are the major beneficiaries. It is vitally important for the flow of goods. The Belt and Road Initiative (BRI) of China passes through Turkey, bringing both ends of the continent of Asia together.

Straits
Turkey controls two of the four waterways in the Middle East, connecting the Black Sea to the Mediterranean Sea together with the Aegean and Marmara seas. These waterways and seas are crucial shipping lanes, mainly for oil and natural gas coming from Russia. They are also the only warmwater access for Russia and the only high sea outlets for Bulgaria, Romania, Ukraine, and Georgia. In times of crisis, these four countries have only Russia and Turkey as alternatives to depend on or they are at the mercy of. Other powers that can be kept out of the region solely by Turkey in times of war.

Rivers
On the eastern end, Turkey controls two rivers: The Euphrates and The Tigris. They are the lifelines for the Fertile Crescent where one of the earliest ever civilizations in the world prospered. Downstream, Syria and Iraq are beneficiaries. Turkey

has built more than twenty major dams on northern portion of these rivers in the past four decades. Water flow is practically controlled with some of the world's biggest man-made lakes which are used to irrigate farming lands in southeastern Turkey, at the north end of the Fertile Crescent. Taming these magnificent rivers has consequences. One, it fuels economic growth in Turkey. Energy and agricultural production increase tremendously. Two, Turkey can regulate how much water Syria and Iraq get, directly affecting their energy and agricultural production, and the social fabric of the people downstream.

b— Geological Ripple Effects

Turkey has two main functions in the world. One, it is a conduit for pipelines carrying energy to Europe. The other, it is a haven for refugees but also a transit point.

Pipelines

Oil and natural gas pipelines from east to west follow the same route. Kazakhstan, Turkmenistan, Azerbaijan, Russia, Iraq, and Iran ship their natural resources via Turkey to Europe. More than 30 percent of the European energy supply depends on this route.

Refugees

Turkish land-bridge serves as the only route for the refugees heading from Asia and Africa to the West. Land-bridge in this case also serves as a floodgate to stop the illegal or irregular mass flow of the refugees and contrabands.

B. The Turkic Race

The Turkic race is a source of strength for the Republic of Turkey. In the past, Turks were a horse-riding warrior nation. They are the reason why there is the "Wall of China." In modern times, they are known for their heroism in wars and for their staunch role in the Western alliance against the Soviet Union.

The Turks have an approximately 2000 year-long glorious history.
Every time one of their empires came to an end, they created another one immediately.
They were never stateless!

* * *

Modern Republic of Turkey is the 17th Turkic state in succession. It was founded despite a concerted effort by the Christian West.

In 1983, Turkey created an additional state, and called it "The Turkish Republic of Northern Cyprus" (TRNC) after carving out one third of the island of Cyprus in 1975 for its Turkic and Muslim brethren living there. It accomplished this against joint threats coming from NATO and the Union of Soviet Socialist Republics (USSR).

In 1991, after the disintegration of the USSR, five more Turkic states gained independence. Today, Azerbaijan, Kazakhstan, Uzbekistan, Turkmenistan, and Kyrgyzstan are registered members of the United Nations. The TRNC is not.

The rest of the descendants of Turks are very scattered across Asia and Europe.

C. Islamic Identity

Turkey is an Islamic country. More than 95 percent of its eighty-million plus population is Muslim. Most of them are Sunni.

Since the 10th century, when Turks immersed themselves into Islam, they also became first saviors and then messengers of the religion by expanding the message of the prophet. They converted many with centuries-long wars.

Their last two Muslim empires—the Seljucks and the Ottomans—are revered as the most powerful and cherished Muslim empires of them all. Together they ruled for a thousand years.

Today, especially since the coming of the Erdoğan regime, Turkey has become a hope for the Muslims of the world, reminiscent of its glorious past. The regime in power cherishes the opportunity to play this role and makes use of it at every opportunity.

Fast-growing Muslim population across the world in the 21st century look for leadership in the absence of Caliphate that was abolished a century ago. Istanbul being the last home of the Caliphate has bolstered Turkey's status for such leadership. Erdoğan, with his political Islamist convictions, for the moment symbolically fills the void as a visionary leader.

2. Growing Pains in the First 100 Years

Great experiences are making even Turkey greater.

Modern Turkish Republic is home to the most celebrated socio-political revolution in history.

It is the longest surviving, maturing revolution.

In contrast, the French revolution never made it more than few years before it was toppled.

Nonetheless, the Republican years were the most difficult.

There were existential threats. The country was in survival mode throughout this time.

Joining the Western alliance in the 1950s saved the country but brought new problems.

1950 through 1980 was a period of an experiment with democracy.

Democracy brought not much as development, but plenty of chaos and anarchy.

The country was on the brink of bankruptcy and dismemberment throughout.

In the end, it not only survived, but also grew stronger.

Ironically, the 1980 coup d'état came like a lifeline.

It put an end to nightmares once and for all. It brought the Islamists to power.

With them, a new wave of challenges emerged and continues today.

A. Republican Years 1923-1950

When modern Turkish Republic was declared in 1923, the US and the Western European powers were bitter enemies of Turks. They had just lost the "War of Liberation" in 1922, waged by Turkey and its founder Mustafa Kemal Ataturk. Ataturk was now ruling the day under the leadership of his Republican People's Party (RPP) led regimes in a one-party parliament.

On the other hand, for Turkey, that was the only thing going well. The country was poor, depleted, war weary. The Turks were fighting wars for eleven years uninterrupted, since the Italo-Turkish War of 1911 in Libya.

The Ottoman institutions were destroyed or paralyzed. To replace them with the Kemalist ideology consisting of republicanism, populism, nationalism, secularism, statism, and reformism was a long and arduous process. Plus, there were objections, resistance, revolt, and disbelief across the board.

Nonetheless, overtime, Turkey did not make the mistake of the WWI during the WWII. It stayed neutral and saved the country from additional catastrophic wars and destructions. But domestically, the results were not as good. At the end of the WWII, RPP paid the price. People voted them out of the office.

Ataturk, the founder, the great statement, and warrior, was long gone too, having passed in 1938.

B. Democratic Years 1950-1980

Many domestic and international attempts tried to derail the progress of the country.

Each coup d'état Turkey experienced, paradoxically made it stronger over time. Its institutions became pillars for democracy. Modernity arrived.

The period began when Adnan Menderes regime came to power in 1950. It was the beneficiary of the Western support, ending the one-party system of RPP. The messy multi-party democratic experiment had its many casualties. It ended with the coup d'état in 1980.

Unlike the Republican years when the leaders focused solely on internal matters, during "Democratic" years, many firsts took place in the international arena.

Korean and Cyprus wars, joining Western alliance, and detrimental spats with three US president were the highlights. But there was also a big tragedy. Menderes became the only casualty of the democracy. He was hanged. His rise and demise will always remain as the legacy of the West with the Turks in modern times.

a— The Korean war

In November 1950, Turkey sent a brigade of 5453 soldiers to the Korean War. They were later awarded the highest honorable citation of the U.S. Army for saving the U.S. Eighth Army and the IX Army Corps from encirclement and the U.S. 2nd Division from total annihilation in the Battle of Kunuri. During the war, Turks lost 717 men and suffered 2413 wounded.

i— Nothing but Praise for The Turks for Their Heroism

G.G. Martin—British Lieutenant General summarized it best, "While the Turks were for a long time fighting against the enemy and dying, the British and Americans were withdrawing. The Turks, who were out of ammunition, affixed their bayonets and attacked the enemy and there ensued a terrible hand to hand combat. The Turks succeeded in withdrawing by continuous combat and by carrying their injured comrades on their backs. They paraded at Pyongyang with their heads held high."

He was not the only one who lauded the historic bravery and skillset of the Turks.

"4500 soldiers in the middle of the firing line have known how to create miracle. The sacrifices of the Turks will eternally remain in our minds," *Washington Tribune*

"The courageous battles of the Turkish Brigade have created a favorable effect on the whole United Nations Forces," *Time*

"The surprise of the Korean battles were not the Chinese but the Turks. It is impossible at this moment to find a word to describe the heroism which the Turks have shown in the battles," *Abent Post*

"The Turks have shown in Kunuri a heroism worthy of their glorious history. The Turks have gained the admiration of the whole world through their glorious fighting in the battles," *Le Figaro*

"We owe the escape of thousands of United Nations troops out of a certain encirclement to the heroism of the Turkish soldiers. The Turkish soldiers in Korea have added a new and unforgettable page of honor to the customs and legends of heroism of the Turkish nation," Emanuel Shinwell, U.K. Minister of Defense.

ii— The Bravery of Turkish Brethren and the Americans

The comments of the American soldiers and lawmakers are even more endearing:

"The heroic soldiers of a heroic nation, you have saved the Eighth Army and the Ninth Army Crops from encirclement and the 2nd Division from destruction. I came here today to thank you on behalf of the United Nations Army,"— General Walton H. Walker, Commander, Eighth Army

"The Turks who have been known throughout history by their courage and decency, have proved that they have kept these characteristics, in the war which the United Nations undertook in Korea," Burner, U.S. Congressman.

"There is no one left who does not know that the Turks, our valuable allies, are hard warriors and that they have accomplished very great feats at the front," Claude Pepper, U.S. Senator

"I now understand that the vote I gave in favor of assistance to Turkey was the most fitting vote I gave in my life. Courage, bravery and heroism are the greatest virtues which will sooner or later conquer. In this matter, I know no nation superior to the Turks." Rose, U.S. Senator

"The Turkish forces have shown success above that expected in the battles they gave in Korea," General Collings, Commander US Army

"The Turks are the hero of heroes. There is no impossibility for the Turkish Brigade," General Douglas MacArthur, United Nations Forces Commander in Chief

* * *

Korean War meant more to the US in the ensuing years in its fight against the Soviet Union. Turkey became a staunch ally defending the southern flank of the Western alliance under NATO practically single-handedly.

But it took three Democrat US presidents to undo what no-one will ever be able to fix again. Presidents JFK, Lyndon Johnson and Jimmy Carter were like 'three strikes and out,' for the US-Turkey relationship to go out of the window within a decade after the Korean war heroism saving US soldiers.

b— The Kennedy Sell-out

When young JFK, the 35th president of the US, came to power, he was basically caught with his "pants down" in the face of Khrushchev regime of Soviet Union.

The reaction of Robert Kennedy, attorney general of the United States, when he learned on Tuesday, 16 October 1962, that Soviet nuclear missiles had been deployed in Cuba, just ninety miles off the coast of Florida, was understandable: "Oh shit! Shit! Shit! Those sons of bitches Russians."[1]

What was later-on to be called the Cuban missile crisis ended up becoming a betrayal of a staunch US ally.

"His letter to Khrushchev on 27 October in which he agreed not to sanction any invasion of Cuba was manifestly effective in getting Khrushchev to back down by agreeing to remove the nuclear weapons from Cuba.

So too was the secret mission he sent Robert Kennedy on that evening to inform the Soviet ambassador in Washington, Anatoly Dobrynin, that in due course the US Jupiter missiles in Turkey would be secretly withdrawn."[2]

Jupiter missiles were in Turkey to defend the US ally against Soviet Union.

c— Johnson's ill-conceived letter

Two years later, Lyndon Johnson sent a letter to his counterpart Turkish prime minister Ismet Inonu. In the letter, as published in NYT "Johnson warns Inonu on Cyprus; Invites him to U.S. for talks—Turkey said to give up plan for a landing."

Sounds innocent! Not to Turks.

---

[1]   https://www.historyextra.com/period/20th-century/
        kennedys-jfk-robert-cuban-missile-crisis-cold-war-america-soviet/
[2]   https://www.historyextra.com/period/20th-century/
        kennedys-jfk-robert-cuban-missile-crisis-cold-war-america-soviet/

By then, "Turkey had massed a force 120 miles from Cyprus for a possible invasion to protect the Turkish Cypriote community on the island from the Greek Cypriote majority," NYT writes.

Invitation for talks was in the aftermath of the Jupiter missiles betrayal. It was a threat to leave Turkey alone against Soviet threat the country was facing.

It was only a decade ago that the Turks had saved 2nd Division from total inhalation in Korea, yet now their brethren of war were putting them in harms-way with no qualm! Turks accepted the letter, nothing less than as a backstabbing.

* * *

A decade later, Turkey invaded Cyprus, disregarding any threat from ally and foe, and took one third of the island, and soon after named it: "Turkish Republic of Northern Cyprus."

d— Carter's Embargo: The Straw that Broke the Camel's Back

Upon invasion of Cyprus, the US regime that was in disarray, immediately imposed embargo on Turkey. Incoming Jimmy Carter, the 39th president of the US some-how owned it.

It was the final nail in the coffin for the relationship. By the time the embargo was lifted three years later, it was already too late. Turkey had long decided that it cannot trust the US anymore and it set the course for independence.

* * *

In short, in a thirty years span, the US had helped bring more democracy to Turkey with multi-party system of Menderes regime. After that, it became best of brethren in war and staunch allies against a common communist enemy. Finally, the US practically lost its ally with a "betrayal," a "back-stabbing," and a "brashness" of three Democrat presidents.

Go figure!

C. Islamic Years 1980-2018

Islamic years in Turkey began with the 1980 coup d'état. American agents took full credit for the regime change. It was just like thirty years earlier when they conspired to bring the pious to power with Menderes regime. Ironically, they were now replacing them with the Islamists.

Reportedly, by 2016, US agents were in favor of another regime change in Turkey. But when the 15 July coup failed, the last cycle of close relationship between the West and Turkey also came to an end, but not the way it was desired by the Western powers.

How co-incidental! Last failed coup d'état attempt was "bonkers" that took place under another Democrat president, Barack H. Obama.

Later, Donald J. Trump, the 45th president of the US, capitalized on the misfortune of his Democrat predecessors and started putting an end to the betrayals, back-stabbings, brashness and bonkers of Kennedy, Johnson, Carter and Obama. Trump within two years after he came to power and extended a friendly and firm hand to Turkey.

By then, in 2018, Turkey had already switched from parliamentarian to the presidential system of government with a referendum, allowing Recep Tayyip Erdoğan regime to consolidate power and make Turkey even more independent.

Turkey was now ready to give its final push and complete its major projects and celebrate the first hundred years of the republic with a Big Bang of accomplishments. The world's longest bridges, biggest airports, state of the art military platforms, highway and high-speed rail networks second to none, each more amazing than another and too many of them to list were making waves domestically and internationally.

3. The Next century

Does not end in 2053 or 2071 but they are big milestones

Where do the Turks and Turkey go in their second century, starting in 2023?

The answer lies in history, dating back couple thousands of years.

But we must also look back at the first hundred years of modern Turkish history.

Finally, we need to visit Erdoğan's progress during his first two decades in power.

Second centuries have always been the better centuries for the past sixteen Turkish states.

If that pattern holds true, then the modern Turkish republic is going to have a great century.

II. Turks and Turkish States in History

Today there are perhaps 135 million Turkic people in the world.

Only about 40 percent of them live in Turkey.

The rest are scattered across Central Asia, Eastern Europe, and the Middle East.

Some of them are also in northern and western China.
They are one of the most widely scattered races in the world.
The Mongols were slightly related to the Turkic groups.
There is one main difference between the Mongols and the Turks.
The Mongols tended to return home after their conquests.
The Turks preferred to stay in their conquered lands.

* * *

Historical Summary

For the Turks, their third one thousand years began with Islamist Erdoğan regime in Turkey.

Throughout their second thousand years, the Turks were at the gates of Europe.

During their initial thousand years, Turks were busy causing havoc throughout Asia.

1. The First Thousand Years

They were in Asia

Turks were horsemen that came from a small tribe in the Altai mountains.

They established many independent states and empires during the first thousand years of their history.

A. Who are the Turks?

The Turks are said to have descended from a small tribe of horseman in the Altai region. Today they are still fierce warriors, living in a secular and Westernized society as a Muslim nation.

"They came from the Altai Mountains in southern Siberia, Kazakhstan, and Mongolia. The first historical references to the Turks appear in Chinese records around 200 BC. Chinese sources in the sixth century A.D. identify the tribal kingdom called Tu-Küe. It was located on the Orkhon River south of Lake Baykal. The earliest known example of writing in a Turkic language was found in that area. It has been dated around A.D. 730."[3]

---

[3]   Source: Library of Congress, January 1995

"The word 'Turk' is derived from the Chinese character 'Tu-Kiu', which means 'forceful' and 'strong.' The Turks were such excellent horsemen that the ancient Chinese called them 'horse barbarians. Turkish women reputedly could conceive and gave birth while riding. They were one of the first groups of people to use saddles with stirrups. This enabled them to swiftly attack their enemies because they could stand up and shoot their long bows while riding.

The Chinese believed these Turks descended from wolves and the Great Wall of China may have been built to keep them out. According to legend a gray wolf led the first Turkic tribes from their homeland in Central Asia into Anatolia.

Turks have been known throughout history for their fierceness and fighting skills. Most of the warriors in the Mongol armies were Turks. Turks also dominated the Mamluk forces and beefed up the Persian Safavid and Indian Mogul armies. Turkic tribes were a threat to the Byzantines and Persians starting in the A.D. 6th century. They absorbed Islam during the Arab invasions which began after Mohammed (SAV)'s death in 632."[4]

B. Is It 220 BC or AD 546?

Does it matter?

According to Turkic sources, it all began with the Great Hun Empire (204 BC— 216 AD). That was also the first of the 16 states, listed in the emblem of the president of the modern Turkish republic, the 17th Turkish state in history.[5]

Other sources say that the Turks had their origin between 546 and 553. The Türks overthrew the Ruruan and established themselves as the most powerful force in North Asia and Inner Asia. This was the beginning of a pattern of conquest that was to have a significant effect upon Eurasian history for more than a thousand years.

The Türks were the first people to use this later wide-spread name. They are also the earliest Inner Asian people whose language is known, because they left behind Orkhon inscriptions in a runic-like script, which was deciphered in 1896.[6]

The first great state which carried the name Turk was the Kok-Turk State which extended from Manchuria to the Black Sea and Iran between the A.D. 6th and 8th centuries. This empire had trade links with China, Iran and the Byzantines and left behind inscriptions and an unusual alphabet on stones in Mongolia.

---

[4] http://factsanddetails.com/asian/cat65/sub424/item2688.html

[5] Source: http://www.allaboutturkey.com/states.htm

[6] Source: Library of Congress, June 1989

The Turkish migrations after the sixth century were part of a general movement of peoples out of central Asia during the first millennium A.D. that was influenced by a few interrelated factors—climatic changes, the strain of growing populations on a fragile pastoral economy, and pressure from stronger neighbors also on the move.

Among those who migrated were the Oghuz Turks, who had embraced Islam in the tenth century. They established themselves around Bukhara in Transoxiana under their khan, Seljuk. Split by dissension among the tribes, one branch of the Oghuz, led by descendants of Seljuk, moved west and entered service with the Abbasid caliphs of Baghdad.[7]

2. The Second Thousand Years

They arrived Europe

Turks arrived West after they beat the Byzantium in 1071 at the Battle of Manzikert.

They settled in the geo-strategic Asia Minor.

"Veni, Vidi, Vici."

Like Julius Caesar said, after winning an earlier battle in Asia Minor.

Turks came, saw and conquered Asian Minor.

They have been the masters there ever since.

A. The Turkic States

Dominant Turkic tribes in the 10th, 11th and 12th centuries included the Uighurs, Khazars, Kipchaks, and Seljucks.

All Turkic tribes converted to Islam except for the reindeer herding Yakuts in Siberia and the Chuvash in the Volga region of Russia, but the wolf mythology stayed with them.

Ninth century stela in Mongolia show young Turkic children suckling from the teats of a mother wolf like Romulus and Remus, and the Osmanli Turks, the forbears of the Ottomans, marched with banners depicting a wolf's head when they conquered their way from Central Asia to the outskirts of Constantinople.

In the 11th century, Turkish tribes began invading western Asia from their homelands in Central Asia. The strongest of these tribes was the Seljuks.

---

[7] Source: Library of Congress, January 1995

In the wake of the Samanids (819-1005)—Persians who set up a local dynasty in Central Asia within the Abbasid Empire—arose to two Turkish dynasties: the Ghaznavids, based in Khorasan in present-day Turkmenistan, and the Karakhanids from present-day Kazakhstan.

Karakhanids are credited with converting Central Asia to Islam. They established a large empire that stretched from Kazakhstan to western China and embraced three important cities: Balasagun (present-day Buruna in Kyrgyzstan), Talas (present-day Tara in Kazakhstan), and Kashgar. Bukhara continued as a center of learning.

The Karakhanids and Ghaznavids fought one another off and on until they were both out maneuvered diplomatically and militarily by the Seljuk Turks, who created a huge empire that stretched from western China to the Mediterranean.[8]

B. The Seljuks

According to The Encyclopedia Britannica, during the 10th century migrations of the Turkish peoples from Central Asia and southeast Russia, one group of nomadic tribes, led by a chief named Seljuk, settled in the lower reaches of the Jaxartes River. It later converted to the Sunni form of Islam.

At his death in 1063, heading an empire that included western Iran and Mesopotamia, Seljuk's two grandsons, Chaghri (Chagri) Beg and Toghrïl (Tugril) Beg, enlisted Persian support to win realms of their own, controlling the greater part of Khorāsān and Toghrïl.

Under the sultans Alp-Arslan and Malik-Shāh, the Seljuk empire was extended to include all of Iran and Mesopotamia and Syria, including Palestine. In 1071, Alp-Arslan defeated an immense Byzantine army at Manzikert and captured the Byzantine emperor Romanus IV Diogenes. The way was open for Turkmen tribesmen to settle in Asia Minor.

Because of Toghrïl Beg's victory over the Būyids in Baghdad in 1055, the Seljuks came to be seen as the restorers of Muslim unity under the Sunni caliphate.

While Alp-Arslan and Malik-Shāh expanded the empire to the frontier of Egypt, the Seljuk vizier Niẓām al-Mulk oversaw the empire's organization during both their reigns.

The Seljuk empire, political as well as religious in character, left a strong legacy to Islam. During the Seljuk period, a network of madrasahs (Islamic colleges) was founded, capable of giving uniform training to the state's administrators and

---

[8]   http://factsanddetails.com/asian/cat65/sub424/item2688.html

religious scholars. Among the many mosques built by the sultans was the Great Mosque of Eṣfahān (the Masjed-e Jāmeʿ).

The Seljuk empire was unable to prevent the rise of the Nizārī Ismaʿīlīs, a Shiʿīte sect thought to be responsible for the killing of vizier Niẓām al-Mulk in 1092. The last of the Iranian Seljuks died on the battlefield in 1194, and by 1200 Seljuk power was at an end everywhere except in Anatolia.

C. The Ottomans

According to Britannica, Ottoman Empire, created by Turkish tribes in Anatolia (Asia Minor) that grew to be one of the most powerful states in the world during the 15th and 16th centuries.

The Ottoman period spanned more than six-hundred years and came to an end only in 1922, when it was replaced by the Republic and various successor states in southeastern Europe and the Middle East.

At its height, the empire encompassed most of southeastern Europe to the gates of Vienna, including present-day Hungary, the Balkan region, Greece, and parts of Ukraine; portions of the Middle East now occupied by Iraq, Syria, Israel, and Egypt; North Africa as far west as Algeria; and large parts of the Arabian Peninsula.

The term Ottoman is a dynastic appellation derived from Osman I (Arabic: ʿUthmān), the nomadic Turkmen chief who founded both the dynasty and the empire about 1300.

3. The Third Thousand Years: Where Will the Turks Go?

They have no need to go anywhere else

In their first two thousand years the Turks always moved.

Unlike the Mongols, they did not return home.

In their next thousand years, the Turks settled in Anatolia permanently.

They never released their hold.

The irony is that the Turks, for the first time ever in their third 1000 years, are changing.

They are venturing to new countries, but they are coming back home afterwards.

Much like the Mongols!

But it took them two thousand years to find their final homeland in Anatolia.

III. Cards Turkey holds

At the centennial of the republic, Turkey holds 3 very important cards.

It also has a whole deck of other cards ready to play as necessary.

One, Turkey has a very fast-growing and very varied economy.

Two, it has a high-tech, fast-growing, high-percentage indigenous defense industry.

Three, it has a socio-political revolution that has not only survived but also matured.

1. A Top 5 Economy

Parity with the UK, France and Germany is not far away.

Modern Turkey is fast-growing.

It is projected to become one of the top five economies in the world.

Reportedly, by 2030, it will rank above Germany, UK, and France in GDP.

A. Turkey Has Markets in Its Crosshairs or Under Its Influence

<u>Europe</u>

Turkey has Customs Union with the EU. It is also a "forever" candidate to become a full member of the union. Its economy has multitude of leverages over countries in Europe. The Turkish banking sector is tightly integrated with Western Europe. Half of its total trade volume is with the EU, and its trade is expected to go over a trillion dollars within five years.

<u>Oil Exporters</u>

Iran, Iraq, and Russia are markets poised to increase the current Turkish total trade volume over time. Turkey buys their oil and natural gas, transports the rest to Europe, and then supplies them back in return with manufactured and agricultural goods.

<u>Middle East and Central Asian Republics</u>

The volume of trade with these countries is still very low, but their Turkic and Muslim heritage make them viable growth markets for Turkish products. They are primarily targets of Turkish military platforms.

Indonesia, Pakistan, Malesia and Bangladesh

Turkey works cohesively with Pakistan and Indonesia. They are main client states for defense industry related procurements ranging from warships to submarines to tanks and attack helicopters to name a few. Malesia and Bangladesh are not lagging behind.

Africa

In the first eighty years of modern Turkey's history, relationships with the black continent were limited to five North African countries, sharing a centuries-long Ottoman heritage together. In the 21st century, Turkey established diplomatic and cultural relationships with the remaining forty-nine African states. Military interactions and new targets on trade volume came after that.

The Americas and Far East

The US is a big trading partner. Recently, in 2019, Trump and Erdoğan agreed to set the trade volume between two countries to 75 billion dollars a year.

Overtures to Latin America are new but fast-growing.

In Asia, Turkey has major partners. From nuclear power plants to high-speed rail networks to tanks, many high-technology projects in Turkey come from Japan and South Korea.

China and India

Turkey also has a special and fast developing relationships with China and India from technology transfer to tourism to nuclear reactors to satellite or missile technologies to name a few.

B. Turkey Has Resources

Water and Continental Shelves

Turkey has vast arable land, big herds of livestock, and a rich historic and cultural heritage that appeal to tourism. It has surrounding seas with shipping ports and rivers with man-made lakes for irrigation.

It is a rich land with many options and possibilities. And there is the progressive Erdoğan regime that is constantly exploring potentials, like building the Panama-canal-like Kanal Istanbul from the Black Sea to the Marmara Sea. A project for the ages!

a— *Natural Resources*

Turkey, unlike other countries in the Middle East, has natural resources of biblical proportions. Rivers and waterways have been there for thousands of years and will continue to be there forever, unlike oil or other forms of natural resources that are limited in size and quantity.

The Fertile Crescent is also a naturally abundant environment because of its two biblical rivers. They have been a food source for the regional population for thousands of years. Turkey is in possession of this one-of-a-kind "bread-basket" for the world that could potentially feed a whole continent alone.

Finally, there is a raw material that has been there all along but technology on earth was not developed enough to use it until the 21st century. Now, when it is understood that it has vitally important role that cannot be replaced by any other, Turkey seems to be the major source by far.

The Fertile Crescent
Turkey includes a large arable portion of the biblical Fertile Crescent. It has the capacity to feed Europe since the completion of man-made lakes and irrigation canals in the aftermath of twenty gargantuan dams over Euphrates and Tigers rivers built since 1960.

Rivers
Controlling the flow of water down the stream or management of exports of food products coming out of the Crescent give Turkey great leverage over the Middle East and to a greater competitive edge in Europe.

Boron
Reportedly, Turkey has an almost exclusive control over the world's most sought-after natural resource that is used in the defense sector. China, India, Russia, the US are the main customers and none of them have significant reserves.

Waterways
Turkey is a gigantic peninsula, surrounded with three seas. It also has an inner sea with two strategic waterways tying it to other international seas.

Continental Shelves
Turkey is the only country with continental shelves in all three inner seas in the region with proven hydrocarbon reserves. Continental shelves of Turkey in the Eastern Mediterranean are the largest among all countries, including Greece,

Turkish Republic of Northern Cyprus, Republic of Cyprus, Syria, Israel, Palestine authority, Lebanon and Egypt. Turkey also splits the Aegean Sea with Greece, and practically controls half of the Black Sea.

b— Man-made or Developed Riches

In the 20th century, Turkey did not have capital but more importantly it did not have a long-lasting regime to complete major projects. Erdoğan regime has been a different experience. It makes promises and then keeps them. Same as Donald J. Trump.

Istanbul Airport is a case in point. The world's biggest project was completed in 5 years. There is no such project in Europe, and it is not possible to finish it there in a decade.

Railways and Highways
Turkey will have the longest high-speed rail network in the world behind China by 2023. Portion of it will also serve the Belt and Road Initiative highway and rail network between China and UK.

Oil and Natural Gas Pipelines
One of Turkey's forays in the energy area is the oil and natural gas explorations on the continental shelves in Black and Mediterranean seas. Oil rigs already started to pop up one after the other reflecting the speed with which Turkey is moving forward. Ever growing Turkish navy is also growing as fast to serve as a bulwark to assure that spoils of the riches in these competitive waters are not compromised.

Kanal Istanbul
Kanal Istanbul is a project to build a 'Panama Canal' next to the Bosporus in Thrace. It is a big project inside a new city to be built in five years. The new city will double Istanbul in beauty, functionality and wealth. Oil tankers, cargo ships and warships will be the main beneficiaries. Waiting lines in the Bosporus will be eliminated. The prospects for Bulgaria, Romania, Ukraine and Georgia on the Black Sea basin will also improve.

In 2018, the tourism sector enjoyed ripple effect of the growing economy and from exposure to international markets. A record-breaking year made Turkey the sixth biggest destination in the world after Italy. Turkey is projected to triple its current forty million tourist capacity in a decade.

Turkey has divided highways, some of the world's biggest bridges, harbors, airports, airlines, resorts, hotels, restaurants, shopping environs, museums. The country is filled with natural and historical sites dating back to the Romans and even earlier. Excavation and preservation of the antiquities are humbling experiences.

More importantly, the Erdoğan regime, like its predecessors Ataturk or Mehmed the Conqueror cherishes the world heritage. In 2018 alone nearly 350 archaeological excavations and around fifty rescue missions were carried out.[9]

C. Turkey Generates Powerful International Brands

Turkey is generating multitude of international brands because of its very varied economy. Most involve high technology and sophisticated manufacturing. There are also major and one of kind military platforms. Construction companies build some of the world's major projects like bridges, highways, airports in Turkey and around the world.

Turkey

Turkey itself is a brand. Erdoğan regime today is welcomed in every country it chooses from Tanzania to Venezuela but also from China to Russia. Until few years ago, most of the African and Latin American countries either did not have Turkish embassy or never saw a Turkish president visiting their country and vice a versa. Turkish brand today stands for a value and an alternative for many products, including as a way to bring modernity and security to a country.

Turkish Airlines

Turkish Airlines is a good example. The number one airline of Europe is expected to get even bigger with the new Istanbul airport now operational. The world's biggest airport is projected to become the main hub of Europe, taking business away from its counterparts in Germany, Holland, and other European centers.

Automotive Brands

Since 2018, approximately 20 percent of Turkish exports have come from the automotive sector. Automobiles, commercial vehicles, and spare parts make up the industry. Turkey recently took a great leap forward in this sector even further. It is in the process of building its first indigenous electric car. The prototype to be ready in 2019. Considering the fact that within 5 to 10 years Europe will turn to totally into electric cars, Turkey will be ready.

Industry and Technology Minister Mustafa Varank summarized the expectations stating that the "primary goal at the beginning is to produce a domestic car.

---

[9]   Source: http://turkisharchaeonews.net/node?page=6

By grouping five indigenous private companies, Turkey uses its competence and capacity to develop the technology with a business model that hopes to create a successful world giant."

Defense-Industry-Related Brands

Currently listed as the 8th biggest military exporter, Turkey is soon expected to become the 5th behind the US, Russia, China, and India surpassing European manufacturers.

Defense industry came a long way since 1975. From military vehicles to sophisticated ordinances, the rate of indigenous production is constantly increasing. Same applies to the exports of small arms, missiles, attack helicopters, war ships, submarines, satellite armed drones. Turkey is also working on larger platforms. It is building its own training and attack planes, as well as 5th generation aircraft, and flattops.

Industry serves mainly Muslim world and other countries looking for sophisticated and affordable systems and platforms. So far four of the top 100 defense industry companies in the world are from Turkey. Their numbers and rankings are sure to increase soon.

2. Top 5 military

Soon to become the Most Powerful from Indian Ocean to Mediterranean Sea

Turkey has manufacturing capacity to build military platforms competitively.

Living in a bad neighborhood, Turkey has opportunities to test them in the real world as well.

Turkey's indigenous platforms are sophisticated and high-tech.

Leading Western military platforms benefit from Turkish ingenuity and competitiveness.

Rapidly developing export markets coupled with overseas bases produce more benefits.

More countries seek Turkish products and welcome Turkey as a strategic partner.

A. Manufacturing Capacity

Turkey has wide-ranging manufacturing capacity from guns and rifles to ordinances to electronics to major land, air, sea and space platforms. They are produced indigenously up to 70 percent. The goal is to reach 100 percent by 2023. It was less than 20 percent only two decades ago!

According to the Brookings Institution, a nonprofit public policy organization based in Washington DC, the capacity of Turkey in the manufacturing is relatively small when China controls up to twenty, the US, nearly eighteen; Japan, ten, Germany, 7 percent of the world manufacturing capacity. Turkey is one of the top twenty manufacturing countries at the bottom of the barrel with 1 percent but rising.

Turkish capacity is projected to pass Germany, Japan and UK in the next decades. In defense industry, the manufacturing growth varies. The potential rise of Turkish economy to 5th slot in the world will bring an equally powerful military to life.

B. Real War Testing Capacity on Land and Sea Targets

What makes Turkish military grow faster and stronger is the technological advances it has gained over the past decade or so. They are tested in one of the worst neighborhoods in the world, full of refugee crisis, contrabands from narcotics to human trafficking to arms to terrorists. They are tested in actual wars in Syria and Iraq, plus in the surrounding seas, benefiting from real-time war scenarios.

For example, Greece has thousands of islands in the Aegean Sea. Turkey recently sent its indigenously built Heybeliada corvette to Greek waters and kept it there for day or so before notifying the Greek authorities about the location of its warship. Not until then Greek navy did not know that Turkish warship was there. It was stealth!

Another example is indigenously built high tech armed drones. Satellite controlled drones are able to stay in the air twenty-four hours and can rise to 27 thousand feet. "Our domestic UAV made its first flight with its domestic and national engine PD-170," Presidency of Defense Industry (SSB) President İsmail Demir said in December 2018.

Meanwhile, studies on the PD-220 engine, which will be an upper version of the PD-170 engine, have also begun. This engine will power up a twin-engine mechanism and with twenty-four hours of endurance at 40,000 feet. Akıncı of Baykar Makina has already started to be manufactured. Set to make its first flight in 2020, the system will carry over 1,000 kilograms of ammunition. Delivery is expected in 2021 after a one-year testing period.

In the meantime, nearly hundred already in service, Turkey deploys drones regularly in the international waters over the Aegean. Every time a Turkish drone is caught on a Greek armed forces radar, minimum two F-16 aircraft are sent to counter them. It costs sixty thousand dollars an hour for F-16 to go after a drone that has four times less cost to fly. In the meantime, Turkey's drone management capacity is being tested while war of attrition costs Greece ever more with each encounter.

C. The Latest and Most Sophisticated Military Platforms

Turkey has gained a lot of experience in the defense industry in the past forty years. In the early days of the modern Republic of Turkey had experimented and built its own military platforms. But by 1950, they came to a halt when Turkey joined NATO. The US started to supply technology and platforms as per agreement. Turkish defense industry remained idle until mid-1970s for half a century.

Since then, Turkey started to develop its defense industry again. Today it produces most of its military platforms on its own, but it also continues to enter into joint projects with allies. Like submarines with Germany, flattops with Spain, attack helicopters with Italy, missile technology with France, jet engine with UK. 10 Turkish companies have supported the development and/or production of Joint Strike Fighter (JSF) F-35. Roketsan and Tubitak-SAGE are two of them.

Lockheed Martin Missiles and Fire Control has partnered with Roketsan, through a teaming agreement, to jointly develop, produce, market and sell the advanced, precision guided Stand Off Missile (SOM-J) for JSFs. They will be carried internally on the 5th Generation F-35 aircraft.

On that note, Turkish missile programs are some of the most developed in the world. Apart from the existing J600-T Yildirim and Jaguar with 250 km range, Toros since 1999 with 100 km and others indigenously developed and mass produced, there are others much longer range. In 2011, the state scientific research institute TUBITAK announced missiles with ranges 930 miles and 1550 miles underdevelopment. With them, northern half of Africa, all of Europe, Middle East will be in reach of Turkish missiles including Moscow. That is not even taking into account the fact that since 2013 and 2015, Turkey has already started to build its satellite launching system (UFS) and to augment its satellite capability effort with Space Systems Integration and Test center (USET) where more than one satellite of up to five respectively reflect how the Turks have made strides across the board.

D. Overseas Military Bases

Turkey has military bases in Albania, Azerbaijan, Iraq, Northern Cyprus, Qatar, Somalia, Sudan, Syria. Each is different in purpose. Some are large bases accommodating navy, air force and land forces.

According to reports, Turkey plans to deploy 60 thousand soldiers in four of its overseas bases, projecting plans until 2022. Two of these bases are said to be in Qatar, one of them a navy base.[10]

According to another report Turkey already has 3,000 troops deployed in its compound in Somalia and is developing a full-scale navy and air base in the Suakin Island in Sudan on Red Sea. It is said that it will be capable of holding some 20,000 military personnel at a time.[11]

Turkey in other words moved from being the second biggest land army in NATO to an overseas military power that has indigenous manufacturing capacity with procurement and delivery means. The progress did not go unnoticed. More and more developing countries nowadays seek strategic partnership with this growing power.

All within a half a century!

3. A Socio-Political Revolution

The only capitalist and Islamist-turned-leftist revolution that is still alive and thriving

Turkey is a by-product of the most successful socio-political revolution in the world.

It evolved with coup d'états that were mostly non-violent.

It tolerated to the "democratic" process, international interferences and the Islamists.

The pillars of the Kemalist ideology stood test of times.

The country survived the pre-Cold War period and then the bipolar world.

Maturing secular state, at the end, reconciled its differences with the Islamists.

Ironically, Erdoğan today is the foremost supporter of the Kemalist ideology.

The country never grew as much in the last two decades when he was in power.

He was able to fend off many attacks including a coup d'état attempt.

The fact that coup came after a large interval from the first four also indicates a finale.

It was a desperate attempt in vain, after Turkey has become a capitalist economy.

As Ataturk predicted: Turkey had reached the "level of the contemporary civilizations."

Did Ataturk mean that Turkey will be progressive, wealthy, powerful, and charitable?

"Separation of church and state" was the first goal that was achieved early on.

---

[10]   http://english.alarabiya.net/en/views/news/middle-east/2018/03/18/
      Turkey-cements-economic-ties-with-military-base-in-Qatar.html

[11]   https://www.middleeastmonitor.com/20180118-turkey-to-deploy-60000-soldiers-
      in-bases-abroad-including-in-qatar/

"The biggest humanitarian donor status," the latest achievement for a fast-growing state.

Today, Republic of Turkey is a domineering economic and military regional power.

Yet, it is also projected to become a global role player that can tilt the balance of power.

It has formidable cards to play as the presumptuous leader of three billion Muslims.

IV. The Cards Turkey Plays

Turkey has some natural cards to play.

One is a "land-bridge". The other is a "flood-gate."

Its geo-strategic location gives the country crucial roles to play.

The international system also imposes additional responsibilities on Turkey.

It has a big role to play in the "balance of power" between East and West.

Plus, Turkey is also obliged to regulate refugees heading West.

To slow the flow, it acts as a "pressure valve" for some countries and regions.

Finally, Turkey is in possession of "American Cards."

Like the US had a century ago, Turkey has a formidable Navy in the making.

It has a TV series industry making big ratings in sixty countries and presence in 135.

The US became a superpower with Blue Navy, Hollywood, and Mighty Dollar.

Turkey having two of the three cards is a sure bet to become a regional power.

1. Special Cards for Turkey to Play

They are the only cards in the world

Turkey is a land-bridge between Europe, Asia and the Middle East.

It is also a floodgate.

A. Land-bridge

Turkey's land-bridge is open to everybody.

It is a land-bridge for natural gas and oil pipelines coming from Russia, Kazakhstan, Turkmenistan, Azerbaijan, Iran, and Iraq heading to European markets. These pipelines allow Europe not to be hostage to the flow of the similar from northern stream via Germany. Plus, China's Belt and Road Initiative passes through Turkey, making use of the same land-bridge.

B. Floodgate

The gates are to regulate the flow. Turkey as a country is a gate for Europe and acts as a gatekeeper.

a— Refugees

Turkey hosts close to four million refugees from Syria since the civil war broke up in 2011. When one million additional refugees from Syria ended up in Europe in 2015, radical right in Germany, France, Holland, and Austria increased their share in their respective parliaments.

Letting some of the refugees continue their path to Europe seems to be a sure bet to bring more challenges there. Holding the gates of Europe is vitally important. Turkey, uncharacteristically, in many people's mind, should be the last country keeping an eye on European gate. But it is true. It is doing it. So far!

b— Arms and Narcotics

Refugees are not the only thing that go back to Europe illegally. Contraband has always been the biggest lure. It is no different today.

2. Cards to Prevent Wars

Turkey is a heavy weight country that has a balancing role in the world.

It also plays a "pressure valve" role for the oppressed of the world.

A. Balance of Power

Middle East has largely been in disarray throughout the past century under Western hegemony. The effects are clear in Europe with the spill over of refugees from Syria.

Balance of power during the bipolar war was a stabilizing factor. Short of that and with the absence of hegemony, more refugees are bound to Europe in times of crisis.

Balance of power in the Middle East will never work when there is no balance of power among East and West. And there has not been one since the dismemberment of the Soviet Union, nor a hegemony since the invasion of Iraq by the US.

Since then, and since the coming of the Erdoğan regime in 2002, Turkey has become the only country in the Middle East that can prevent wars between two nations. It already flexed its muscles twice to display its military and economic capacities and political will power.

In 2018, when Saudi Arabia, Bahrain, UAE and Egypt threatened to overthrow the regime in Qatar, Turkey interfered, and cool heads prevailed. Again, in 2018, second refugee crisis from Syria was prevented single handedly by Turkey, working with Russia and Iran.

In the 21st century, it is no longer the question of if Turkey were to act as a balance of power in the region. More independent Turkey with a dominant economy and military is already making selective forays across the region and more so around its border regions. So far, no other power is willing or able to stop its limited and measured attempts.

But what is not sure how far should Turkey interfere to the problems of the Middle East. Also, how selective it should be and how the West should align with Turkey and fast! After all, the Middle East is more like a place where a never-ending big family infighting continues until a big brother interferes.

In the absence of the US hegemony, and absence of a balance of power between East and West in the world at large, disarray will continue to be the norm for the foreseeable future as a legacy of the West.

B. Pressure Valve

Turkey relates to many countries through common history and religion.

Turkey, with its resources, can and must play the role of "pressure valve" for the Muslims of the world, otherwise the mass of humanity by 2030 will be even more difficult to manage. Time is now to regulate the growth and march of Muslim waves towards the West.

a— Pressure valve works when history matters

Turkic historic ties go back 2000 years. Many Turkic states ruled much of Asia and Europe for centuries at a time. The last one, the Ottomans were on three continents and more than six centuries. Approximately, one out of four countries today listed at the United Nations lived at one time under Turkish suzerainty. Most cherish their history with modern Turkey of today.

Currently, there are six other independent Turkic nation-states, all sharing the same historic heritage with Turkey. They are Azerbaijan, Northern Cyprus Turkish Republic, Kazakhstan, Uzbekistan, Turkmenistan, Kyrgyzstan. Turan, meaning a Turkic union, is the word that unites them all. Today, these seven have set up varying relationships among them, increasing their exposure and cooperation in many areas. Military exchanges or joint projects are also becoming significant.

Beside these independent countries there are also autonomous Turkic States across Europe and Asia: Republic of Nakhichevan, Republic of Tuva, Republic of Tatarstan, North Ossetia (Alayna) Federal Republic, Crimean Autonomous Republic Tatar Autonomous Administration, Adige Federal Republic, Altai Republic, Bashkiria Federal Republic, Saha (Yakut stan) Federal Republic, Karakalpak Turks and Karakalpak stan, Kara cay-Circassian Republic, Kabardian-Balkar (Malka) Republic, Sin can/Uighur Autonomous Region (Eastern Turkistan), Republic of Chechnya, Chuvash stan, Dagestan Republic, Gagauz (Gokoguz), Hakas People and Hakasia (Hakas Republic), and Hakas Federal Republic.

Furthermore, there are Turkish communities around the world: Western Thrace Turks, Bulgaria Turks, Kosovo Turks, Macedonian Turks, Afghanistan Turks, Ahiska Turks, Derbent Turkmens, Khazar and Karay people, Turks living in Idyll-Ural Region, Caucasus Turkmens, Kaskay Turks, Sanjak Turks, Kumuk Turks, Melancon People, Turks in Mongolia, Aright People (Altai Turks), Nogay Turks, Turks living in Romania, Turks living in Iraq, Iranian Turks, and Turks living in Syria.

Finally, there are bulk of emigrants mainly living in Western Europe. There are millions of them in Germany, Netherlands, Belgium, Switzerland, UK, Italy, and France.[12]

Turkic pressure valve works in many parts of the world when Turkey interferes. It happened in the dismemberment of Yugoslavia. It also worked in the Caucasus when Chechens and others were fighting the Russian Federation. It certainly worked in Cyprus when Turkey separated two Cypriots, splitting the island into two separate entities. Turkey helped stopped the bloodshed in Nagorno-Karabagh. It is doing military incursions in northern Iraq and northern Syria to save Turkmens from the wrath of Kurdish militia known as PKK and YPG. It also works to a certain degree with Turkic minorities within Russia and China without interfering with the domestic affairs. Much more can be done, but Turkey's role clearly makes difference to prevent wars.

b— Pressure valve works when religion becomes an issue

Religiously, Turks connect with even larger masses around the world. The Ottomans were the last Muslim empire that not only protected the Muslim religion but also expanded it. It was an empire of the Sunnis which made up more than 90 percent of the Muslims.

---

[12]   https://www.turksoy.org/en/turksoy/about

Turkey is a Sunni Muslim majority country. Today, it plays a leadership role among the biggest segment of Muslims, numbering more than one billion people. Soon they will go over two billion. Turkey, with resources, and especially with Erdoğan regime in place, can motivate and rally most of these Muslims to varying degrees.

Turkey demonstrated its capacity, coupled with the political will power of the Erdoğan regime. When the Trump Administration declared Jerusalem as the capital of Israel, Turkey was not only able to convene the Organization of Islamic Conference (OIC) and the General Assembly of the United Nations and pass resolutions condemning the unilateral US declarations. Turkey went even further and countered them having majority of countries by big margin declaring Jerusalem, the capital of the Palestinians. With these initiatives Turkey also served as a pressure valve and prevented upheaval turning into violence when hysteria takes over.

The plight of the Raghavan Muslims in Burma is another example. Erdoğan repeatedly kept their cause in the news and continues to do that.

Turkey in 2018 became one of the biggest humanitarian donor countries in Africa. Turkey in the past few years established relationships with nearly all countries in the dark continent, approximately half of them have Muslim heritage, making them feel kinship with Turkey.

As described by the wife of a British ambassador in the 1800s, posted in Istanbul, "the Turks live the life a different way than the Westerners or Easterners and for sure much different than how the Middle Easterners or Africans live."

Yet there will always be Voltaires who would hate the lifestyle of the Turks. It is a matter of taste and other factors. Such people exist everywhere.

But for lots of Muslims, modern Republic of Turkey is a symbol of rising modernity, but also significant economic prosperity and military strength that have tangible and intangible ripple effects on them.

Strong Turkey with a progressive Erdoğan regime is simply a form of pressure valve for large Muslim masses that are naturally aggravated by the likes of Voltaires who would always show disdain towards Turks and for that matter Muslims in general.

3. American cards

Turkey replicated two of them

Turkey has nowadays a navy, like the Blue Navy of the US in the early 1900s. It has TV series making big ratings in more than 60 countries around the world. But it does not have a mighty dollar like the US has.

These three cards made the US a superpower.

Turkey has two of the three.

They should make Turkey a domineering regional power.

And it already is.

A. The Navy

Naval power played a big role to project the US economic might worldwide. Theodore Roosevelt was the second of three Republican presidents with a vision to project US power beyond borders to far reaches around the world. He figured to use the US Navy. He started to articulate a theory that America's greatness depended on the robust deployment of sea power.

As president for nearly eight years, Roosevelt strove tirelessly to develop the navy as the "big stick" of an increasingly ambitious U.S. foreign policy. Working with Congress and the service itself, he increased the size, armament, amour, speed, efficiency, and overall capacity of the Navy and its vessels. The squadron system gave way to modern fleets, with coaling stations.

Roosevelt deployed naval assets to cultivate American power, including in 1903, when he sent naval vessels to ensure that Panama would secede from Colombia—paving the way for the Panama Canal, which enabled the US Navy to concentrate its battle fleets quickly.

Shortly thereafter, he earned a Nobel Peace Prize by successfully mediating the end of the Russo-Japanese War in 1905 at the Portsmouth Navy Yard with the deft support of key Navy assets.

Roosevelt's deployments culminated in the cruise of the Great White Fleet, sixteen battleships of the Atlantic Fleet that sailed around the world between December 1907 and February 1909—sending a clear signal that the US had global reach and ambitions.

Roosevelt's legacy as a naval strategist is linked closely to the rise of the U.S. as a great power. More than any other individual, he was responsible for creation of the modern, blue-water U.S. Navy and its deployments to promote an ambitious foreign policy—in the Caribbean, Asia and ultimately in Europe.[13]

Roosevelt sought to demonstrate growing American military power and blue-water navy capability. Hoping to enforce treaties and protect overseas holdings, the United States Congress appropriated funds to build American naval power. Beginning in the 1880s with just ninety small ships, over one-third of them wooden and therefore obsolete, the navy quickly grew to include new modern

---

[13]   http://www.theodoreroosevelt.org/site/c.elKSIdOWIiJ8H/
b.8344389/k.75CD/The_Naval_Strategist.htm

steel fighting vessels. The hulls of these ships were painted a stark white, giving the armada the nickname "Great White Fleet" John Mack Faragher [et al.] Out of Many: a history of the American People. Prentice Hall, 2012. p. 574.

a— Win some lose some Turkish naval history

Turks learned over many centuries the importance of having naval power and employing it smartly. Both the Ottoman Empire and the modern Republic of Turkey have significant naval victories and defeats that determined the fate of the 16th and 17th Turkish states, respectively, in history.

In the 16th century, the Ottoman Empire decided to become a naval power in the Mediterranean Sea. It built a formidable navy. But at the naval battle of Lepanto, Holly League navies defeated the Ottomans to end the dream.

The Ottomans rebuilt their navy quickly. In 1571, they embarked to take the island of Cyprus from the Venetians and they did. The conquest of Cyprus meant controlling eastern Mediterranean. During the Ottoman reign, when Cyprus was in the Ottoman hands, Egypt was also in the Ottoman control. Soon entire Mediterranean Sea practically turned into an Ottoman lake.

Then Sadr Azam of the Ottoman Empire, what is a prime minister of today, stated that "when they defeated our navy, it was like they shaved our beard, but when we took Cyprus, we actually cut their arm."

Cyprus remained under Turkish rule until 1878 when Great Britain assumed the provisional administration of Cyprus. In 1914, when the Ottoman Empire entered the First World War, Cyprus was unilaterally annexed by Great Britain.

Turkey returned to the island and took one third of it in the northern section where Turkish Cypriot community was in majority, a century later in 1975.

Currently, Turkish navy has a formidable presence in its surrounding Black, Aegean, and Mediterranean seas. The next step would be a Theodorian step forward and to send the Turkish navy away beyond the region.

b— Turkish navy in the 21st century

After two decades into the 21st century, Turkey is at a crossroad and knows the vital importance of 'Navy First', like Theodore Roosevelt discovered almost exactly a century ago.

History in their mind and the role of the US Navy vividly impacting the international policies in their region, Turkey concludes the role and future of its navy, accordingly.

Turkey has a three-prong approach to materialize it. One, via submarines that can stay under water longer periods. Two, with flattops that can project air power and facilitate troop deployments or humanitarian help. Three, with more sophisticated and powerful destroyers, frigates and corvettes, and superfast attack and patrol boats that navigate well in seas in the region and beyond.

Turkey since 2000s has increased development of indigenous ship building industry and has already built numerous navy vessels on its own with the latest technology, power projection, stealth capabilities and speed. Next in line are: first of two flattops, first of four frigates and first of six submarines to be launched in 2019.

The rest to be completed by 2023 with additional large and smaller platforms to give the navy capabilities in Red Sea, Persian/Arabian Gulf, and Indian Ocean, as well as far reaches of the Mediterranean beyond the island of Crete.

Currently, Turkey has the biggest and most powerful navy in the eastern Mediterranean Sea. In 2019, Turkey flexed its muscles in the sea and conducted two naval exercises within two months. First was called "Mavi Vatan," meaning Blue Homeland, encompassing 463 thousand kmsq. It was a mammoth undertaking with 103 warships. The next one was even bigger covering the same territory with more than 150 warships. The exercise was conducted in three surrounding seas at the same time. No military exercise in such scale has ever taken place in the region to date.

B. Motion pictures

Hollywood was good for the US economy, same as the US Navy was. But that was the first half of the last century. By 1980s, Hollywood was no longer helping the US image outside. Rather it was depicting many ills of the American society.

Hollywood lost even more and faster when other countries began investing into their movie industries, capitalizing on the decaying image of the Hollywood. The vacuum was filled by numerous countries from Britain to India, China, Japan and S. Korea.

Turkey also made progress. Turkish TV series took off. Today, more than sixty countries prefer Turkish soap operas or historical series. They help spreading the Turkish brand in 135 countries, in last count.

a— Hollywood

Hollywood propelled the US power abroad expanding the American culture across the world. The effect of the US movie industry to the growth of the US economic and military power cannot be ignored. People around the world learned about the American way and wanted to imitate it with American products. Coca Cola sold more. Marlboro sold more. So did American cars.

i - American Westerns and WWII Movies

Hollywood grew big with American Westerns. They glorified American life and values all around the world with cowboy movies. "Spaghetti Westerns" were great images, like nothing else in the world. It was all good.

Then came the WWII movies that glorified the American power and might. People learned more about the American values and deeds. With these positive images, the world welcomed America and Americans.

Then came the other war movies from Vietnam and Iraq, and other movies depicting US soldiers in dire straits like in Somalia. Hollywood was no longer adding to the American cause, rather they were hurting the American banks and franchises because they were soft targets for terrorists who hated American capitalism.

ii— Soap Operas and Other Social Issue Topic Movies

It was the same story with other Hollywood movies and TV series. Some were great to promote American ideals and good life, including American exceptionalism.

But when Hollywood turned to show the American greed and vanity, people around the world reacted accordingly. These movies were now hurting the American brand.

In short, Hollywood first contributed positively to the great American image, only to kill that same image in the latter part of the last century as fast.

b— Turkish TV series

The Turkish series have attracted great interest in many markets, especially in the Middle Eastern countries but also in the Latin American markets. Reportedly, they air in more than 135 countries and they are second to US series, bringing increasing export earnings expected to become billion-dollar industry soon.

While the selling price of the USA's most expensive series in the Middle East was about thirty thousand dollars, reportedly, Turkish series started to sell for four times of that.

In particular, the series that contain Ottoman and Turkish culture such as "Resurrection Ertuğrul" and "Payitaht Abdülhamid" are great examples to promote Turkish culture to the world.

The Resurrection, for example, depict the Seljuk and Oghuz Turks, recent history of Turks in Anatolia. It appeals to large swaths of Muslims and non-Muslims. They enjoy them because they are familiar with the story lines.

Turks come up with original stories that their Western counterparts would not touch because they would not have big audiences for them in the West.

In other words, Turkish TV series first make the story lines popular in local markets nearby where they will be well received. After that, they expose them to other markets, mainly with the likes of Netflix, You Tube, and others, increasing their popularity even further, expanding Turkey brand.

C. Mighty Dollar

Dollar is the last of the American cards, but Turkey does not have a replica.

Dollar may no longer be mighty as it used to be, but nonetheless it is still in a class of its own. That is why the US continues to be the only superpower in the world while everybody else can pretend to claim other prizes, including Turkey.

a— Mighty Dollar made US a superpower

Rule of Dollar allowed the US to become a superpower, and still dominates and will continue to remain the major monetary currency for the world as we know it.

In World War II, much as it had during World War I, the U.S. benefitted from its late entry into the fray. It spent much of the early part of the war shipping exports to the allies and collected much of their gold as payment. After the war, it was impossible to reconstitute the gold standard mostly because the U.S. owned almost all the world's gold.

So instead of basing the world monetary system on gold, the advanced economies based their currencies on the U.S. dollar. The dollar was still linked to gold, meaning foreign government central banks could, in theory, redeem exchanged dollars for U.S. gold whenever they wanted. Under this system—the post-war arrangement known as Bretton Woods—the exchange rates to the dollar were fixed at a certain price, but there was some leeway for devaluation if necessary.[14]

---

[14]   https://www.theatlantic.com/business/archive/2014/11/
how-the-dollar-went-from-a-simple-bank-note-to-the-worlds-currency/382725/

b— *Then it became a universal currency*

All countries agreed for the Dollar to become the universal currency simply because of the size of the economy which at one time was half the planet's economy.

Furthermore, under the Bretton Woods system, most countries exported more than they imported. As a result, they ended up with growing piles of dollars. They needed a place to put these dollars. The only financial market big enough to absorb them was the market for U.S. Treasury securities. In other words, these countries were all lending money to the U.S.

That encouraged the U.S. to run large deficits and build up its foreign debt. Eventually foreign lenders began to doubt, rightly, whether it could cough up all the gold they were theoretically entitled to. That's why president Richard Nixon snipped the last strand of a linkage between gold and the U.S. dollar in the early 1970s.[15]

c— *Nowadays, it declines in currency reserves*

The U.S. dollar's share of currency reserves reported to the International Monetary Fund fell in first quarter of 2018 to a fresh four-year low, while euro, yuan, and sterling's shares of reserves increased, according to the latest data from the International Monetary Fund.

The share of dollar reserves shrank for five consecutive quarters as the greenback weakened in the first three months of 2018 on expectations faster growth outside the United States and bets that other major central banks would consider reducing stimulus. Still the dollar has remained the biggest reserve currency by far.

Reserves held in U.S. dollars climbed to 6.499 trillion dollars, or 62.48 percent of allocated reserves, in the first quarter. This compared with 6.282 trillion dollars, or 62.72 percent of allocated reserves, in the fourth quarter of 2017. The share of U.S. dollar reserves contracted to its smallest level since reaching 61.24 percent in the fourth quarter of 2013, IMF data released late on Friday showed.[16]

---

15   https://www.theatlantic.com/business/archive/2014/11/
      how-the-dollar-went-from-a-simple-bank-note-to-the-worlds-currency/382725/
16   https://www.cnbc.com/2018/07/01/reuters-america-u-s-dollar-
      share-of-global-currency-reserves-fall-further-imf.html

d— Lately it was weaponized to its own detriment

There have been efforts to replace the dollar as the reserve currency for some time—China even blamed the dollar's international role as one of the causes of the financial crisis in 2008. The problem is that no other currency has stepped forward as a good replacement.

What's changed? The weaponization of the dollar by Washington.

When Trump re-imposed sanctions on Iran last week, he warned that any company doing deals with the Iranians in dollars would also be subject to sanctions. Several Russian companies are also under U.S. sanctions. Lavrov said Russia already uses local currencies in trade with China and Iran and that several other countries are also thinking about doing the same. China has been active in setting up trade deals in its own currency, the renminbi. "I strongly believe that abuse of the role the U.S. dollar plays as an international currency will eventually result in its role being undermined," Lavrov said.[17]

e— It was also undermined with Euro

The dismal performance of the Turkish lira (down 38 percent to the U.S. dollar in 2018) and the Russian ruble (down 14 percent) is strong evidence of how even relatively low-octane U.S. sanctions or the threat of harsher ones can hurt an economy. But could the U.S. be going too far with the weaponization of its economic advantage? Could its aggressive use of sanctions end up undermining the dollar's global dominance?

To listen to the loud noises coming from Ankara and Moscow, that's exactly what's happening. "We are preparing to trade in our local currencies with the countries that we have the largest trade volume such as China, Russia, Iran, and Ukraine," Turkish President Recep Tayyip Erdoğan said in response to the U.S. administration's doubling of import tariffs on Turkish steel and aluminum and personal sanctions against Turkish officials. Russia, Turkey and Iran aren't strong enough to challenge the U.S. dollar's dominance.

Both Russia and Turkey have dramatically reduced their U.S. debt holdings in recent months, but that was a mosquito bite to the U.S. since their investments were dwarfed by those of countries such as China, Japan, and Brazil. It's even harder for them to shift a global paradigm in which most trade—theirs, too—is invoiced

---

[17]   https://www.forbes.com/sites/charleswallace1/2018/08/14/
are-russia-and-china-trying-to-kill-king-dollar/#181f72b87948

in dollars. They simply don't have enough pull to change this. Shifting trade from dollars to euros would create a new dependence on Western democracies.[18]

f— China's Renminbi into play but with not much pull

That pretty much leaves China, as interested as the three mavericks in undermining what it sees as the dollar's unfair advantage. Despite having raised the renminbi's share of its trade settlements from zero in 2010 to 25 percent in 2015 and making it the second most popular currency in the world for trade finance (ahead of the euro), China faces an uphill battle in winning global share for its currency. In June 2018, according to Swift, the payment facilitation service, the renminbi's share of global payments reached 1.81 percent compared with 39.35 percent for the dollar.

For now, the Trump administration can act with impunity, imposing sanctions right and left: Even China's enormous pull isn't enough to get the anti-dollar bunch where it wants to be—in a world where the U.S. is powerless to punish them economically.[19]

---

[18]   https://www.bloomberg.com/view/articles/2018-08-20/
      dollar-power-turkey-russia-iran-can-t-go-alone-on-currency.

[19]   https://www.bloomberg.com/view/articles/2018-08-20/
      dollar-power-turkey-russia-iran-can-t-go-alone-on-currency.

CHAPTER THREE

ERDOĞAN

Since the turn of the Millennium, Turkey is identified with one man.

Recep Tayyip Erdoğan.

He came to power in 2002.

He leads the Justice and Development Party, aka AK Party (AKP).

Since then Erdoğan won more than a dozen successive elections.

Today, he continues to be in power as the president of the country.

He is projected to remain president until 2028.

By then, Turkey is expected to become top five economy and military in the world.

He is now considered the most accomplished of all twenty-seven previous leaders of the republic.

His legacy may even equal the founder of the republic, Gazi Mustafa Kemal Ataturk.

I. Gazi Mustafa Kemal Ataturk and Recep Tayyip Erdoğan

Modern Republic of Turkey was founded by Gazi Mustafa Kemal Ataturk in 1923.

He was president until his passing in 1938.

Successive Turkish leaders kept the republic intact until Erdoğan arrived.

They were all Muslims, governing a secular republic.

Once they were elected to their post, they also became part of the establishment.

Most came from margins of the society or Anatolia.

Erdoğan is no exception.

He is now part of the Turkish establishment.

He is a pious Muslim.

He is governing a secular state.

1. Pre-Erdoğan Years 1923-2002

Leaders in Turkey came to power with popular vote and left in free and fair elections

The path from Ataturk to the arrival of Erdoğan took three cyclical periods.
A span of ninety years was full of tests and trials and transformations.
From separation of 'church and state' to liberal economy to the political Islam.
In the first cycle, Ataturk led the revolutionary republican leaders.
Second cycle was the democratic period and lasted thirty years.
Third period was progressive.
That is when openly Islamist leaders became prime ministers.
One even became president of the country.
Turkish Armed Forces remained the guardians of the secular state throughout.
When three cycles are completed, secular Turkish state was at peace with itself.
It was also more democratic.
It was ready for the Erdoğan regime.

A. The revolutionary leaders 1923-1950

The period began with Ataturk. He became president in 1923 and stayed until his passing in 1938. He ruled the early days of the modern republic under Republican People's Party (RPP). He has become the eternal leader of the country, beloved by most.

Before his passing he tried once to switch from one party control to multi-party system. When he realized that the country was not ready, and would fall into chaos, he switched back to business as usual until the time was right.

He was not there to witness the maturity of his country in 1950 when it switched to the multi-party system. He died young. Some would argue he would have been proud to see the progress Turkey, becoming a perennial power. Some others wished he had lived longer to bring the country to parity with the civilized nations of the West sooner.

After his passing Ismet Inonu became the president. He kept Turkey out of WWII. There were shortages. He imposed wealth tax. He was no longer popular. A movement on the right began and Democrat Party was formed under Adnan Menderes to challenge the reign of RPP.

B. Status-quo leaderships 1950-1980

Secular republic gave a survival fight during a thirty-year cycle called "democratic process."

In 1950, Adnan Menderes came to power as the leader of the Democrat Party with US support. The popular vote ended the reign of the People's Republican

Party after twenty-seven years. He became the prime minister. The country entered into multiparty system for good. Menderes, with US backing, seemed to follow a path to prosperity. But soon, he felt he was no longer independent. And he decided to change course and tried to look for alternatives in the international arena.

Menderes paid dearly for his mistakes. He was hanged in 1960 after a coup d'état, reportedly with the help of the US inspired agents. In a sense, in the age of bipolar world, a country with such strategic location and role to play had no place to become independent. After all, Menderes had chosen to waiver only few years after the country was admitted to NATO when Stalin, then the leader of the mighty Union Soviet Socialist Republics (USSR) had planted his eyes on fledgling Turkey proper.

Next series of Turkish leaders like Suleyman Demirel and Bulent Ecevit, two of the most prominent and longest serving prime ministers, were in a sense succumbed to the difficulty of handling the democratic process. The chaos and anarchy in Turkey went through the roof during their reign. The Turkish Armed Forces interfered again in 1971 when country was totally broke.

Some argued that the Turks never learned how to govern themselves in a democratic environment. Some others justified the domestic governance problems for being in a difficult neighborhood. The countries in the Middle East and in the Balkans were under autocratic rules. To have a democracy between two regions where two world wars had started, and nuclear war exchanges came close to taking place when no one had heard about democracy sounded like a suicide to many.

In the ensuing years, when more than thirty people were dying a day because of the so called left and right terrorism, it was the worst of times. Chaos and anarchy took their toll and brought the fledgling republic to the eve of dismemberment. Yet, no one in the country had understood at the time that that was part of the process. Afterwards, it is widely reported that the international forces in conjunction with some among the Turkish establishment were fabricating conditions ripe for the third coup d'état.

In September 1980, a coup d'état promptly ended the democratic experiment in Turkey. It suddenly gave the country a breathing space. The plan behind the coup was to bring to power the Islamists against the growing communist danger emanating from the "evil empire" Soviet Union, then as the US president Ronald Reagan put it. Though the goal of the brilliant US inspired planners and their Turkish co-conspirator were to play the Communism card, they apparently never realized or did not care that they were turning the country to its legitimate rulers, Erdoğan like Islamist regimes of the future, and for good.

C. Out of box leaders 1980-2002

This period was dominated by two Islamist leaders.

The first, Turgut Ozal, eased into official leadership carefully and tenderly. He paid attention to optics. He was a pro-American politician with strong religious convictions. He immediately passed bills lifting the commonly known 163 and 164, limiting religious expression in the country. Yet, Ozal was not an open or active advocate of religious community. He knew his place in history. He was an Islamist, but he did not need to rub it in.

The second was Necmettin Erbakan. He was altogether opposite of Ozal. He assumed the role of going out bluntly, stating what everybody knew all too well. He was an Islamist leader and preached it openly and actively. It was a remarkable time in history for the secular republic, tolerating a leader attacking to the very principles of the republic. Nonetheless, he was peacefully hurried to leave his post to his co-habitant.

Erbakan was prime minister only one year where as Ozal remained in power for a decade. The establishment was able to tolerate Erbakan only a short period where as Ozal was embraced because these two leaders in a sense were fulfilling their role in history. While Ozal was getting the Islamists through the door for the first time, Erbakan was celebrating openly and happily once inside even if it was for very brief period.

At the end, these two Islamist leaders played their role in the rise of political Islam in Turkey as they should have played. Some would say it was choreographed. The first Islamist would ease the fears of the general public and act like if he is part of the establishment while the next would assert the identity of their purpose.

In summary, the pious Turks of the 1950s were finally in power and the establishment was tolerating them.

2. Erdoğan years: 26-year uninterrupted journey

The longest serving leader of modern Turkey
It starts when AK Party wins the national elections in 2002.
It lasts until 2028.
It includes pre-presidential period from 2002-2018
It also includes presidential period 2018-2028.
Erdoğan took the country for a referendum in 2018.
People approved the switch from parliamentarian to the presidential system.
The vote was 51.41 percent for the change.
In the ensuing presidential elections, Erdoğan received 52.5 percent of the vote.

AK Party also won most representatives in the Grand National Assembly of Turkey. President Erdoğan has since the required minimum majority to pass bills.

A. Transformation of Erdoğan 2002-2018

Erdoğan's AK Party came to power in 2002 when it won the first national elections that it entered. Since then, it did not lose another election. It won some by close margins that was enough to stay in power consecutive years until 2018.

Abdullah Gul became the prime minister in 2002. The third Islamist to reach the highest office. Gul regime was the time to fight if a fight was necessary from an Islamist perspective. Fight it was. The establishment had to tolerate for the first time in history of the republic an Islamist party coming to power with full majority.

Gul becoming prime minister also meant paving the way for Erdoğan to replace him next in 2003 as prime minister and for Gul to be appointed as a candidate for president in 2007.

Turkish Armed Forces reacted promptly with an email no less! First, when Erdoğan became prime minister in 2003 and again when Gul was elected president of the country in 2007.

Were they adopting to the changing times is open for debate? Optically, the military not leaving its barracks and sending a warning via email looked as if it was adopting to the times. To some it was also reflecting how the secular republic was maturing. It was an extraordinary development.

From Erdoğan's perspective, the goal was accomplished. The fights have been fought. Now it was the time to make peace with the rest of the country.

B. Starting another decade with Erdoğan 2018-2023

In 2018, there was a referendum in Turkey whether to replace the parliamentary system with presidential or not. People voted yes, despite coordinated campaign against it, coming also from the US and Western European sources.

Then, there was a presidential election. Erdoğan became the first president of the new system, never relinquishing his post. He will be at the helm until 2023. Until the centennial of the republic.

C. A new beginning with Erdoğan 2023-2028

Erdoğan is eligible for another term of five years as president. At this time, it looks like it is a sure bet that he will be reelected. Turkey has 2023 targets. If they are met, there is no way that Erdoğan will not be reelected. Chances are for those targets to be met are 1000 percent. Yes, they are one thousand percent. Most targets are expected to be completed long before—in the next two years or so, by 2020.

II: About Erdoğan

Erdoğan in his earlier years in power almost never made attribution to Ataturk.
Yet a decade later, he has solidified his tenure and concentrated his power.
He nowadays frequently addresses to Ataturk.
He gives him due respect when appropriate.
In a sense, he also became a mainstream political leader of the republic.
Ironically, he became part of the establishment Ataturk created.
Erdoğan is the fourth Islamist that rose to the highest echelons of power.
He became the master of the electoral process in the modern Republic of Turkey.
He has won more elections in a row than all his predecessors.
Hence, he became the epitome of the Islamist movement in Turkey.

1. Erdoğan became part of the establishment

Erdoğan came to power through electoral process in place.
Overtime, he became part of the establishment.
He followed a revolutionary path like Ataturk did and continues on the same path.

A. Erdoğan abided by the rules and norms

Erdoğan came to power in 2002, abiding by the rules and norms that were established long before he was around. He adhered and adopted the paths of his predecessors one step at a time. He proved himself to masses time and again, in many ways but primarily by winning successive elections that will keep him in power until 2023.

Since 2018, after he became the first president of the newly established presidential system, Erdoğan continues the same revolutionary path and acts as part of the establishment Ataturk started after they Young Turks first made name for themselves in the late 1800s with the same ideals.

B. Erdoğan is a revolutionary and part of the establishment

Revolutionary in the modern Turkish republic means being against the Ottoman empire. Yet this is only true because the republic replaced the empire out of necessity.

In reality, Young Turks and Ataturk were the officers of the empire that had no choice but to create a new Turkic republic when their Islamic empire was withering away.

How is Erdoğan different than any of them when he pursues similar Turkic path alongside being deeply entrenched into Islamic faith? Weren't Young Turks Muslims or pious? What about Ataturk? Didn't he want to keep Caliphate in place until the international system forced him to abolish it? Doesn't that make him a believer or in faith as much as anybody or like Erdoğan?

a— Erdoğan is part of the establishment

Erdoğan has become part of the so called modern Turkish establishment after nearly two decades in power. In modern Turkey, establishment means, adhering to the principles of Kemalism. It is the ideology of the founder Ataturk and consists of six pillars: Republicanism, populism, nationalism, secularism, statism, and reformism.

In 2018, to argue if Erdoğan is part of the old establishment or extension of it or an altogether a new establishment is not relevant. After all what is the modern Republic of Turkey? It is a revolutionary republic in progress.

b— Erdoğan will follow revolutionary path

Modern Republic of Turkey is almost a century old, and most successful, still enduring, and evolving socio-political revolution in the world today. For those in the know, if you are part of a socio-political revolution you are it, a revolutionary. So is Erdoğan, so long as there is the modern Republic of Turkey alive and kicking.

After ninety-five years since it was created, in 2018, the fact that the Republic of Turkey continues to evolve, and even in full throttle in the past two decades under Erdoğan regime, it is nothing more than a melting pot in full progress.

People are moving from villages to small cities, from small cities to bigger cosmopolitan centers, from the poor neighborhoods of the biggest cities to limelight, to prominence, to wealth, to political power. In other words, they are moving from the margins to where the action is into the so-called modernity, and in full blast.

In short, those, who were in the margins of yesterday, have all become the establishment of the new today.

2. Erdoğan is not the first or last Islamist president of Turkey

Erdoğan earned his way to leadership in a democratic system.

He lived in the margins throughout his early years.

He arrived at prominence after hard work and long walk.

He took the mantle of previous leaders from Ataturk to other Islamists.

A. He was not even in the margins

In the 1980s, when Turgut Ozal, the first ever Islamist that came to power as the prime minister and then president of the country, Erdoğan was beyond the margins of the modern Turkish society. He was living in one of the least desirable neighborhoods of Istanbul called Kasimpasa, much like the very early days of east end in New York City.

a— He moved to the margins

Erdoğan became part of the margins of the modern Turkish society in the 1990s when he entered local politics and rose to become the mayor of Istanbul. He was against the Turkish establishment then, that had abolished the caliphate in 1924.

Secular republic had replaced the religious Ottoman Empire and had left much of the population in the margins. The new modern Turkish society was emerging, only those with resources and proximity were able to witness and to taste it in some circles of the big cities, like Istanbul and Ankara.

Not until 2000s, most of the eighty million Turks did not have much opportunities to improve their lives. They were simply in the margins like Erdoğan was with limited opportunities.

After 2002, the fortunes of this "silent majority" improved. Erdoğan became prime minister in 2003. He was now able to take his followers to new heights. It was time to transform millions from margins to the mix of the society, living the good life. The republic was fast growing, maturing and prospering. He was able to empower them.

b— Erdoğan finally arrived after two decades

After two decades into the Millennium, a whole new generation of Turks were now in power, enjoying all the glamour and glitz that came with it. They were now no different than the establishment of the old anymore. They were it, like Erdoğan. They had finally arrived.

B. Erdoğan followed the tried path to success

Many Turkish prime ministers or presidents followed the same path to success. Who is to say that they were pious or Islamists or part of the establishment before they arrived?

In the modern republic, in Istanbul or Ankara, nobody was obligated to bring their piety into open. No one was requiring them to make their private lives public. They learned that in the secular modern Republic of Turkey, religion was a private affair. In the buildings of the secular state it was more apparent. Over there, they were witnessing what secularism was. The duality of the system and the lifestyle was before them to live, learn and enjoy.

What Emma Lazarus said, "Give me your tired, your poor, your huddled masses," she imagined the Statue of Liberty saying, "yearning to breathe free." In Turkey, this call applied to those yearning to come to Istanbul and to Ankara to become part of the establishment and witness this duality. In the countryside, the experience was not as clear because there was not much government institutions or universities where duality was most present.

Yet, they came to Ankara and Istanbul in hordes. But they kept their religious beliefs in check voluntarily. Even though, they knew they were to end up first in the margins in some of the roughest of all neighborhoods like Kasimpasa, where minorities like Jewish, Armenian, and Greek were also living. There they endured until their time came to become part of the newly being established modern Turkish society.

III. What Erdoğan is not

Erdoğan is not anti-secular or anti-Christ or anti-Ataturk.

He is not anti-Caliph either!

Yet he also did not claim at any one time that he wishes to be a Caliph.

At least not until yet.

1. Not anti-secular

During Erdoğan's first decade in power, public opinion in Turkey was against him.

Majority thought that he was to replace the republican regime with a religious order.

There were couple major signs for fear mongering to go hysterical.

One, Erdoğan was incarcerated for ten months by the Turkish military establishment.

He was considered too pious to become a leader of the secular republic.

Two, Erdoğan was against the Turkish media.

The media was bias about his religious views as too radical.

Public opinion about Erdoğan's intentions and purpose in the short term were off.

Erdoğan was not in power to replace the republican regime out right.

But he was for the modernization of the structure of the state.

Erdoğan accomplished both goals.

He consolidated the military power in July 2018 rather than replacing the regime.

He forced ownership change in Hurriyet, the admiral of the Turkish media earlier in May.

One before the presidential elections in June, the other right after.

There were no cries of wolf or protest of any kind formally, quietly, or violently.

Six months later, in Turkey everything was still business as usual.

Secular republic was intact and political Islam was continuing its role of governing. There was no visible or noticeable or real change in the country.

Nothing was like fear monger bullhorns made up to be.

Secularism was alive and well.

A. Pacification of the military

Erdoğan had to consolidate the government according to the Western European norms.

Two years to the day after an attempted military coup sought to oust him in 2016, Erdoğan moved to stamp his authority on Turkey's armed forces and issued a decree that put the general staff under the sway of the defense ministry.[20]

Erdoğan swiftly did exactly what the European Union wanted him to do! He happily put the Turkish military in civilian hands. The irony was that this was the same military that was in concert with the globalist Europeans who were hoping to see the coup d'état in Turkey would end Erdoğan's reign.

But Erdoğan was lot smarter than everybody else. He not only made the military less likely to revolt against his regime by putting it under civilian authority, but he also appointed the very four-star general, the Chief of the General Staff of the Turkish Armed Forces that was in charge during the coup d'état in 2016 as the Defense Minister in charge.

It was a brilliant move. General Hulusi Akar was from the "Dogu Kanadi" group of the Turkish Armed Forces (TAF). They were the favorites of the People's Republican Party (RPP), the main opposition party of Erdoğan, the "so-called"

---

[20]   https://www.ft.com/content/4e273880-8823-11e8-bf9e-8771d5404543

secularists of Turkey. He was also the choice of the most people in the country for the Minister of Defense.

More importantly, the self-appointed guardians of the secular republic within the TAF preferred someone from Dogu Kanadi at the helm. They tended to be less open to socialization with their foreign counterparts unlike the "Bati Kanadi."

Furthermore, it was the Bati Kanadi that was behind the 15 July 2016 failed coup d'état. They were the ones who were in bed with Fettullah Gulen (FETO), the cleric who is living in Pennsylvania and blamed by Erdoğan to be the culprit of the coup d'état. RPP and HDP, the Kurdish Party of Turkey were also their ally inside the parliament.

Akar, in short, on a good day, was supposed to have been favorite of FETO, RPP, HDP, and a secularist, hard-core opponent of the Islamists. Yet, he was Erdoğan's choice for the post, and it was a perfect union.

Erdoğan was simply showing how he could easily be open or tolerant to secularists.

Reportedly, Erdoğan as a great strategist had figured this dynamic right in the middle of coup d'état. Apparently, he let Akar stay with the revolting officers long enough to find out who were the conspirators afterwards.

True or not, it makes lots of sense, looking at the final results like a Monday morning quarterback.

B. Civilization of the free press

The other problem Erdoğan took an issue with was none other than the free press. He was in the belief that in order to have a civil society, there needed to be a civil discourse. The media in Turkey, according to the constituents of Erdoğan, were hysterical when an Islamist have risen in the polls or god-forbid came to power.

So, Erdoğan had prioritized long before 2002 that the first thing he was going to do was to go after Hurriyet, the admiral of the free press in Turkey.

Soon there was no more an issue to discuss except for the cry-wolfs among the Western media when it was reported that the "Dogan Media Group," the parent company of Hurriyet, was sold to a so-called pro-government Turkish conglomerate.

"It was a move widely seen as likely to further limit the independence of the Turkish news media."[21]

The West needed the free press in Turkey as an agent of change or control or influence. At least that is what Erdoğan thought about it. He simply thought that the concept of free press was an instrument to interfere internal affairs of Turkey.

---

[21]   https://www.nytimes.com/2018/03/21/world/europe/turkey-media-Erdoğan-dogan.html.

By 2018, Erdoğan knew all too well this was the last vestiges of EU or the US based anti-Erdoğan forces.

Yet in Turkey people knew what the transfer of ownership from the Dogan Group to the Demiroren Group meant.

Big nothing.

It was a common knowledge in Turkey that the Demiroren family was and is as secular or as religious as the Dogan family has ever been.

Furthermore, having lived in a progressive Erdoğan regime for nearly two decades and prospering throughout, everybody in Turkey has turned pro-government other than the "usual suspects" that made up about 49 percent of the country at any one time.

By the way, Ataturk also had his own 49 percent to deal with from time to time in his heydays!

C. The state is secular, but individual can be pious or Islamist

What is clear is the fact that Erdoğan never claimed that he is anti-secular. Not until he is to announce that he is anti-secular no one can claim that he is.

Like in the case of Ataturk, no one can claim that Ataturk was not as pious as any other Turkish prime minister or president that came to power in the secular republic before Erdoğan.

On one hand, all leaders of the modern Republic of Turkey were Muslims. They were all secular, simply because no one declared that they were anti-secular even though speculations were always abounded that some were.

No one would ever know, would they? After all, being atheist or pious is not a talking point. They are state of mind, way of life, private matters, practiced in one own's privacy.

On the other hand, it is widely believed the fact that secularism is the definition of the state, not the people, like Erdoğan argues regularly these days. He also argues that Ataturk also meant to say the same when he declared that the state is secular.

2. Not anti-Christ

Erdoğan is a pious Muslim.

Like all other Ottoman sultans were.

Like all prime ministers or presidents of the modern Turkish republic were.

He is not anti-Christ.

None were anti-Christ.

A. There is no anti-Christ Muslim Turk in Turkey

A Muslim Turk can never be anti-Christ because Islam does not permit it. In Christianity, the reverence may not be the same, but Muslims respect all prophets before Mohammed (SAV).

That is even more true for Sunni Muslims which most Turks are. As for the Ottoman sultans that hated the Christians when they were waging ferocious wars against them in the Middle Ages and beyond! Well, they were fighting religious wars. That's why those times were called the "Middle Ages."

B. Yet, Anti-Christ is said to come from Antioch, Turkey

There are biblical references that there is an anti-Christ in horizon, and it is from Assyria, which is thought to be Antioch, a city within the south eastern boundaries of Turkey proper of today.

> Isa 10:12 Wherefore it shall come to pass, that when the Lord hath performed his WHOLE WORK upon mount Zion and on Jerusalem, I will punish the fruit of the stout heart of the king of Assyria, and the glory of his high looks. Isa 14:25 That I will break the Assyrian in MY land, and upon my mountains tread him under foot: then shall his yoke depart from off them, and his burden depart from off their shoulders.

3. Not anti-Ataturk

Erdoğan is not anti-Ataturk.
Why should he be?
No smart leader would be.
He knows how to benefit having Ataturk on his side.

A. Erdoğan benefits from Ataturk

Erdoğan publicly acknowledges that Ataturk is the founder of the modern Republic of Turkey and he gives him due respect when appropriate. He visits his mausoleum and addresses or praises him no less no more than another Turkish leader that led the country in the past century had done.

a— Erdoğan takes hit for praising Ataturk

Yet no sooner Erdoğan brings his guard down, he finds himself not only he is attacked but much to the surprise of many he is also put together in the same basket with Ataturk.

A nineteen-year-old woman in Turkey's western province of Uşak was arrested on charges for insulting Mustafa Kemal Atatürk, the founder of the Republic of Turkey, and Turkish President Recep Tayyip Erdoğan, the Hürriyet newspaper recently reported.[22]

b— Erdoğan is for Kemalist principles

Much to the chagrin of many, Erdoğan is not an anti-Ataturk. On the contrary, Erdoğan ever continues to keep the vision of Ataturk alive and well. Six fundamental pillars of the Kemalism, Republicanism populism, nationalism, secularism, statism, and reformism, are in place, regularly reinforced, and reinvigorated where applicable by the policies of Erdoğan regime.

Development of the defense industry is a clear example of how statism is applied. Nationalism is always in full force with gigantic Turkish flags posted in unbelievably high flag polls in greater numbers every time one visits Istanbul and the rest of Turkey. The symbols of republicanism and secularism are everywhere. EU will attest how reformist Turkey has been since 1960 application for membership was submitted.

B. Erdoğan Marches to His Own Drum

There is a saying: "marching to the beat of your own drum." It is so true for Erdoğan. For example, as recently as, on November 2018, in a ceremony commemorating the 79th anniversary of the passing of Mustafa Kemal Atatürk, the founder of the Turkish Republic, President Tayyip Erdoğan delivered a speech which surprised many in Turkey.

Slamming those who said he usually referred to the founding father as Gazi Mustafa Kemal only, which means "war veteran Mustafa Kemal," without mentioning his surname "Atatürk," which means "Father of the Turks," until a short while ago.

---

[22] https://www.turkishminute.com/2018/11/15/young-woman-arrested-for-insulting-ataturk-and-Erdoğan/

Erdoğan said the following:

"Certain people are writing a lot of scenarios because we referred to Atatürk as Atatürk. If his name is Gazi Mustafa Kemal Atatürk, what could be more normal than calling him this?

Are we going to leave it [Atatürk's legacy] to the monopoly of those circles who are Marxist in rhetoric but fascist in soul?

We will not let an amorphous party like the CHP [the main opposition Republican People's Party] hijack Atatürk from our nation.'

'Our nation has an eternal respect for the Gazi. There is not the slightest hesitation concerning the respect of our nation for Mustafa. Our nation does not have the slightest problem with Kemal.

We know very well that our nation has no difficulty with the surname Atatürk, which itself gave him this surname.

So, why has there been a debate about it?

The answer is that those circles who favor coups, juntas, tutelage systems and who are hostile to the values of this nation have been trying to hide themselves under the guise of Atatürkism [the term usually used in Turkey for Kemalism]."[23]

4. Not Anti-Caliph, but Not a Declared-Caliph Either – Also Not YET!

A Caliph is a religious Muslim leader acting as a political leader.

The Caliphate is system of governance and a replacement for the electoral process.

It takes place where there is disarray, anarchy, calamity, and no hope of peace.

The Arab world of today seems to be the place where it may be most needed.

Turkey does not need it because it has had a well-functioning system in place for the last 100 years.

Egyptians first yearned for it in 1926 when Turkey abolished the Caliphate in 1924.

Nowadays a Saudi leader is bringing it up loudly and officially.

Does Saudi Arabia have a problem with governance and electoral process?

Or is it a mistake by a new leader desperate to hold on to power in the face of calamity?

---

[23] http://www.hurriyetdailynews.com/opinion/murat-yetkin/and-Erdoğan-praises-ataturk-122325

A. What is Caliphate and Caliph?

Caliph is a religious leader fulfilling a political role. Caliphate becomes the system of governance in the absence of electoral process for the appointment of the Caliphs.

a— Caliph

Caliph was the person acting in Muhammad (SAV)'s place after his death, i.e. Four Caliphs came in succession from 632 to 661.

Many people claimed to be a Caliph in modern history since it was abolished. They were all false prophets because last Caliph ruled between 1922 and 1924.

The Ottoman Sultan Selim called himself Caliph in 1517. Later sources claim that the Abbasid Caliph transferred his dignity to Selim I. In the 18th century the importance of being Caliph had grown stronger for the Ottoman Sultan and started to call himself the protector of the Muslim religion. Some influence did the Ottoman Caliph and Sultan have. With the fall of the Ottoman Empire, the Sultan held on to his title of Caliph for two more years, until his office was abolished in March 1924 by Atatürk.

b— Caliphate

The Muslim community faced problems of governance and appointment of leaders after Muhammed (SAV)'s passing in 632. Caliphate meant to fill the gap. The Rashiduns, the Ummawiyss, the Abbasids dynasties declared themselves as Caliphates and their leaders ruled as Caliphs from 661 until 1517. The Ottomans ended Arab hold to Caliphate when they conquered Egypt in 1517.

Caliphate in the modern times at best can fulfill the role Papacy plays in Vatican. If the Muslim community one day decide to do so, it becomes possible. The most logical place for Caliphate to reside would be its last residence. Istanbul was that place before Ataturk abolished Caliphate. Reportedly, Turkish parliament, then, never ratified his executive order.

So? It must still be active but abolished!?

B. Erdoğan never claimed to be a Caliph, nor does he need to

Turkey has a democratically elected functioning process for almost a century. Erdoğan came into a sophisticated system of governance and elections. He improved the system, making it effective further with a referendum in 2018. Turkish citizens voted 'Yes' and elected him the president of the new system.

Erdoğan is not anti-Caliph. No Muslim would be anti-Caliph. Caliphs are short of being prophets. They are mostly revered. Erdoğan is no different. He revers them like any Muslim would.

On the other hand, Erdoğan never declared, that he is a Caliph or wants to be one, but also not yet. Moreover, there are no plans to establish a Caliphate in Turkey or any other Muslim country where there is a functioning electoral process.

Implying that Erdoğan is a Caliph, wants to be Caliph, or will be a Caliph is an insult and disrespect for the pious and the 17th Turkish state. And Turks take notice of such insults and they never forget who makes such claims and would bring it up in due process.

C. Some Arabs Might Believe That They Need the Caliphate

The Arabs are in disarray. Like in the 7th century, Damascus is in flames. Desperation and calamity make people yearn for a higher power to save them. Like then and nowadays in Syria and Iraq where governance and legitimately elected systems demolished, people claiming to be Caliphs made appearances.

Some Arabic countries wish to have the Caliphate back ever since Ataturk abolished it in 1924. Egyptians tried to bring it back soon after two years.

The fact that some leaders in the Middle East and beyond who do not like Erdoğan and the power that he exercises as a domineering regional leader. They attack him for having ambitions to become Caliph. With that, they show how much they are worried from Erdoğan's power and achievements. Yet, their reference also reflects yearning a need for Caliphate to endure their own rule over Muslims to an extent.

a— The Egyptians

A congress in Cairo in 1926, that tried to reestablish the Caliphate, did not manage to succeed. Important Muslim countries did not participate, and the resolutions agreed upon did not result in real actions, even if they expressed to be in favor of a Caliphate. Since then nothing has been done much, due to nationalism in different countries. There are no more Caliphs around the world today.[24]

b— A Saudi

Mohammad Bin Salman (MBS), the Crown Prince of Saudi Arabia, refers to Caliphate and Caliph more often than most leaders in the Middle East. He gives the impression either he is yearning for something or something is bothering him.

---

[24] http://www.allaboutturkey.com/halife.htm

MBS, also recently, acquired new attributes like "complicit" after Saudi journalist Jamal Khashoggi was murdered and then dismembered with a "smoking saw!"

Before that MBS was also called, reportedly, a "conspiracy theorist," among other things.

i— A Conspiracy Theorist?

Could Mohammad Bin Salman (MBS) be one of these conspiracy theorists? He is calling Recep Tayyip Erdoğan "Caliph Erdoğan." MBS can be called a conspiracy theorist among other things as far as recent news coverages are concerned.

US Senators believe he is more than the Crown Prince of Saudi Arabia. After meeting with CIA director, Republican senators say Saudi Crown Prince Mohammed bin Salman is "complicit" in journalist's murder.

Recently, Saudi Arabia's powerful Crown Prince Mohammed bin Salman has described Turkey as part of a "triangle of evil" along with Iran and hardline Islamist groups, Egypt's Al-Shorouk newspaper reported on Wednesday, March 7, 2018.

The Saudi prince also accused Turkey of trying to reinstate the Islamic Caliphate, abolished nearly a century ago when the Ottoman Empire collapsed. His reported comments reflect Saudi Arabia's deep suspicion of President Tayyip Erdoğan, whose ruling AK Party has its roots in Islamist politics and who has allied his country with Qatar in its dispute with Saudi Arabia and some other Gulf states.[25]

ii— Confused on Islam?

In harsh but indirect remarks addressed to Saudi Crown Prince Mohammad bin Salman, Turkish President Recep Tayyip Erdoğan has said the Saudi official does not own the Islamic faith.

Speaking at a major investment conference in Riyadh on October 24, 2018 bin Salman had vowed to return Saudi Arabia to "a moderate Islam." President Erdoğan said after that that the notion that there was a "moderate" Islam and an "immoderate" one had been invented by the West to "weaken" the faith.

"The term 'moderate Islam' is being lathered up again,"
Erdoğan said in his remarks.
"The patent of 'moderate Islam' belongs to the West.
There is no 'moderate' or 'immoderate' Islam; Islam is one.

---

[25] https://www.reuters.com/article/us-saudi-turkey/
saudi-prince-says-turkey-part-of-triangle-of-evil-egyptian-media-idUSKCN1GJ1WW

The aim of using such terms is to weaken Islam."
"Perhaps the person voicing this concept thinks it belongs to him.
No, it does not belong to you,"
President Erdoğan said, without referring to Mohammed bin Salman by name.

While the official ideology in Saudi Arabia is Islam, an ideology known as Wahhabism is preached by government-sanctioned clerics in the country. That same ideology is practiced by the Takfiri terrorists wreaking havoc in the Middle East region and beyond, as well.

"They (the Saudis) say 'we will return to moderate Islam,"
but they still don't give women the right to drive.
Is there such a thing in Islam?
I guess they will give this right when they turn to the moderate one,"
Erdoğan said, jokingly.[26]

C. Back to Caliph Erdoğan

Would it be outrageous if Caliphate were to be officially reinstituted, some ask?

a— It is a bad idea if it is to replace secular Turkish state

If Caliphate were to mean getting rid of the secular republic, the system of governance and electoral process in modern Turkey then it is wrong because there is no need for Caliphate to come back on that role. There is a well-functioning system of governance and appointment of leaders in Turkey for a century.

Currently, in Iraq and Syria, the conditions are so atrocious that it may seem to some like it is the last hope and best way to find relief and peace. But not in Turkey. A country on a path to become the top five economy and military in the world does not need help from God, but it is good to have God within thoughts.

b— It is actually very good to have it for many other reasons

Having Caliphate actually makes dollars and sense. In the age of competitive economies, it can generate additional funds and economic activities.

For Turkey, actually it is a great idea. Turkey has the number one airline in Africa and Europe and equally competitive stand in Asia. Lots of tourists can make use of the airline to visit the "Caliphate City."

---

[26]   https://www.presstv.com/Detail/2017/11/11/541772/
Turkey-President-Erdoğan-Mohammad-bin-Salman-Saudi-crown-prince-moderate-Islam

i— The Vatican Is Making Lots of Money

The GDP of the Vatican is around 300 million dollars per year. The GDP per capita of the Vatican City citizens is around twenty-one thousand dollars per year. They are the 18th wealthiest in the world in last count.

Modern Caliphate, like the Holy See for the Catholics, makes sense. So long as life goes on forward like Ataturk foresaw it, based on Kemalist ideology with political Islamic regime fulfilling the desire of the majority, why not have a "Caliphate City" nearby. There are more than fifty other Muslim majority countries and nearly two billion Muslims that can cherish it.

Turkey entertained forty-million tourists in 2018. It became the sixth biggest destination in the world. With a Caliphate City there is no reason tourism not to double sooner than later. It will double anyway within five years. Turkey has the biggest airport in the world in Istanbul and one of the biggest airlines in the world which flies to more destinations than any other airline in the world. Surely, Turkey as a Caliphate seat can afford charitable donations to ensure that poor and huddle Muslim masses can also cherish what is theirs to enjoy in Istanbul.

ii— Hope for All the Fast-Rising, Oppressed Muslims

A Caliphate, together with Vatican, can fulfill the needs and aspirations of the world's soon-to-be eleven billion people. After all, governance and the electoral process cannot run everything. States have too much to worry about and to watch out for too. Human beings have their lives to live too.

At this time, an increasing number of countries are obliged to build walls to regulate the inflow of refugees. Having a Caliphate is not a problem. Having fast-rising numbers of Muslims turning into refugees when wars break out are everybody's problem.

The Erdoğan regime has already set itself up as a relief mechanism for Muslim masses across the world. Together with a Caliphate City, they can do wonders raising the spirit of masses.

iii— Only Erdoğan & Turkey, the "gamechanger" can do

Reportedly, there may be an argument that when Ataturk abolished Caliphate in 1924, the Turkish parliament never ratified the executive order. Hence, technically it may not have been abolished but optically, then, it was satisfactory to the Brits who needed a document to act on to subvert Muslims in the subcontinent where they were revolting.

Does Erdoğan have the right to reinstitute the Caliphate one day if he solely decides? Who knows what the Turkish constitution says, and what the conditions will be if, and when, a decision like that is to be taken?

Very successful Erdoğan can reinstitute Caliphate if he sees it fit solely because Caliphate was last in the hands of the Turks and it was in Istanbul. But the bottom line is, if someone were to be sanctioned to revive it, it is Turkey that would have the logical path to it.

Logic says!

IV. Who is Erdoğan?

Erdoğan is Islamist. No question about it.

Nothing is wrong with that. Nothing to worry either.

Being Islamist is no different than being a pious Jewish or Christian.

Lots of leaders in the world are pious, or Muslim, or Christian, or Catholic, or Jewish.

Erdoğan is also Turkic.

He envisioned 2023, 2053, and 2071 as milestones.

Muslims of the world cherish these dates.

But Turks also celebrate them as an achievement of their race.

Finally, Erdoğan is for modernity.

And he is realistic like most Turkish leaders have been.

How do you tell?

They survived. Didn't they? And now they are in global prominence.

1. Islamist

Erdoğan is the true, tested, trusted leader of political Islam in Turkey.

He defends it against everybody, every time, and everywhere like any pious should.

He does the same as a president of a Muslim country as well.

He knows all too well that the state that he leads is secular and republican.

He also knows that it is a Muslim majority country.

Erdoğan reacts promptly every time he hears someone oversteps the boundaries.

He does not discriminate when he criticizes.

A. Erdoğan's diatribe against a religious elite

Erdoğan is pious. He is Islamist but he is also against bigots.

a— Erdoğan calls religious preacher "illiterate"

The commandments of Islam can and will never change, President Recep Tayyip Erdoğan has said, amid criticism over his earlier comments on the necessity for an "update" of Islamic regulations.

"It is wrong for some individuals, who have no relation to the realities of life, to utter some words and confuse people. Nobody has the right to accuse our religion."

Erdoğan said at an event in Ankara on March 9, 2018.

He had criticized specific preachers on March 8, following Social Fabric Foundation head Nureddin Yıldız's controversial comments about violence against women.

"Women should be grateful to God because God allowed men to beat women and be relaxed."

Yıldız said on March 3 in a video posted online, stirring outrage.

Erdoğan also blasted Yıldız as "illiterate" on March 8, without directly citing his name.

"You cannot implement provisions dating back to 14th or 15th centuries … Carrying out the regulations and traditions of a specific society at a specific date can only spoil them," he said.

b. Erdoğan on Religious Reform

One day later, he underlined the importance of 'adapting' religious practices to current historical and social conditions.

"We do not seek reform in religion, which is beyond our capability …
Our holy Quran has and will always have words to say.
Its commandments will never change. But the independent reasoning derived from them, the developed rules and their implementation, will surely change according to time, conditions and possibilities,"
Erdoğan said.

Erdoğan also reiterated his call for the Directorate of Religious Affairs (Diyanet) to take a more active role in addressing the issue.

"I do not have the authority to speak on such matters. But as a president, as a Muslim, and as a person who has responsibility, I cannot tolerate such discord brought to my religion," he said.

"We cannot ignore the stain and the shadow that such people's random words about women and youths have brought to Islam. Nobody has the right to cause such confusion and caricature our religion as such."
he added.

"The understanding that tries to depict Islam as a religion closed off to change and the understanding that attributes deviancies
that have nothing to do with Islam to our religion only serve the same aim,"
Erdoğan said.[27]

B. Erdoğan reacts to criticism when he hires non-Islamists

When there were complains that Erdoğan was hiring non-Islamists over Islamists to his governments, he said that he was not looking for disciples for a Dervish order, he was looking for the qualified government officials.

Erdoğan continued his criticism saying that friendship with cause is an important matter.

"If you are committed for a cause with a friend,
then you go with that friend until grave, not until the marketplace.

Some of these people we started to walk with as friends.
They came with us until the marketplace
and then they suddenly jumped off the train.
This is not acceptable.
There is no deviation from the cause.

They say we are ignoring the Islamists,
and, in their place, we are bringing on board the non-Islamists.

In a political party, to separate people as Islamist and non-Islamist is not right.
We are not looking for disciples for a Dervish order.

In a political party one has to be honest, principled,
and one must love his nation and country,
and one must comply with the principles of the party.

---

[27] http://www.hurriyetdailynews.com/
centuries-old-islamic-provisions-cannot-be-implemented-today-Erdoğan-128491

But some decided on what is right and what is wrong on their own
and started to select people that adhered to their beliefs. Nobody has a right to judge
others like that. I don't have that right.

Don't bring the eternal life to the daily life in making judgements."

2. Turkic

Erdoğan and his followers like to refer Turkey as the "New Turkey."
In their view, Turkey is a rising power.
It has left behind the trappings of Ataturk's pro-western republic.
And they expect this power to emerge as a regional hegemon.
They are yearning for a restoration of the Turkish power that drives AKP today.

A. Erdoğan a nationalist like Ataturk

The party's Islamism has long been co-opted by its desire to adopt and own the state and its structures in Turkey. Having finally eliminated all his enemies—the "deep state," the secular military, and finally the Gulenists—Erdoğan has consolidated enough power to reshape the military, the bureaucracy, security services, and education.

But he has not fundamentally changed the core of Turkey's state philosophy or national security doctrine—he just put himself at the center of the decision-making process. AKP's earlier instincts to challenge the Kemalist republic's establishment views on Kurds, on relations with Europe, and democratization have long been replaced by complacency.

On most national security issues, AKP's outlook today is no different than the former secular establishment. The party has even lately embraced Ataturk as a symbol—referring to Turkey's founder as a savior who reversed western designs on dividing Turkey. AKP supporters like to draw a direct line from Ataturk to Erdoğan.

Erdoğan has walked away from the decade-long peace process with the Kurds (the separatist Kurdistan Workers Party, or the PKK) in 2015 and assumed hardline positions on the Kurdish question in general—not only inside Turkey, but in Syria and Iraq as well.

His speeches are peppered with praise for Turkish and Ottoman history and he now attends events like commemorations for the battle of Manzikert, which mythically opened the gates of Anatolia to Turkic tribes in 1071 and started its "Turkification" when Byzantium was defeated.

A decade ago, Erdoğan, the Islamist, would have had nothing to do with a ceremony glorifying Turkish ethnicity. Today, Erdoğan, the nationalist, is eager to witness the re-birth of the Turkish Empire.[28]

B. Turkic heritage

Turkish history starts with Great Hun Empire Teoman 220-216 BC, according to the official records of the republic. Followed by three other Hun Empires, namely West, European, and White. Gokturk Khaganate 552-745 established them in the Asian Steppes and allowed them to come across rising Muslim Arab Empires in Iran when they started to convert to Islam.

Another five empires followed suite—Avar, Hazar, Uygur, Krahanli, Gazne before Great Seljuk Empire ruled Anatolia from 1040 to 1157 when Byzantium was first defeated in the Battle of Manzikert in 1071, beginning the conquest of Anatolia.

While the Seljuk empire was eventually replaced by the last and the biggest Turkish empire, the Ottomans, the Turks formed another four empires, mostly in Asia, namely Harezmsahlar, Altin Ordu, Timur, and Babur.

The Republic of Turkey today is tied to all these Turkish empires, all sixteen of them. In short, Turkish history is the culmination of all 2238-year-old history. Give or take few years or decades.

Presidential Emblem of the Presidency of the Republic of Turkey reflects this reality formally. It is composed of a sun with eight long and eight short rays surrounded by sixteen stars; it is named "the Presidential Seal." The sun represents the infinity of the Republic of Turkey and the sixteen stars represent the sixteen independent great Turkish empires in history.[29]

Establishing many powerful states in history, Turkic people have made outstanding contributions to the development of human civilization. Turkic states played a crucial role throughout history in enabling political, commercial, cultural and societal communication and interaction from the East to the West, and from the North to the South in the Eurasian geography.[30]

---

[28]   https://www.hoover.org/research/Erdoğan-nationalist-vs-Erdoğan-islamist

[29]   https://www.tccb.gov.tr/en/presidency/seal/

[30]   http://www.turkkon.org/en-US/messages-from-the-founding-presidents/299/311

C. Seven Turkic states of our times

In present, there are seven independent Turkic states. They are Kazakhstan, Uzbekistan, Kyrgyzstan, Turkmenistan, Azerbaijan, Turkey, and The Turkish Republic of Northern Cyprus. The last one is created and recognized by Turkey at will in the 1970s when Turkey was at its weakest in economic and military strength, and the Western dominance in the region was most powerful.

Author Hugh Pope lived in Turkey many years, puts it in a perspective.

"Now with six different independent states
all trying to create new Turkic identities.
I call them Turkic; they would call it Uzbek or Turkman, but it is Turkic.

And even if you ask someone like President Nazarbayev of Kazakhstan
'What are you?' and he says,
'I am a Turk.'

And you look at him slightly oddly because Turk now means a citizen of Turkey.

He says,
'No, not like that.
We sent armies from here 500 years ago,
a thousand years ago, to conquer Turkey.
They married the local population, and now they're called Turkey.
But the real Turks are still here in Central Asia, and it's us.'"

D. Reinforcing Turkic heritage

It was a natural phenomenon that the Cooperation Council of Turkic Speaking States (Turkic Council) was established in 2009 as an international intergovernmental organization, with the overarching aim of promoting comprehensive cooperation among Turkic Speaking States. Its four founding member States are Azerbaijan, Kazakhstan, Kyrgyzstan, and Turkey the potential for common development amongst its member states.

Although it brings together a group of countries, the organization does not take an exclusive approach. On the contrary, by promoting deeper relations and solidarity amongst Turkic *speaking* countries, it aims to serve as a new regional instrument for advancing international cooperation in Eurasian continent, particularly in Central Asia and Caucasus.[31]

Uzbekistan will join the Cooperation Council of Turkic-Speaking States, Uzbek President Shaukat Mirziyoyev said on April 30, 2018 during Turkish President Recep Tayyip Erdoğan's official visit to the country.[32]

For the first time, in September 2018, Hungarian Minister of Foreign Affairs and Trade Peter Szijjártó took part in the meeting of Cooperation Council of Turkic-Speaking States as an honorable guest.[33]

Erdoğan summed it up where the Turks and Turkic people are standing, and they should be heading in his recent speech at the Turkish Conseil meeting in Kyrgyzstan. Describing the Turkic Council, which he said is the product of shared efforts, vision and dreams, as the symbol of a joint ideal, President Erdoğan stated:

"What today gathers us together is not only our language, history and culture but also, our desire and will to build a secure and prosperous future together. It is a must for us to join forces to advance our prosperity, succeed in our development attempts, and effectively deal with the problems we are faced with.

Emphasizing the importance, they attach to the Turkic Council working in coordination with the Organization of Islamic Cooperation, the Economic Cooperation Organization and other multilateral platforms, President Erdoğan said:

"In this regard, we also want the Council to obtain an observer status at the United Nations. Moreover, we also support the member states' efforts to deepen their cooperation with Euro-Atlantic organizations."

3. Modern

Erdoğan is living in the modern age, not in the past. His regime speeded up the rise of modernity and the role of Turkey in the world. It is reaching out to as many countries as possible around the world to demonstrate and share its economic and military achievements. It is also seeking cultural exchange and providing humanitarian aid when necessary.

---

[31]   http://www.turkkon.org/en-US/general_information/299/308
[32]   http://www.hurriyetdailynews.com/uzbekistan-decides-to-join-turkic-alliance-during-Erdoğans-visit-131109
[33]   http://kabar.kg/eng/news/ministerial-meeting-of-turkic-council-takes-place-in-bishkek/

Erdoğan movement in a sense in its second decade in power is no different than where the modern Republic of Turkey was heading in its early days when it was founded in 1923.

Simply put, since Erdoğan came to power, Turkish economy grew three times faster than it ever did before, making it one of the bigger economies of the world. Its military also ranks in the top ten and rising fast.

If past fifteen years is any indication, the presidential system Turkey adopted and made Erdoğan its first president will surely speed the economic and military growth trend. With that 2023 goals will surely be attainable for a greater Turkey.

The economy grew three times bigger. Bosporus has, first ever, two tunnels like Lincoln and Holland in NYC, and one more bridge like the Golden Gate in San Francisco, in the Bosporus alone, since Erdoğan regime came to power in 2002.

And that is only the tip of the iceberg. One of the world's longest bridges, Osman Gazi is already operational in the inner sea Marmara, while the world's longest is scheduled for opening in 2023 over the Dardanelles.

Comparatively, in the previous thirty years, Turkey was able to build only two bridges of equal grandeur over Bosporus. Divided highways were 200 kilometers long in total. Since 2002, 2000 more kilometers were added. There was no high-speed train system in the country. By 2018, there were 500 kilometers, and thousands more kilometers are under construction. Turkey will have the second longest network in the world after China by 2030. It will have nearly ten thousand km long high-speed network.

Export numbers and number of tourists visiting the country are other indicators of accomplishments for the Erdoğan regime. Modernity is not limited with these major projects but hundreds other local projects. Imagine a country where there is a hospital, university, stadium, airport within 100 kilometers to every corner and individual. Plus, each one of the eighty-one provinces of the country to have numerous other projects to display from green areas to rehabilitated zones in cities. Erdoğan regime is the sole builder of them all.

4. Realistic

Erdoğan knows all too well that the modern Republic of Turkey is not built in a day or by one person or will be led by one person forever.

It took a century to arrive to this point and with many leaders taking their turn with free and fair elections. There were twenty-seven prime ministers since 1923. In Turkey there were always narrow victories. No regime ever came to power by ever wining 60 percent of the vote.

Until 1950 during one party system when CHP/RPP ruled being exception, rest of the 20th century was a struggle for regimes to remain in power for a year or two on average. When Turgut Ozal regime came to power in the 1980s, it was the first time since Adnan Menderes regime of the 1950s after thirty years, a regime was able to stay in power for almost a decade.

Of course, all that changed when Erdoğan regime came to power in 2002. Since then Erdoğan won all elections, by a very slim margin. Him being called dictator, autocratic, Caliph is outrageous. He won every election in the past two decades but never like in any communist or other so called democratic or autocratic regimes.

In Turkey, no one came to power with 90 percent of the vote, not even with 60 percent. More often than not, the majority party in the Parliament received about 40 percent of the vote on the average. Winning elections when tens of political parties participating the race with wide ranging agendas, time and again coming on top with the biggest percentage is a hard-earned achievement anywhere at any category.

V. What the future holds

For those in denial, the future is bleak because they cannot stand Erdoğan.

For his loyal supporters, the future is very rosy.

For the rest: it is the same old, same old.

But the reality is Erdoğan is aware of his legacy.

That is what matters.

1. Worrying Too Much About Erdoğan Does Not Help

Worrying about Erdoğan too much does not help.

It is also not necessary.

In international relations, Erdoğan is a reactionary leader.

He reacts and counter-reacts as necessary.

He is much like Donald J. Trump.

He will counter punch if you punch him or if you are about to punch him.

He is "Kasimpasali."

He will not let anybody out-maneuver him.

Period.

What transpired in 2010 is a reaction?

When a Turkish entity came under attack, he reacted when people died on that ship.

So, he reacted much more forcefully than he might have perhaps!

But didn't he react when civilians were killed outright by soldiers?

Any leader would react when a civilian is killed by a soldier.

No solider of a modern country should be killing any civilian anyway.

It is the norm of modernity the West established for everybody to adhere, isn't it?!

A. Are they making too much about 2010 incident?

2010 marked a turning point for Turkey, according to an article published under "Turkey's transformation, Islam, nationalism and modernity" in *The Nation* magazine.

"For decades Turkey had been America's darling: a secular, democratic Muslim country that was both a member of NATO and an ally of Israel, with which it had signed a defense pact in 1996 and enjoyed close military and commercial ties.

Tensions had occasionally flared up over Cyprus, Iraq and the Kurdish and Armenian issues, and Ankara's courting of Russia, Syria and other Western bugbears had been a growing source of disagreement. But never, till this past May in 2010, had Turkey's fundamental orientation come into question. Then, in the span of a few weeks, Turkey became a black sheep."

Yes, Turkey was cast as a black sheep because it was then in the interest of powerful international groups to make it so.

Simply put, when a soldier kills a civilian, not to mention eight of them, including one Turkish-American aboard the lead ship in the flotilla, the Mavi Marmara, no matter what the circumstances are, not acceptable.

We all witnessed how "a military jury acquitted a decorated Navy SEAL of premeditated murder Tuesday in the killing of a wounded Islamic State captive under his care in Iraq in 2017, after another US soldier admitted the murder." Considering these seals were in a declared war zone, yet they are still questioned for their actions. It is the times we live in when a human life matters the most under any circumstances.

There has to be a pause when a civilian is killed with a military bullet. Period.

B. Has "Erdoğan turned Turkey eastward to a veritable revolution?"

Others insisted the West had nothing to do with it: they attributed Turkey's eastward turn to a veritable Islamist revolution, led by Recep Tayyip Erdoğan, the head of AKP and Turkey's prime minister.

"Gone, and gone permanently, is secular Turkey," wrote Michael Rubin in Commentary last summer. It has been replaced by an "Islamic Republic" that is our "enemy." Lest it pass American weaponry and intelligence along to "Hamas, Sudan, or Iran," he suggested, Turkey should be kicked out of NATO. He equivocated on this last point, but he wasn't kidding.

C. Are they taking too short a view of Erdoğan's Turkey?

"The underlying problem with these explanations is that Turkey's reorientation is simply the product of resentment or a revolutionary turn toward Islamism is superficial and to take too short a view.

Each contains a grain of truth: the former, that Turks resent being treated shabbily, as benighted supplicants at the altar of Brussels, and are angry about the destabilization of Iraq; the latter, that Erdoğan is a pious Muslim and a blowhard who sympathize publicly and sometimes histrionically with the plight of the Palestinians and likes to throw his weight around.

But to fixate on a few recent incidents and ascribe outsize importance to them is to imply too great and too sudden a change, and to cast the situation in too dire a light. Turkey's transformation has far deeper roots, and a far broader basis, than either of these pat explanations acknowledges, and it is not intrinsically threatening to the West," says the same argument in *The Nation.*

D. What about the charges leveled against Erdoğan?

Opinionated inuendo that appear in the Western outlets do not really educate the Western audience that needs to make the right judgement about Turkey & Erdogan for its own future.

Here below examples of reports that vacillate on Erdogan, his intentions, thinking, beliefs, tactics and so on.

"This isn't to say that all the charges leveled against Erdoğan are false. He is an Islamist, albeit not an extreme one; his rule is heavy-handed; and his speech and behavior are often rough."

"Erdoğan has managed to sideline, neuter or cow his secular opponents, and his party's pursuit of EU membership is obviously, though perhaps not only, tactical."

"But it's undeniable that Erdoğan is genuinely popular, and that his party has twice won national elections, by wide margins, whose outcomes no one seriously contests. To comprehend Turkey's transformation, one must understand the sources and nature of that support."

As the convoluted arguments try to examine what may have transpired during Erdoğan's rule in volatile times, without talking to Erdoğan himself, the findings do not help a bit for anyone to understand anything. If the goal is to confuse them. Then, yes!

Simply put, judges and jury aside, the reign of Erdoğan can simply be explained by the results. Where Turkey was before his reign and what Turkey has achieved since he came to power? It is out there for everyone to see and judge without the "fake news of today" because Erdogan is still the same old, same old and Turkey is many times better off then yesterday. Even their adversaries in the West admit, when the truth be told!

2. Same old, same old

After almost two decades in power, Erdoğan is same old, same old.

He is still the leader of the political Islamist movement in the country and beyond.

He is still the president of modern Republic of Turkey, running with the ideals of Ataturk.

Erdoğan regime today actually became the strongest vanguard of the republic.

Ironically it is true, much to the bewilderment of many in Turkey and the Western world.

Erdoğan regime is also the champion of the Muslims everywhere.

Unlike the common belief, he does not need have to be a Calif to enjoy the glory.

In his first sixteen years in power, Erdoğan could have replaced the republic with new order.

He could have proved the suspicions of many that he wanted to get rid of republic.

On the contrary, Erdoğan completed the sixteen-year cycle from 2002 to 2018 with strength.

In 2019, he is standing tall to champion both the secular republic and the political Islam.

The West must feel good that Erdoğan is the leader that can tame the Muslim masses.

The West must also get used to the fact that he will be around for another decade.

The Middle East too must feel good that there is a leader like Erdoğan to lead Muslims.

The Middle East must also understand that strong Turkey is good for the ummah.

Secular Turkey that transformed from a religious empire is a good sign for everybody.

It is an assurance that Turkey will stay in its borders and benevolent regional power.

In other words, Turkey is still the same old, same old, after two decades with Erdoğan.

3. Aware of his legacy

Erdoğan is aware of his legacy.

He is the most accomplished leader of the modern Republic of Turkey.

Even Ataturk, the founder of the state could not achieve as much on economic front.

He was, then, bogged down with wars—existential problems.

Erdoğan achieved economic growth and the rise of the military power.

On top of that, he brought the presidential system to make the republic even stronger.

It was the ideal of many of his predecessors, when Turgut Ozal first loudly expressed it.

It was him that did it for the republic by bringing political Islam to power alongside too.

Simply put, Ataturk's legacy was to create the 17th Turkish state in history.

Erdoğan's legacy became to right the ship, for the 17th republic, in the second century.

After all, no state with centuries long journey does not evolve.

Erdoğan knows that he is on the right path because of the criticism he hears worldwide.

Reportedly, President Emanuel Macron of France believes Europe will fall even further behind Turkey, if Erdoğan were to stay in power for another ten years. Thus, EU must be vigilant against Turkey.

Chancellor Angela Merkel of Germany had to admit the trajectory that Turkey is in, pointing at how fast Turkey built the world's biggest airport in Istanbul and the fact that now it is set to build its indigenous automotive sector. Thus, something must be done.

They are not the only leaders who have validated Erdoğan's accomplishments loudly, albeit sarcastically and clearly with no well wishes. President Trump, president of China, prime ministers from Africa or the Middle East are on the record as well.

The following statement genuinely and frankly summarizes Erdoğan's legacy in the eyes of the Western leaders, in the aftermath of the 15 July 2016 failed coup d'état against Erdoğan.

"If we were able to bring Erdoğan down,
Muslims would have-lost and we would have von.
Plan fell through because of Erdoğan and Turks.
Forty-year long setup was over in four hours."

Erdoğan is well aware of what the Western leaders have said or how they feel about him. Accordingly, he puts it in a perspective looking at Ataturk when he also was subjected to the same type of treatment. Hence, he feels vindicated of his legacy.

VI. How does Erdoğan go forward?

Erdoğan moves forward by saying "no" to American methods and "yes" to alliance.
He is firm with the Western Europeans, short of ultimatum.
He lets the West know that the use of "free press" as a tool no longer admissible.
He integrates Arabs to Turkish foreign policy objectives selectively.
He embraces Russians with measure in number of areas.
He works with Iran, but he has no illusions.

1. American methods vs alliance with the US

Erdoğan increasingly will oppose to some of the American methods.
He will not tolerate Western use of free press as a tool of foreign policy objectives.
Nation-building or resorting to a coup d'état or bullying will face heavier consequences.
On the other hand, Erdoğan will continue to cherish most of the other American values.
Tolerance, religious-freedom, free-and-fair-trade will be welcomed enthusiastically.
Strategic alliance based on mutual trust, respect, and dignity will be cherished.

A. Freedom of Press

a— Purely an American concept

Freedom of Press is purely an American concept. Before the thirteen colonies declared independence from Great Britain, the British government attempted to censor the American media by prohibiting newspapers from publishing unfavorable information and opinions.

Freedom of the press—the right to report news or circulate opinion without censorship from the government—was considered "one of the great bulwarks of liberty," by the Founding Fathers of the United States. Americans enjoy freedom of the press as one of the rights guaranteed by the First Amendment.[34]

When Freedom of Press became one of the pillars of the new republic, it also began defining the core values, beliefs, and traditions of the US. The American media accordingly became the instrument, representing independence, equality, informality, and directness of the American culture.

b— European culture is a completely different animal

As these virtues became unique to the US, the Western Europe remained the same. The media there represented the diverse cultures of the old continent. In other words, Freedom of Press clearly reflected characteristics of the countries in their media outlets.

c— Turkey is more like Europe nothing like the US

Modern Republic of Turkey adopted the long-established European trends, including norms and regulations in the development of its media industry. Over the decades, the media in Turkey became not much different than the European media but nothing like the US media. The concepts of Freedom of Press and media over time clearly reflected more and more deep routed elements of the rich Turkish culture.

Today, it is composed of many nationwide and independent print outlets and television networks. They operate under the norms and regulations of the Western European media. They are in the company of thousands of local dailies, radio stations and television stations. Freedom of Press is bountiful, widespread and touches everybody across the country.

---

[34] https://www.history.com/topics/united-states-constitution/freedom-of-the-press

* * *

The problem arises when the concept of Freedom of Press is exploited as a foreign policy instrument to push Western ideals, norms, and values over Turkey. Erdoğan regime rejects the double standard. On one hand, Turkey feels it is part the West hence it should be treated with similar temperament. On the other hand, Erdoğan regime feels that there is outright bias against Turkey that he leads.

Considering the state of the US media is today, defending the wisdom of Freedom of Press has even bigger dilemma. When either half of the media in the US is blaming the other half as fake, the concept of Freedom of Press loses the grounds it stands on.

In other words, in the US, since 2016, there is no longer a media that formed the basis for the Freedom of Press that properly functioned all along since the British rule. The country is nowadays kind of split into two. Each side is claiming to represent the truth while blaming the other side as non-American.

So, the question is, when the media no longer has a universal role within the United States which one of the two media could have legitimacy or credibility to impose the virtues of the Freedom of Press onto others domestically, not to mention overseas?

B. Nation-building

The other commonly known and criticized American method has to do with overnight nation-building attempts, complementing US foreign policy objectives. In the Middle East, coup d'états have been widely used with varying results in the long run.

In Iran, 1953 coup d'état came back to hunt the US in 1979. Today, the single biggest problem, that the US faces, is the Iranian regime that came to power with vengeance and soon to celebrate its 40th year anniversary.

In Turkey there were four or five of coup d'états in one century. According to some others, the number was around seven or eight. The last one was an attempt that failed on July 15, 2016. It was a first in Turkey. All others were successful. Last two were via emails, of all things, Turkish Armed Forces were keeping up with times!

Erdoğan regime is the by-product of the coup d'états in Turkey over many decades. The only difference is that Erdoğan ironically believes the US inspired coups have no more place in Turkey now that number of them were instrumental for his coming to power in the first place.

In other words, there are two regimes in power in the Middle East today that were not supposed to be there, but they are because of the Western inspired coup d'états. The revolutionary Islamist Iranian regime and the political Islamist regime Erdoğan in Turkey have begun their journey with 1953 and 1980 coup d'états respectively. Both are firmly marked in history as unintended by-products of the US foreign policy objectives.

Unintended consequences have turned Iranian regime at the least into an existential threat in the region against many states. Turkey, on the other hand, matured as a benevolent domineering regional power still firmly allied with the West. The only thing that changed is that "Realpolitik" replaced "Catch-22" as "modus operandi" between the modern Republic of Turkey and the West.

2. Ultimatums or Realpolitik in dealing with the Western Europeans

Erdoğan is firm with the European Union and demanding straight answers.

Yet, they sound like ultimatums.

No one in the West raises its voice back because Westerners think what if Erdoğan walks out again! Most remember the walk-out in 2012 when Erdoğan left the stage in Davos, Switzerland.

Reportedly, another no so pleasant encounter took place behind closed doors. Erdoğan was invited to a meeting with leading Western leaders but as a surprise guest.

Not until than no leader of a Muslim country was ever part of such meeting. But this time, Putin and Obama without telling others had invited Erdoğan to join.

The other Western leaders were shocked to see a Muslim joining their private meeting. But what happened afterwards was even more shocking when Erdoğan ignored norms.

He first insulted Sarkozy about Algerian revolution and Rwanda massacre. Then he turned on Zapatero about the Alhambra decree.

Holland was not spared either with Srebrenica massacre in former Yugoslavia. Germany with Nazis and Putin with Chechen wars also received their share of blame.

Putin and Obama had decided together to bring Erdoğan into the mold. He was only there to represent all the Muslims and to play the game! But he was not playing it…

Did everything reported here happen?

It does not matter if it did or not.

But there is a big likelihood that it would have happened exactly like that.

If there was such a private gathering and if Erdoğan were to be invited.

Like it could have happened with Donald J. Trump.

Erdoğan is not the kind that adheres to established norms.

But since Erdoğan is not in a position to give ultimatums, what is his end game?

Realpolitik! It looks like Realpolitik is back again.

But this time it is between secular Turkey and the West.

Unlike the Communists of the past, political Islamists are the counterparts.

A. Ultimatums

Erdoğan would like to see European Union decide on Turkish membership to the union of the Christian club. He would like to see a "yes" or "no" as an answer. He is fine with either one of them.

"No hard feelings!"

He says.

Call it ultimatum or not, indecision he does not want. In 2019, he stated that if there is no definite answer from the EU, he would like to go on a referendum to determine if the membership application Turkey to the EU should continue or be withdrawn.

Since the relationship with EU countries turned to normal after a two-year spat in 2018, Turkey first time flexed its muscles again later in the year. It demanded that no members of media should be allowed to attend a joint press conference of two leaders of a country unless approved by both sides.

Call it ultimatum or not, in the ensuing state visit to Germany, some members of German media voluntarily decided not to attend the press conference in order not to put Chancellor Merkel on the spot. No other noticeable bravado took place since then as far as news reports to date.

B. Realpolitik

The West is not the West of the old. It is no longer the 20th century. It is no longer the bipolar world. There is no more US hegemony in the Middle East like there was before 1991. There is no trace of formidable Western Europeans in the Middle East anymore.

Plus, the West has its own domestic governance problems on both side of the Atlantic. New economic realities are apparent. There is an economic parity between the US and the rising China and India on one hand. Turkey is in parity with the Western European powers on the other hand.

Turkey is in a position to negotiate the future from the point of strength. It is better for the West to be on the same page with Turkey today than when Turkey will have even more leverage against the European states in the coming years. Time is on Turkey's side with Erdoğan's regime in power.

Plus, the West has issues to resolve within. The future of NATO and PESCO is a competition to the detriment of the West. Ironically, Turkey comes in as a balancing act.

Finally, the prospects regarding Russia's leverage over the Western Europe and China's over the US are even more pressing problems. Having Turkey as an asset rather than as a burden is the new reality in the face of larger problems.

Not that the Middle East still isn't an ongoing problem and that the refugees will not continue to become the mother of all problems, they are nonetheless on the back burner for the moment. At this time, the West has to overcome the current and more urgent problems like nuclear North Korea or the Iranian nuclear deal's sunset clauses. All the while, China trade deal with the US also hangs like the sword of Damocles.

In view of all these complexities, Turkey appears to be the only viable alternative for the Western civilization to rely on. Realpolitik makes more sense with Turkey at a time when everything else seems to be precarious for the West.

3. By integrating with Arabs

Some would say, thank god modern Turkey is there to take care of the problems.

Some others would argue that Turkey is the problem, nothing else.

The reality is that Arabs mostly relate to Turkey historically but also geographically.

Turkey complements them and brings them more good whether they admit it or not.

Erdoğan nowadays is personally connected to handful leaders in the region as a Turk.

He employs multi-layered approach against those that are not yet on board with him.

Most Arabs will side with Turkey over time for variety of reasons.

Turkic race, Muslim religion, fast-growing economy, and powerful military play role.

They know that absence of the West, balance of power and hope also are the reasons.

And conditions fueling terrorism and migration will never be eliminated without Turkey.

A. Close friends of Erdoğan

Erdoğan will take care of some of these terrorism and migration problems with the help of friends. Many leaders across Middle East and Africa side with him these days. Their numbers are constantly increasing because he has lot to offer them and he actively seeks their participation.

In Qatar, Sudan, and Somalia, Turkey has military presence but more importantly Erdoğan has personal relationship with their leaders. But there are also others in Kuwait, Oman, Yemen, Lebanon, and Jordan.

Then there is another set of them in North Africa.

B. Multi-layered approach for others

Erdoğan has three leverages that he can use if and when they become necessary. First two are water and oil pipelines. Turkey never weaponized them. It never uses them for coercion. The third, by nature, requires give and take anyway. As Erdoğan puts, it is Win-Win.

Water for those in down-stream is an effective reason to work with Turkey in the north.

Oil pipelines coming from Iran and Iraq heading west are important leverages.

Defense industry and technology coupled with the very diversified fast-growing economy that recently made Turkey to become the biggest donor country in Africa are the others.

a—Water

Water is the future of the Middle East, and the source of the Euphrates and Tigris in the region originate from the Turkish mountains in Anatolia. Not that Erdoğan leverages water flow from Turkey to Iraq and Syria as foreign policy tools, having them under his belt is a leverage, nonetheless.

Half of the Crescent is in Turkey, the rest is split among Arab states. Turkey in the northern part of the Crescent has the upper hand. That has been the history of the region and nothing can change that.

Flow of natural resources, people, and goods via highways, high-speed trains, pipelines over Turkey to Europe are other realities that bring three continents closer to one another via Turkey. Turkey simply has lots of leverages to put in play as a land-bridge for countries like Iran and Iraq to ship their natural resources to Western European markets via pipelines.

c— Win-Win

Two decades into the millennium, Turkey has even more to offer to its brethren Muslim countries and others in need. It has now an indigenous defense industry and high-tech technologies that innovate and manufacture the latest, and one-of-a-kind war ship platforms, attack helicopters, tanks, drones, missiles, intelligent ordinances, small armaments.

All at competitive prices as an alternative what the Westerners or the Russians and the Chinese could supply. And they come without license restrictions and with technology transfer. Russia used to be the suppliers of many client states that Turkey is in a position to supply with alternative products, especially involving military platforms.

3. Having Russia as a transactional friend instead of an eternal enemy

Defense industry in Turkey has advanced so far that now Turkey feels self-confident, so much so that once what was a Russian bear is nowadays a cuddly bear for Turkey.

Erdoğan rose to power in the region by challenging Russia first with a Zero-Sum game.

Turkey outright shot-down Russian military aircraft over the Syrian border region.

But a year later, Erdoğan and Putin buried hatches and mended bridges.

Neither fell into a trap when both sides viewed it first as a Western conspiracy.

In the meantime, the US needed a miracle after the disastrous Iraq invasion.

Unfortunately, Obama made matters worse by pulling out of Iraq prematurely.

Obama did more damage to the US interests with policies in Syria and Iran.

He naturally created a vacuum that was quickly filled by Russia and Iran.

The disastrous mistakes of the US left no alternative for Erdoğan but to enter Syria.

It was now lose-lose for the West, and Turkey had no option but to work with Russia.

Soon it was clear to both Turkey and Russia that it was beneficial to become friends.

Together, they were able to strike a three-way balance of power with EU.

For Turkey it is better to be amiable with its northern neighbors Russia and EU so that Turkey can focus on more urgent developments elsewhere, starting with Iran.

4. Remembering history when it comes to Iranians

Turkey and Iran have a border that stood test of times since 1514.

There were no wars, yet the relationship was never stress-free either.

Turkey and Iran always competed on all-fronts, some were not friendly exchanges.

For example, nuclear Iran will be the sole reason why Turkey will go nuclear.

Balance of power has to be maintained between two countries like it is in Syria, when Iran is siding with the Bashar Al Assad regime.

The Iranian regime reflects its combative nature also against Saudi Arabia.

The protectorate of Mecca and Medina will always be in the crosshair of Iran.

The warnings from Turkey went on deaf ears of Bush-43 and Obama administrations when it objected the invasion of Iraq and insisted on removal of Assad regime in 2012.

Yemen war became the closing act when, in 1970s, Lebanon was the opening salvo.

In between, invasion of Iraq and the quagmire in Syria must have never been allowed.

Iran capitalized on all Western miscalculations to date and making steady advances.

Today Iran is no longer within the 1514 borders simply because of West's mistakes.

The Turks kept Iran in control for four centuries.

The West could not hold Iran in the same place for one single century.

Now, Iran today is an existential threat for the West.

Turkey finds itself torn between two worlds.

5. Living with Europe on equal footing

Yet the reality is that Erdoğan has to live with the West.

But it is also another reality that the West cannot do without Erdoğan.

Times have changed, not only because political Islam came to power in Turkey.

Times have changed because there will be parity between Christianity and Islam soon.

The world will have equal number of people from both religions.

Western Europe and Anatolia will be the bastions of the two leading religions. Social values will require tolerance and accommodation at close circles.

Economic and military coordination will have to increase to prevent crisis like exchanging visa-free walking rights to Turks, versus land-bridge guarantees, so that refugees can be managed and the 'pressure valve' will work as intended.

A. Exchange a bridge and a gate for walking rights

Erdoğan is ready to commit Turkey full-fledged into a land-bridge and a gate-keeper role for the West. In return, he demands further integration with Europe.

Land-bridge brings energy flowing through pipelines. Gates keep refugees out and bring them to EU in a regulated fashion.

Last century, Europe needed Turkey as a leverage against the communist threat from north. This century although the threat from north did not disappear alto-gether, Turkey became independent and with lots of leverage against EU.

President Dwight D. Eisenhower said it best to put it into perspective after Turkish brigade saved the 2nd Division of the US forces from the complete anni-hilation in Korea.

"No doubt the strongest and most reliable protector of European civilization is the Turkish Army."

Erdoğan had already saved Europe twice from a total annihilation by stopping single-handedly the second time when in the first crisis one million of the five mil-lion refugees ended in Europe while the rest was kept in Turkey.

Suddenly, the demands to integrate Westernized Turkey into Europe more tightly no longer seems like an ultimatum or brinkmanship by Erdoğan, rather it has become "Realpolitik" at best.

B. Brinkmanship has no place

For Turkey and Erdoğan and the West, there is no place for brinkmanship or ulti-matum in the 21st century.

Turkey is well situated in the middle of three continents with a fast-growing economy and military. Erdoğan having completed a sixteen-year cycle in power and came out stronger after being tested many times over domestically and inter-nationally. Now they are the power of two, facing the same global problems that the West is facing, starting with the refugees.

Unlike the 20th century, Turkey does not have all powerful Stalin in the north rather interdependent Putin's Russia at peace with its southern neighbors Turkey and EU alike. Nor there are the globalist Clinton, Bush, and Obama trio with its blunders or the bonkers of Kennedy, Johnson, and Carter to worry about. Plus, nationalist and realistic President Trump is a timely replacement.

The leadership in EU is another matter in view of Angela Merkel walking out and Emanuel Macron is looking for his groove after Brexit. Yet, the changing times will not permit Western Europeans to make mistakes. Bullying, having never worked against Turkey, brinkmanship of any kind will have severe repercussions in the face of refugee crisis to deal with. Hungarian prime minister said it best after a wall was erected between Croatia, Slovenia, and Hungary, that the wall worked but only with the help of Turkey cooperating.

It took two years for the European leaders to realize their fatal mistake. By 2018, they reconstituted their relationship with Erdoğan. On the face, Erdoğan seemed to have no hard feelings against them. He hosted Merkel, Macron and Putin in a foursome summit in Istanbul on refugee matters in Syria.

Yet, the reality is that the Western Europeans can be sure of one thing. Turkey and Erdoğan, the power of two will not resort to a zero-sum game in the absence of an existential threat, but they will surely play Realpolitik from here on every step of the way.

CHAPTER FOUR

POWER OF 2

Modern Republic of Turkey and Recep Tayyip Erdoğan: together they are the Power of 2.

The former is a secular-republican nation-state.

The latter is the leader of a political Islamic regime in power.

They are a viable tandem. More so, game-changers.

One represents the state of heart. The other, mind of a nation.

Together, they have set target dates, fulfilling mutual faiths.

They address universal needs, starting with the huddled masses and their deeds.

To save civilizations, they will lead billions with a superpower or alone.

But, domestically and internationally, they will always act as power of 2.

I. Game-changers

Turkey and Erdoğan are game changers today.

They are, for Turks and Muslims, both within country and beyond borders.

They were "one" during the Ottoman Empire.

But they lost one another during the birth of the modern Republic of Turkey.

After eight decades of separate lives and growth period, they are united at the top.

In the last two decades, they have reconnected tightly again.

Now they are ready to go forward with the faithful.

It is time to gather the flock that was idle since the Ottomans faded away.

1. Heart and mind of Turks and Muslims

Power of 2

Republic of Turkey is no longer the fledgling secular state.

It is created a century ago from the ashes of the Ottoman Empire.

A religious empire and the 16th state founded by Turks in history.

It lasted six centuries and ruled in three continents.

President Recep Tayyip Erdoğan is not at the helm by chance.

He has arrived after a challenging, arduous and life-long journey, and a political process.

He is leading the 17th Turkish state to new heights none of the previous sixteen reached.

Together they have become heart and mind of Turks but also Muslim masses.

A. By product of the US

Islamists came to power in secular, yet Muslim majority Turkish republic in the 1980s, mainly, as a result of the US foreign policy objectives in the region. Erdoğan emerged as the true, tested, and trusted leader of the movement ever since.

Of the three other Islamist Turkish leaders that preceded him, one died in office, the other was forced to leave with a political coup, the third served his term in full first as prime minister then as president of the country.

B— Fear of the West vs hope of the East

Coexistence of secular Turkey and Islamist Erdoğan spread fear in the West and a sense of hope in the East.

Economic and military growth of Turkey and consolidation of power by Erdoğan are spurring more interaction among Muslim states and increasing overseas overtures, respectively. Turkey grew three times faster in the last twenty years than in the previous seventy-five years and opened more than two dozen new embassies most of them in Africa.

Erdoğan won more than a dozen nationwide general elections, including a referendum to switch the system from parliamentary to presidential, giving him more powers.

C. Insignificant for the US

Yet, Turkey & Erdoğan tandem is still a fledgling phenomenon for the US. They are more of a nuisance than a threat.

In the Middle East and beyond, even though the tandem is not yet presenting significant challenge or for that matter, much damage to the interest of the Western regimes in place, ever growing independence of Turkey from the West is a growing concern for the US.

D. Big deal for the European Union

For the EU, the presence and continuing growth and strength of the tandem is a significant development. Erdoğan & Turkey are both a threat and opportunity that it cannot ignore and does not want to ignore. For EU, they are game changers.

E. Game-Changers for the Rest Too

For the rest of the European, Middle Eastern, and North African countries, Turkey is the main engine and Erdoğan is the driver they cannot do without.

Russia and China, and to a lesser extent India, view this tandem as an alternative, a strategic partner, and gives them a leverage they did not have before. How they will benefit or how long they will work together are the other questions with no guarantees. But that is beside the point.

Dozens of other countries in the rest of Africa and Latin America, on the other hand, view the Turkey and Erdoğan combo with interest and with a hope they could not have imagined, coming their way, suddenly appearing out of nowhere.

They are simply game changers for most of them.

2. Union of secular state with political Islam

100 years in the making
Ataturk founded the Turkish Republic in 1923 out of nothing.
Then, it became a project to build a secular state.
Modern Turkey had to be converted from a religious empire.
At first, the task was separation of church and state.
Then, it became establishment of religious freedom and expression.
Finally, it turned into co-existence of secularism and Islamism in harmony.

A. Meet the Islamists

Modern Republic of Turkey was sixty years old when it welcomed the first true Islamist leader. Turgut Ozal became the prime minister of the country. By then, Turkey was a full-fledged secular republic.

Ozal experiment was a prelude for the secular Turkey-Erdoğan tandem. It lasted about a decade. It worked very well. Turkey opened itself to the Turkic world for the first time. Turkey also got even more closer to the West, the US in particular.

It was like the early days of the Adnan Menderes regime in the 1950s. Menderes had appealed to the pious living in the countryside. Together, they came to power.

Modern Turkey started to collaborate with the US. As a result, it became more democratic, went to war in Korea siding with the allies, and was admitted to membership in NATO. Its economy started to improve.

Ozal regime made further progress in the country. More foreign investment came. Turkey became more liberal and more tolerant about religious expression. Turkey also cooperated with the US on creating a no-fly zone in northern Iraq for Kurds. Ozal allowed the US aircraft to use Incirlik airbase for sorties to enforce a new regime, north of the 36th parallel in Iraq.

In other words, the modernity that had started with the Young Turks in 1908 in the waning days of the Ottoman Empire, took off with Ataturk in its earlier days of the modern Turkey. After that, baton was passed to leaders that opened arms to the pious and the Islamists that delivered.

B. Walk with the Islamists

When Erdoğan's AK Party came to power in 2002, there was already tried pathway to build on. Menderes and Ozal regimes lasted a decade each and they had left great marks behind. They both had improved economy. They had also opened the country to more international relations. Yet, lion share went to the domestic developments. It was glaringly clear for Erdoğan that he had to make the adjustment.

Erdoğan took Turkey to new heights immediately. He built three times more in his first sixteen years what others could not since 1923. The achievements of the Erdoğan regime in the international arena were equally impressive. He reached out to Muslim countries. Plus, he established relationship with African countries as well as making forays into Latin America. Finally, Turkey-Erdoğan tandem were everywhere in the world. Ataturk's project to build a secular state was now walking with political Islamist regime and making waves with gargantuan domestic projects and impressive international overtures.

3. Going forward

In October 2018, Erdoğan made a statement in a meeting with religious officials, addressing Muslims soon to outnumber other ethnic and religious groups with almost three billion people.

"Turkey, with its cultural wealth,
accretion of history and geographical location,
has hosted diverse faiths in peace for centuries,
and is the only country that can lead the Muslim world."

In view of the rising Muslim reality and statement from Erdoğan, the importance of the religious symbols like Caliphate gains prominence, yet in secular Turkey not everything is religion.

A. Home of the Caliphate

When the role of Istanbul for the Muslims, the current non-existent status of the Caliphate, and the recent actions of Erdoğan regime regarding Muslim causes around the world are examined, Erdoğan's statement makes even more sense.

Erdoğan is talking from the heart of Islam. Istanbul has been in the minds of the Muslims of the world. Erdoğan is only reviving it after a century. The Ottoman Empire once ruled large swathes of the world's predominantly Muslim regions from Istanbul, the capital of the empire, known as Constantinople, until 1453 when Turks took it from the Byzantines. It is a city known to the world for a long period as a safe haven for diverse religious groups.

Since the Ottoman sultans laid claim to the title of Caliph of Muslims, the city was elevated to the same status, like Mecca and Medina and Jerusalem have been. Even though the Caliphate was abolished by the founder of the Turkish Republic, Mustafa Kemal Atatürk, in March 1924, the city never lost its luster in Islam.

Erdoğan and Turkey will surely continue to use the high place Istanbul holds among Muslim masses of the world more and more. More and bigger mosques will continue to be built. The city will shine even more gloriously as the brightest star of the faith.

Some view this development as the radicalization of Islam in Turkey. In fact, it is the natural progression of Istanbul in the face of rapidly rising Muslims all around the world. Muslims need a direction. When they look at Istanbul, they see it as the last home of the Caliphate. The new and bigger mosques and other architectural marvels like the biggest airport, subway system, bridges, tunnels reflect changing times and bring hope to masses. Muslims of the world realize that their prayers are answered.

That is why when Erdoğan engages with Muslim countries, he always holds the conferences in Istanbul. The last one was when he led the fifty-nine-member state meeting of the Organization for Islamic Cooperation in protest against Israel's killing of Palestinian activists.

One school of thought would surely say Erdoğan unfairly is using the symbolism of Istanbul to further elevate his own status worldwide. The opposite end would argue that Erdoğan and Turkey with Istanbul are playing the role of a "pressure valve." In reality, Turkey & Erdoğan represent the glory of a Muslim majority state and how it can be a great example and sign of hope for Muslim masses in the contemporary world today.

Some who are disgruntled with Turkey & Erdoğan are missing the point. When Byzantines lost the city to the Ottomans, it had only forty thousand people living in it instead of 400 thousand in its height. The first thing Mehmet the Conqueror did was to increase its population. Six centuries later, Istanbul is still one of the most prosperous, cosmopolitan, enjoyable and cherished cities of Europe today like London, Barcelona, Amsterdam, or Paris are.

As for the most recent municipal elections that brought to power after twenty-five years rule of Istanbul by Islamist mayors, the answer is nothing much has changed or will change.

Metro Istanbul was forty-five kilometers long at the turn of the Millenia. Since then, in the fifteen years span from 2014 until 2019 when the new mayor from opposing party took over, AK Party led regimes built another 200-kilometer-long new metro line. The ongoing projects will increase the metro line for another 300 kilometers by 2023. In other words, new mayor will oversee the expansion of the Metro Istanbul to 517 kilometers, making the world's longest within four years. New mayor having solely the power to implement what the Istanbul City Council has passed will continue the same path for Istanbul's growth according to the majority still firmly in the hands of AK Party.

Meanwhile, even bigger projects like Kanal Istanbul or superhighways and high-speed train networks or world's first three story rail and road tunnel under Bosporus, third for Istanbul will continue as planned as part of projects under the domain of the Erdogan regime in Ankara. Simply put, Istanbul will march towards its 2053 goals uninterrupted.

B. Not everything is religion in Turkey or for Erdoğan

Turkey will celebrate in 2053, the 600th year anniversary of Constantinople becoming Istanbul. It is not a religious holiday. It is a Turkic, nationalistic achievement.

2071 is the 1000th year anniversary of the Battle of Manzikert. It is another Turkic celebration. The day the Turks arrived West. Some would insist that it is the day Muslim Turks defeated Christian empire Byzantine. Correct yet, for Turks it is a Turkic achievement first.

Overall, Turkey yearly celebrates four national and two religious-holidays. For Turks, race and religion are equally important values yet nationalism always comes first between two because of two main reasons. One, there are big masses on earth that cherish Turkish heroism. Turks do not mind sharing the spoils of glory with the rest of the world, especially with the Muslims. Two, Turks believe in themselves as a race that they can achieve or have achieved most everything even without spiritual help.

That is the essence of the secular republic Ataturk founded. Ataturk did not come up with the secular republic for any reason other than he was a Turk first. As a Turk, he always believed that he and his soldiers will win or die. There was no other alternative for him or them when survival was at stake. Ataturk, at the battlefield, never used the name of god or the faith of his soldiers to galvanize them. He only relied on their Turkishness. He appealed to their Turkishness.

It is also apparent with the Caliphate. The Ottomans took the Caliphate in 1517, yet not until the 18th century when the Ottoman empire was on a continuous decline, the sultan decided openly to use the Caliph role to keep the empire together.

That is also the reason why Young Turks appeared in history. They rejected that the Ottoman empire would rely solely on religion to keep a state alive instead of blood and gut.

Erdoğan regime and Erdoğan himself are no different. He is Turkic first and Islamist second but at this time it does not matter if optics show him, he is Islamist first, Turkic second. He already achieved everything he needed to achieve and ingrained himself into the Turkish history. Now he has the freedom to use leverages, including the Caliphate as he sees it feet, at his own luxury.

II. The source of strength

Power of 2 takes its strength from the power of 3.

Anatolia, Ataturk, and AKP have the back of Turkey and Erdoğan.

First comes Anatolia.

In 2071, Turks will celebrate the 1000th year anniversary of coming to Anatolia.

Since then they never left the region. Will they pledge to stay for another 1000-years?

Second is Ataturk.

In 2023, his republic will celebrate its centennial.

A hundred years is never a small feat.

It will be a moment of pride for a whole lot more than eighty-one million of its citizens.

Third is the AK Party (AKP).

Recep Tayyip Erdoğan created it in 2001.

It is the longest ruling regime of the republic.

What Ataturk's RPP Party created is brought to the finish line by Erdoğan's AKP Party.

Anatolia, Ataturk, and AKP touches many people.

Each appeal to a differing group of people.

Nationalist Turks and Turkic republics care about Anatolia.

They look at Anatolia as the center of the modern Turkic life.

Ataturk appeals to the majority of the Turks in Turkey.

His socio-political revolution is also celebrated with those yearning for modernity worldwide.

AKP does not belong to Erdoğan anymore.

It is becoming a purpose greater than a mortality.

It has already achieved similar heights like RPP, as an institution and a symbol.

The source of strength for the tandem is the immortality of Anatolia, Ataturk, and AKP.

When the time comes AKP and Erdoğan will become one.

Like Ataturk and RPP became one and Turkey and Anatolia have always been.

1. Ataturk's republic made history

100-years old

Modern Republic of Turkey is socio-political revolution that stood the test of times.

Turkey & Erdoğan cannot be understood without homage to Mustafa Kemal Ataturk.

A. The greatest leader of the 20th century

Atatürk rescued the surviving Turkish remnant of the defeated Ottoman Empire. He is one of the great figures of the 20th century. He galvanized his people against invading Greek forces who sought to impose the allied will upon the war-weary Turks. He repulsed British, French, and Italian aggressions.

He founded the modern Republic of Turkey through existential struggles. He is revered forever by Turks. He succeeded restoring pride in their Turkishness. He created a modern state that would grow into a viable secular democracy.[35]

---

[35]   https://www.britannica.com/biography/Kemal-Ataturk

B. 17th Turkish state in history

Modern Republic of Turkey came out of its first turbulent century stronger. Its institutions have come of age. At 2023, it will celebrate as a domineering regional power with political Islam led by the Erdoğan regime.

2. Anatolia's Manzikert changed history

The Battle of Manzikert ended the role of Byzantine as the gatekeeper of Europe.

It replaced it with modern Republic of Turkey a thousand years later.

In the interim, the Ottomans threatened Western civilization for good part of 900 years. In 1683, the Turks came as close as Vienna. They took Constantinople in 1453.

Finally, they settled in Anatolia and smaller portion of Thrace after WWI.

A. Byzantine was the gatekeeper

The Byzantine Empire was a vast and powerful civilization. Its origins can be traced to 330 A.D. It became the "New Rome" on the site of the ancient Greek colony of Byzantium. It was a dedication by the Roman emperor Constantine I. The western half of the Roman Empire crumbled and fell in 476 A.D. The eastern half survived for 1,000 more years, as a military buffer for Europe. It spawned a rich tradition of art, literature and learning.[36]

Byzantine played a major role in the Balkans and Russia. It successfully kept the Arabs and the Muslims out of Europe for centuries. In 1071, the empire seemed invincible. It had reversed many years of decline under a series of energetic emperors. It had recovered territory that had been lost to its enemies. It had morphed into a powerful political and military force.

B. Manzikert Changed the Gatekeeper

The Battle of Manzikert fundamentally reversed this upward trend. It led to the decline of the Byzantine Empire. As Byzantine collapsed, Turkish Muslims gradually gained control of Asia Minor. Muslims took control of the Christian holy lands. European countries responded by launching the Crusades. The Battle of

---

[36] https://www.history.com/topics/ancient-middle-east/byzantine-empire

Manzikert is one of the most important in medieval history. Its repercussions can still be felt today.[37]

Turks never relinquished control since they won the Battle of Manzikert in 1071. First 900 years, they were an existential threat to the Western civilization. But, in the 19th century, the empire was considered as the "sick man of Europe" by the West.

C. Turkey became the new gatekeeper

In the 20th century, the empire was replaced with a secular republic. Overtime, it became an ally of the West.

Manzikert, today, is a town in Anatolia, Turkey. Since 2002, Turkey started to play a different role for the West. It was no longer defending the southern flank of NATO against a Soviet Union. It had now assumed the role of the old Byzantine. It was successfully keeping the Muslim refugees out of Europe.

3. AKP made Turks and Muslims rose to prominence again in history

Time to make Istanbul capital again after 100 years

Some predict, Erdoğan regime will change course in 2023. AKP also set visions for 2053 and 2071. Some in the AKP follow a path along the lines of the Kemalist ideology. Some others are visionary, focusing on Turkic and Islamic realms Ataturk left out.

A. Great legacy in the making

AKP will have a great legacy for itself. Like the world's longest bridge, world's biggest airport, world's second biggest high-speed train network, the biggest refinery of Europe- Middle East-North Africa, Europe's biggest tunnels, world's first three story tunnel, and world's longest subway system.

There are hundreds more either completed or to be completed projects by 2023. They are remarkable achievements small and large. They will go in history as the legacy of AKP and Recep Tayyip Erdoğan. When he is long gone, he will be remembered like Ataturk with these accomplishments, statues to his name.

---

[37] https://dailyhistory.org How_did_the_battle_of_Manzikert_ (1071) _change_the_Byzantine_Empire%3F

B. Building on Ataturk's legacy

AKP has targets to reach for 2023 and 2028. They will be milestones for 2053. If the progress of the past two decades continues at the same pace until Erdoğan completes its second term as president, Turkey could be on a plateau no one envisioned until now.

President Macron of France said it best when he elaborated the fact that Turkey will be ahead of Europe economically and militarily if Erdoğan were to stay in power for another decade.

No matter what, the 600-year anniversary of Istanbul in 2053 should be a grandiose event. Erdoğan like regimes will surely elevate it to new heights by then, like Ataturk did to the secular republic in the first hundred years.

What is a sure bet is the fact that the Ataturk's Kemalist legacy will continue to pave the way for the Erdoğan like political Islamist regimes to lead in the future.

In short, Erdoğan type regimes smartly will cherish original pillars of modern Republic of Turkey to reach higher plateaus. Ataturk's legacy will be there, but Turkey will be a lot different than what it has been in the 20th century.

III. The future

Secular Turkey, together with political Islam, will no longer be anchored to the West.

But more important than that, they will become game-changers.

By 2023, Turkey will be producing most of its defense industry needs indigenously.

Accordingly, Turkey with Erdoğan regime in power will exert influence worldwide.

The West must reflect and decide how to adjust and work with the "New-Turkey."

The US must ally with the New-Turkey over land routes and sea lanes.

New-Turkey together with Erdoğan will be a welcome news for most Muslims.

They will join forces and play a larger role in the balance of power worldwide.

1. 2023 is only five years away

In less than five years, modern Republic of Turkey will start its second century.

By then, it will be an economic giant, totally independent, and a military power.

It will be able to lead spiritually large portion of Muslims worldwide.

It will exert influence over the land routes and sea lanes between China and Europe.

It will project power in the Mediterranean Sea and in the Indian Ocean.

It will have great leverage over the Middle East, North Africa, and Central Asia.

A. Growing Muslim world

In the 21st century, one out of three people in the world is projected to become Muslim. Muslims will look for leadership and they will find it in the Turkey-Erdoğan tandem.

Turkey and Erdoğan will be ready to play a prominent role by 2023 as a secular Turkish nation-state, but also as a leading political Islamist regime in power in the world. They will be able to address many issues, involving Muslims countries small and large.

a— Year removed from 2024

2024 is the hundredth year anniversary when the Caliphate was abolished. The role of Turkey and Erdoğan will be significant during the centennial. The last seat of the Caliphate was Istanbul. By then, Istanbul will be like a new Mecca for Muslims to visit, especially when the Caliphate becomes the focal point. Turkey and Erdoğan will surely cherish the opportunity and tremendously gain from the exposure.

b— Istanbul is at their crosshair

Istanbul, by 2023, will already be twice as big and as powerful as it is today. The significance of 2024 for the Muslim world will further boost its status.

The world's biggest airport, the world's longest subway system, Kanal Istanbul, three-story high next tunnel under the Bosporus will make Istanbul like no other city in the world. No city in the world will be able to claim to have four of the world's biggest infrastructures, like new wonders of the world.

In 2018, Turkey became the number six biggest destination in the world with forty million tourist per year. Turkey is likely to climb the ladder further in the coming years. Istanbul will continue to be the main attraction, but Turkey has lot more to offer regarding Anatolia. From the Roman Empire to Byzantine from Mesopotamia to Aegean to Cilicia to Pontus to Manzikert it has thousands of years of history dating back to biblical times.

The road to history and culture passes through Istanbul. Istanbul is not only a Paris or London but also a gateway to another world as far as Noah on one end, St. Paul on another, not to mention it is the only land-route to Jerusalem or Mecca and Medina.

The Crusaders will tell you.

B. China looms like a gigantic opportunity and a problem

By 2023, Turkey does not have to worry about the Crusaders but what is transpiring in the Central Asia steppes. How to deal with or handle China will be the task.

a— Mix bag of the Belt and Road Initiative (BRI)

The BRI will be fully operational in the 2020s. If it works well, every state from China to the UK will benefit, some will prosper more than others. Central Asian republics will be the biggest beneficiaries. Yet not everything is as rosy because in the region there are deep rooted problems that may show their ugly face.

Between China and Central Asian republics cooperation will surely increase. But, so will the tensions, immediately. Despite interdependency, Turkey and Erdoğan will be vigilant about China's treatment of Turks and Turkic republics in Central Asia. China meanwhile will exert increasing pressure along the "Silk Road" states to control the BRI. Variety of forces may come to play to break the flow.

When and if China interferes or worse tries to control the Central Asian republics to that end, Turkey will object. In the absence of balance of power between East and West which can only be possible with US presence and participation, conflicts will escalate easily. In any case, irrespective of Russian influence in that region, Japan, Turkey together with the US should be able to keep China in check and problems from getting out of hand.

b- Turkic power to keep China in check with the US

Not that China itself will not be dependent on the cooperation of the Muslim states overall to maintain its economic dominance of the world. After all, the BRI will be at the mercy of Muslims. Silk road is totally composed of Turkic states and their Muslim brethren like Pakistan, Afghanistan, and Iran.

The soon to be completed Karakoram highway to Gwadar port in Pakistan will give China access to the Indian Ocean. The BRI over Kazakhstan, Azerbaijan, and Georgia will reach Europe via high speed rail network in Turkey, soon to be second longest in the world only to China. More than ten thousand kilometer-long divided highways in Turkey will also contribute greatly for the goods and services to complete their journey between Beijing and London in fifteen days.

Turkey will not only use its leverage over China but will also come to the help of the Turkic republics in the Central Asia economically and militarily when necessary. Turkey most likely will find the US on its side; after all, establishment of the balance of power between the East and the West is vitally important.

C. Continental shelves will become contentious new problems

Balance of Power will also serve elsewhere to prevent full scale wars. In the eastern Mediterranean, continental shelves will soon be contested throughout. In the Black Sea, they are settled equitably among countries bordering the sea.

Yet, there will still be tensions that can get out of hand. The US, the EU, Russia, and Turkey will be the major contestants throughout the region. China will not remain idle either considering what is at stake.

a— EU and US will compete to have a bigger say

PESCO and NATO will protect EU and US interests respectively when natural resource explorations increase in the Mediterranean and Black seas. Balance of power between EU, Russia, and Turkey will shift with the US coming into play with a heavy hand.

b— Muslim navies will dominate seas

In the Indian Ocean, the emergence of ocean-going powerful navies will create tension. Pakistan, Indonesia and Turkey will have large naval forces patrolling the ocean. India will also have a large navy as will China in addition to the Western navies, led by the US.

In the Indian Ocean, continental shelves will be in the back burner. The main battle will be on top of the water. Refugees and shipping lines will dominate the agendas.

2. Time to reflect for the West

2023 is only a few years away.

The West must acknowledge that Turkey will be domineering in the Ottoman territories.

Christianity on the other hand will be nearing parity with the Muslims.

Erdoğan will seek its second term as president.

Montreux Agreement over Turkish straits will end.

New regimes and regulating waterways will come into play.

Turkey will open Kanal Istanbul and the world will change like never before.

A. Independent Turkey

By 2023, Turkey will have three types of indigenous engine technology in mass production. One of them will be for tanks. Turkey already has 600 hp engine in test run and in the process of developing larger engines suitable for main battle tanks. Second, jet engine for a 5th generation fighter plane is under development. Turkey, having already developed its own helicopter engine in 2018, has started the work on a supersonic jet engine. Finally, Turkey is already building submarines that will be able to stay under water longer than two weeks without nuclear reactors on board.

When Turkey completes these three projects, it will be completely independent and will be able to fulfill a lot more export orders without restrictions because it will not be limited with licensing agreements. Turkey currently is able to build the best of the best tanks, warships and fighter planes, along with electronic ordinances and radars and missile systems. Indigenous engines are the last pieces of the puzzle for total independence.

B. Back in the Ottoman territories

Growth of the defense industry, coupled with the indigenous engines on land, air, and sea will give Turkey upper hand militarily in the region and beyond.

At the hundredth year anniversary of the modern Republic of Turkey, the West must look back what transpired in the region in recent past and how Turkey came out as the sole domineering power again.

The West must also observe how Turkey will adopt itself to the changing times in the region and continue to adopt to modern times. The wars and conquests for Turkish states are in the past.

The process of modern Republic of Turkey becoming a "New-Turkey" already started in northern Iraq and continues in the northern Syria in smaller scale. Unlike anti-Turkey hysteria in the world, Turkey will not return in the form of the Ottoman Empire of the past.

3. Regime change

Turks have played major role in history for the past two thousand-years.

They played their role with the new regimes they set in their environment.

When modern Republic of Turkey was founded the regimes were set by the West.

It is very natural for the independent Turkey to set the old regimes right.

But changing conditions in the world also require other new regimes to take a hold.

Belt and Road Initiative, refugees, increased shipping require new regimes.

But what is urgent for Turkey and Erdoğan are the regimes on the straights.

Plus, Turkey is surrounded with three seas where security is paramount.

That is why Turkey builds Kanal Istanbul as a start to resolve the problem in Bosporus.

Hazardous shipping going through fifteen million population requires more regulations.

Modern times require modern measures not only on the straits but also on the seas.

Hence Turkey put in place "Mavi Vatan" in 2019 for the first time.

Declaring an economic and military zone in the surrounding seas was necessary.

Protection of natural resources rights and shipping lines without conflicts was the aim.

Together with Kanal Istanbul, Mavi Vatan is a clear concept of a regime change.

Turkey and Erdoğan will enforce it as a benevolent and domineering regional leader.

A. Resetting the old regimes right

In 2023, modern Republic of Turkey will see to it that the international regimes evolve with times.

Turkey has always been for the territorial integrity of sovereign states. It has always been against nation-building since the day it was created and will continue as such under Kemalist regimes. Erdoğan adheres to the Kemalist regimes like all preceding Turkish regimes have since Ataturk.

But in 2023, Turkey will take the lead in setting number of international regimes right. One of them manages the navigation on the Bosporus. Kanal Istanbul project will require that change. It is expected to be completed by then. It is a replica of the Panama Canal.

Kanal Istanbul will create a new man-made water way between the Black Sea and Marmara Sea, parallel to the Bosporus. Oil tankers will navigate through this Kanal so that the Bosporus can be used for the rest, non-hazardous shipping. In the past oil tankers have caused catastrophic accidents because of the treacherous currents create dangerous currents and drafts. Kanal will have no current. The water level will be regulated and managed.

Montreux regime has been regulating the traffic in the Bosporus since 1936.

B. New regimes

Other regimes may also come into play in the Aegean and Mediterranean seas to regulate further soon to increase economic activities due to natural gas explorations.

Presence of increasing number of warships protecting drilling rights in the region will also require new regimes. Accommodating smooth commercial operations and preventing conflicts turning into full-fledged wars will become priority.

New regimes are also inevitable because population in Africa will double. Large masses will migrate north towards Mediterranean from deep inside the continent. Asia will also see population increase by another billion in thirty years. Indian Ocean will be no different but full of refugees heading West. Europe will be their final destination.

New regimes in the waters on both side of the Middle East will regulate the changing dynamics. The Belt and Road Initiative will also increase shipping traffic, so will the growing number of Muslim navies.

C. Mavi Vatan

Turkey has launched the largest maritime drill in the country's history, testing its war fighting capabilities in the Black Sea, Aegean Sea, and eastern Mediterranean simultaneously. Dubbed "Mavi Vatan," or "the Blue Homeland," the exercise lasted eight days from February 27 until March 8 in 2019. 103 military vessels and thousands of soldiers conducted operations in 462,000 square meters in three seas surrounding the country.[38]

Turkish Minister of Defense Hulusi Akar said, "In the context of good neighborly relations and international law we are trying to improve the confidence building measures and bring the level of our relations to a better level."

Two Romanian and two other Russian warships participated in the exercises in the Black Sea. Romania stated that the "bilateral training actions involving the Romanian Navy are part of the set of measures to deter threats and risks to the security of NATO states, adopted at the Brussels Summit in 2018."

Russia announced that "the crews of two vessels of the Novorossiysk naval base of the Black Sea Fleet—patrol ship Vasily Bykov and minesweeper Valentin Pikul—have held joint Turkish-Russian exercise PASSEX with the crews of corvette Burgazada and minesweeper Akcay." They worked on interoperability between the two naval forces in the Black Sea and conducted a passing exercise in possible mine

---

[38] https://www.jpost.com/Middle-East/Turkey-launches-Blue-Homeland-naval-drill-582048

danger areas. On March 6-8, Turkish warships were in the port of Novorossiysk with a business call as part of national naval exercises dubbed Mavi Vatan-2019.

a— Turkey sends signal with imposing military games

In many aspects, this is not a standard annual wargame played by the Turkish Naval Forces. When nations stage grandiose military games, it is usually a kind of a signal.

There was one such major exercise the Turkish Navy had held in June 1998, Turkish naval elements spread over the Mediterranean. One group was deployed east of Malta and the other west of Crete before launching a virtual battle with the participation of the Turkish air force. That was the largest exercise ever held by the Turkish navy in the Mediterranean and was meant as a response to the tension with Greece at that time.

The Turkish media say the exercise is actually a message to the Eastern Mediterranean Gas Forum (EMGF), a coalition formed recently by Egypt, Israel, Cyprus, Greece, Italy, Jordan, and the Palestinian Authority. The alliance plans to explore energy sources in the eastern Mediterranean Sea, including disputed areas. This show of force on the maritime domain will surely be closely watched by these nations. More than %80 of all corvettes, fast attack craft, and patrol boats, currently not deployed to a mission are taking part in this exercise. An impressive %93 of all frigates have sailed away. To keep so many ships for ten days at sea requires also a good and strong logistical support. The test of the logistical support that Turkey can provide to its deployed forces is one of the important issues of this exercise.

A more important part of the exercise will be the port visits made by the Turkish warships. Between the 6th and 8th of March, forty ports will be visited by sixty-seven participating naval units, seven of which are foreign ports.

Turkish warships will visit, Bulgaria, Romania, Ukraine, Russian Federation, Georgia, and the Turkish Republic of Northern Cyprus. The simultaneous visits to the Black Sea riparian states have a high symbolic value. Turkey is the only nation that can perform such a diplomatic show of force. It is not a small event to do port visits in five different nations at the same time.

In conclusion, this exercise is a military drill to turn the concepts of Turkish Armed Forces into doctrines as indicated by Mr. Metin Gürcan, an independent security analyst. This exercise is a political act to show that Turkey will protect its interests on the high seas.[39]

---

[39]   https://turkishnavy.net/2019/02/27/what-does-the-exercise-mavi-vatan-mean/

b— Message from Turkey to drillers in the Mediterranean

Greek media have reported that the drill is taking place amid plans by Ankara to dispatch a second drilling ship to areas around the divided island of Cyprus later this week after Turkey's Foreign Minister Mevlut Cavusoglu said the country would begin drilling for oil and gas near Cyprus in the near future.

"Let those who come to the region from far away, and their companies see that nothing can be done in that region without us. Nothing at all can be done in the Mediterranean without Turkey, we will not allow that," he said.

D. Erdoğan, Western ally Turkey taking the mantle

Stern warning from Minister of Foreign Relations of Turkey is a sure sign of how Turkey taking the mantle in its waters. When Erdoğan seeks his second term as president, most of these new regimes in these waters will be in place. If not formally, they will be there in practice. As a domineering regional power, Turkey, under the leadership of the Erdoğan regime, will set the new course for the region.

Regime change is necessary for independent Turkey to function properly. The regimes that were set a century ago one sided by the West can no longer survive. There is already new dynamic in the region that the regimes have to adopt and adjust. Otherwise clashes will escalate easily into outright wars every time a small conflict or disagreement arises.

Times have changed economically, militarily, demographically, geographically, historically so must the regimes. The US would prefer the change simply because as the only superpower regimes that serve the greater good would serve the only superpower. Plus, when balance of power in the world is a priority, having a soft belly where Turkey is, full of little skirmishes taking the attention away, is never a good sign.

Having an adamant long-time ally taking the lead is also crucial. Secular Turkey with political Islamist regime in power dealing with Muslim refugees in mass is the right choice. Economically and militarily dominant benevolent and tolerant old-time ally make it a viable and logical choice.

Otherwise what are the alternatives?

The Arabs are in majority in most of the southern end of Turkey and they are in disarray. China, India and Russia as well as Western European powers and other powers from overseas will compete for the riches of the region. Turkey will not be the only country trying to protect its interest. The Arabs will also be sucked into the regime change developments.

Next extension of "Mavi Vatan" may very well be visits to the northern shores of Africa, Red Sea, and the Indian Ocean. After all that is how the US established the "Monroe Doctrine" right after the "Great White Fleet" sailed across the globe. There is no reason why grater Turkish navy not to visit all of its Arab brethren in the old Ottoman territories with a friendly port call.

Most of them will welcome the port call. It will be symbolic, but symbolism will play a significant role considering the disarray and dismal conditions the whole region is in.

CHAPTER FIVE

ARABS

In the Middle East, currently there is an Arab problem.

It is constantly recurring, and it is preventing modernity from taking root.

Maybe the Arabs are in flux when they are left alone.

But problems also continue when they are under hegemony.

Now the US is clinging barely in Syria and mostly relying on Saudi Arabia.

Plus, the Western Europeans are practically out of the region. It is time for anew.

Meanwhile, most Arabs want to be left alone, like the rest of the Middle East.

But for a new beginning to start, there must be some final adjustments to be made.

First, the 20th century legacy must be erased from the region altogether.

Turkey can and must take the lead and must be supported by the US.

It starts in Syria, then comes Iraq, only after that nuclear status of Iran can be tackled, saving Fertile Crescent and Levant, then burying the grave mistakes come in order.

Otherwise, there can never be a clean slate for the 21st century.

Water, oil, refugees, rebuilding, continental shelf issues are waiting like a dark cloud.

Independent Turkey will be the single biggest player that has interest in everything.

It will also have capacity and political will with Erdoğan regime to act on it.

Will Turkey indulge itself to involve beyond the Fertile Crescent in the region?

It will prefer to act with the US but also with the Russian Federation to a limited extent.

But the US has to decide before China and India move into the region.

Joining Turkey and abandoning Saudi Arabia will be the change of the century.

It will make all the difference in the world and for the right reasons.

The US will rise again in the region, and powerful against China across the globe.

I. The rulers of the Middle East

Arabs lived in the Middle East until Turkish horsemen arrived in the 10th century.
Turks are still next door. They are formidable as ever, a thousand years later.
The Westerners came to the Middle East, second time a century ago.
They already look dissipated after a mere century.
One is still there for thousand years, the others only a century.
Yet, the Arabs blame everybody but themselves.

* * *

The difference between the Turks and the Westerners is simple.
The Turks came into the Middle East from north, and directly to Bagdad first.
Before that, they also secured their standings in Anatolia.
The West did not have that choice when they dismembered the Ottoman empire.
The modern Republic of Turkey was still holding strong to Anatolia.
Despite that, the Westerners continued their migration to the region in the 20th century.
The West simply ignored a very important aspect of the Middle East.
Bagdad and Damascus were the heart and mind of the Arabs.
Without them healthy and functioning, the rest of the body had no chance to survive.
The Turks learned this fact naturally over the centuries.
The Romans may have had a similar experience in the first millennia.
But apparently, they did not share it with the rest of the Christianity.
Instead, the West ignored history and forced its hand.
It imposed a hegemony in the region.
The result was a total failure and catastrophic devastation for all concerned.

1. 7th century Arabs

Arabs always lived in the Middle East as a majority.
They are in the Arabian Peninsula, but also from Indian Ocean to Mediterranean Sea.
They ventured to China and to Madagascar on the western shores of Africa.
Then they extended across the northern shores of Arica to Morocco.
They went east towards Central Asia in pursuit of nomadic tribes.
They were in the northeastern mountains and the beginning of the Asian steppes.

There, they first met with Turkic tribes, and they converted them to Islam, some claim by force, by massacring them with no mercy for centuries.

2. Turkish rule

The Turks in the 10th century sought to resolve the Arab problem.

They moved into the Fertile Crescent.

In 1517, they took control of the whole region and brought the Caliphate to Istanbul.

They established a new era in the Middle East under the Ottomans.

3. British mandate

Britain failed to fill the void left by the Ottomans after the WWI.

With the Ottoman Empire destroyed, Russia paralyzed by foreign intervention and civil war, and French influence limited somewhat by their minor military role in the Middle East, Britain's military success made it the dominant power in the region. The resulting settlement, which fostered an instability that continues to be a source of conflict today, generated much controversy at the time and has continued to do so ever since. The legacy of Britain to the region was to divide it into what today Middle East is composed of; Iraq, Palestine, Trans-Jordan, Syria, and Lebanon.[40]

4. US hegemony

The US has emerged as the master of the Middle East in the 20th century.

But the US began on a wrong foot, with wrong methods and strategies.

The US elected to establish relationships with three regimes that did not exist before.

It recognized Saudi Arabia in 1037, Israel in 1948, and Iran in 1953.

They were supposed to be the bedrock of the US foreign policy in the region.

Instead, they ended up becoming a "Bermuda Triangle" that still hunts the US.

The results speak for itself.

Saudi Arabia today needs the most security and one of the furthest from modernity.

Israel is no more secure than its early days when it was declared a nation-state.

---

40   http://www.bbc.co.uk/history/worldwars/wwone/middle_east_01.shtml

Iran, in the meanwhile, became the eternal threat to Saudi Arabia and Israel.

II. 20th century lessons

The West left the Middle East in disarray even though it had a hegemony.

Now, Turkey and the US must retake it and put it back in order.

Saving Fertile Crescent is the first order of business.

When Bagdad and Damascus are burning how could the rest live free and in peace.

Mediating in the Levant is the only way out.

241 US marines should not be left slayed there in wain.

Finally, the grave mistakes must be buried!

Saudi Arabia, Iran, and Israel have to find their rightful place in the Middle East.

1. Folly of the Fertile Crescent

Fourteen years of war and seven trillion dollars later, there is nothing to show for in Iraq!

And that is only a part of the calamity in the Middle East!

Bagdad and Damascus have always been the center of the region.

Unless they are under control, there will never be peace in the rest of the Middle East.

But to have a say and bring order in Iraq and Syria, Turkey must be in the mold.

It holds the only entry point to the region in the north where the riverheads are.

They flow north to south and their water brings life to the whole region.

The folly is that the West came for oil, but it never realized water's importance.

A. Fertile Crescent at the mercy of Anatolia

The road to the heart of the Middle East starts from Anatolia.

It may not make sense unless history is examined.

It is a harsh reality and cannot be avoided.

The price to pay is always big and catastrophic.

Euphrates and Tigris rivers flow north to south. So, does, the floods. But more importantly, invading armies.

The Middle East has always been invaded through the Fertile Crescent. Whoever controlled the northern end of it, basically ended up controlling the entire region. The Persians did it. The Turks did it. The Mongols did it. The Ottomans did it.

The road to Iraq today goes through modern Turkey where the top end of the Mesopotamia, the entry point to the region lies.

The Fertile Crescent was in the hands of Turks since they settled in eastern Anatolia at the begging of the Millennium. Turks eventually took the full control of the region in 1517 by invading entire region from Levant to Egypt to Horn of Africa to both ends of the Arabian-peninsula along the Gulf and Red Sea. An empire that straddled three continents for 500 years understood well the importance of the Fertile Crescent. It is still true today.

At the end of WWI, when the Western powers forced Turkey to its current borders, their primary interest was to keep the oil fields to themselves. They saw it as the future. They left the river heads to Turkey in exchange. It was a fatal mistake.

Oil may be there for few centuries, but biblical rivers have been there for thousands of years. In the interim, the Turks built world's biggest man-man lakes and two dozen major dams to hold the water flow for irrigation. Half a dozen of these dams is sizable. Like Hoover Dam, some are world's biggest projects that can hold most of the water flow hostage if need be.

That is one simple but also one of the main reasons why there is no more Western hegemony in the Middle East.

B. Crescent, heaven or hell?

Yes, and yes, with and without Turkey.
The Crescent has to be considered in one all.
Iran, Iraq, Turkey and Syria cannot be evaluated separately.
They sit on a geography, split into four countries.
The more divided they are, the more complicated they become.
The less divided they are, the bigger problem they become.
That is the other folly of the Crescent.

In Iraq, much to the chagrin of many, it proved that the US made a mistake by not keeping Turkey on board before going after Saddam Hussein in 2003. When the US pulled out in 2014, many lives and much money were lost and there was nothing to show in return. What happened in Iraq is telling. The US first shot himself on the foot in 1980 and then committed suicide in 2003.

The US should have never used Iraq as a proxy against Iran right after the Islamic revolution there. Saddam Hussein of Iraq attacked Iran in 1980, one year after the Iranian revolution, with the blessing of the Bush-41 administration. Iraq never had a chance against much bigger, more populous, and economically and militarily stronger Iran. The attack only further weakened Iraq after eight years of killing fields. When it was over there was no credible bulwark against Iran's expansion in the area. Simply put, the US shot himself in the foot.

In the meanwhile, Iraq faced further setbacks. Israel bombed Osirek nuclear facility. The hero of the Arab world was left like a wounded animal. He, then, resorted to chemical attacks against the Kurds, a softer target that had betrayed him by aligning with Iran during the war. He was now a pariah in the international community.

After that there was a double suicide in the Middle East. The first was committed by Iraq. A depleted economy had left no alternative but to go after easy pecking oil rich neighbor. Iraq invaded Kuwait. The other was committed by George Walker Bush when he invaded Iraq in 2003.

At the end, the US never understood the folly of the Fertile Crescent. One, the ropes were always in the hands of Turkey. Through Anatolia was the only way to take Bagdad and the Turks were against the invasion and they did not permit access over their country from north.

Two, if Bagdad, the heart of the Fertile Crescent, is hurt, the pain will be felt all around it from Iran to Syria. Today, Iran is the nightmare of the region and beyond with its nuclear program. Syria is in a civil war that brought in Russia and Iran as major players and pushed Western powers out.

Is Crescent heaven or hell? Heaven, if modernity, peace, and security can flow in from north uninterrupted and undisturbed. Hell, if Bagdad is not alive and well.

2. Levant, a slippery slope

What could be more important, consequential, deadly than the Fertile Crescent?

The answer is the Levant.

Syrians, Lebanese, Israelis, Jordanians, and Palestinians live there.

Druze, Maronites, Alleviates, Hizballah, or the likes, are also there.

Balkans known to be the slippery slope where two world wars started.

Like the Levant, many ethnic groups live there, invaded by incoming waves.

Yet, the world has never come close to a nuclear war as much as the Levant.

The US and the USSR came face to face in 1973 crisis between Egypt and Israel.

Also, the region is engulfed with Lebanese civil war that started in 1975.

The Syrian civil war that started in 2011 may be the last act.

In Lebanon, today there are no traces of US presence for almost a half century.

In Syria, the US forces were not in a tenable position as of the end of 2018.

They were clinging to an isolated part of the country, surrounded with unfriendly forces. As if Lebanon like calamity was waiting to happen, until Trump came like a White Night.

The US marines paid a heavy price for an ill-advised US deployment in Lebanon then.

A suicide bomb killed many of them when they were part of a UN peace mission there.

The Ottomans ruled the very region for four hundred years.

They never deployed troops were the US marines were deployed.

They must have known something.

The US should not have learnt it at the expense of 241 young American lives.

3. Grave mistakes

The grave mistakes in the Middle East started with Franklin D. Roosevelt.

A dozen US president contributed to the problems of the Middle East since then.

No one knows who to blame but Truman said it best when he recognized Israel.

"I don't have any Arab constituents, but I have tons of Jewish."

When the US created a "Bermuda Triangle," it was a bad amen.

What they did then would come back and hunt the West with a vengeance.

The recognition of the Kingdom of Saudi Arabia in 1937 was to protect the oil rights.

The recognition of the state of Israel in 1948 was because Truman needed votes.

The recognition of the Shah of Iran in 1953 was another with an outright coup d'état, no less!

They were supposed to have been the bedrock of the US policy for ages in the region. Instead, they formed a "triangle" that US could not get out of without getting hurt.

A. Bermuda triangle

Saudi Arabia, Israel, and Iran make the ultimate mother of all Bermuda Triangles. It is impossible to discern who hates who more or who is closer to who. Yet, they were all supposed to have been the best friends of the US at one time.

Instead, Saudi Arabia puts the US in a bind, Jamal Khashoggi being the last case but not an exception. 9/11 and Osama Bin Laden being the other end of the extreme, reminds the saying, "if you have friends like that who needs an enemy…"

Israel on the other hand continues to be a pariah state despite decades long support. Israel still receives foreign aid from the US, four billion dollars on last count. Plus, there is unwavering support in the US Congress. Yet, it is still the most endangered state in the region.

Iran, having become the existential threat to both Saudi Arabia and Israel should come as no surprise. Historical factors have been ignored. There was plenty of time to have dealt with in the past century, instead the West ignored history and "kicked the can" so to speak until now. It is time to reckon with the past policies.

Like President Trump keeps repeating regularly when applies, the previous presidents of the US should have done their job. Unfortunately, some have done practically nothing, some others did what they thought was the right thing turned out to make matters more complicated and worse.

a— An Absolute Monarchy in Modern Times

The modern Saudi state was founded by Abd Al-Aziz bin Abd al-Rahman Al Saud in 1932. To build the state, Abd Al-Aziz had to join forces with the Ikhwan, strict Wahhabi Sunni Islam supporters, in 1912. After that, he took over the most precious Najd and Hijaz, the home of the Muslim holy cities of Mecca and Medina. Then Saudi Arabia discovered oil, which brought the Americans to the region.

Yet, one day, when Saudi Arabia executed forty-seven people, including dissident Shia cleric Nimr Baqr al-Nimr, seemingly in a deliberate effort to inflame tensions around the Middle East, it led a number of Americans to ask a question:

"Why are we allies with these people?"

But it was not the only time, and acts like these continue regularly, unabated.

"There's not a smoking gun, there's a smoking saw,"

said Senator Lindsey Graham, R-S.C., referring to the bone saw that investigators believe was used to dismember Jamal Khashoggi after he was killed by a team of Saudi agents inside the country's consulate in Istanbul on Oct. 2, 2018.

When the US recognized and then supported Saudi Arabia throughout the century, it was there genuinely and with all good intentions. Yet, it was Saudi Arabia's responsibility to keep up with the modern world, reach maturity, and not internationalize internal problems. Nothing of that took place until now despite all the bountiful wealth the country enjoyed for many decades.

Instead, in the 21st century, Saudi Arabia is a country that needs support of much smaller countries like UAE or Bahrain or Israel even though it never recognized it as a legitimate state in the first place. A contradiction for the ages, that causes more damage than brings benefits to all involved, including the US directly and indirectly.

i— For the Sake of Oil

In 1938, a joint US-Saudi venture, eventually called ARAMCO, found truly staggering reserves. The US government wanted to protect its companies and their investments, especially when America was in dire need of crude oil during World War II. In 1943, FDR declared the security of Saudi Arabia a "vital interest" of the United States—despite the Saudis' official neutrality in the Axis-Allies conflict.

Yet, the answer, as it turns out, is more complicated than you might think. The relationship, one of America's longest running in the Arab world, began in 1933, centering on oil exploration. But, during the Cold War, it became more about fighting communism, and after that about preserving a political status quo in the Middle East that seemed to serve both nations' interests quite well.[41]

ii— Wahhabism

When Afghanistan came under Soviet control in 1979, the House of Saud saw an opportunity to project itself as the global defender of all Muslims. This view coincided with the Cold War aims of the US, which saw the Saudi desire to weaponize Islamist ideology as tactically useful in the West's struggles against the Soviet Union. As later described in testimony before the US Senate Judiciary Committee, and listed on the late King Fahd's website, Saudi Arabia spent four billion dollars per year on mosques, madrassas, preachers, students, and textbooks to spread the Wahhabi creed over the following decades.[42]

Muhammad ibn Abd al-Wahhab, founder of "Wahhabism," an austere form of Islam, was preaching a return to "pure" Islam. As a result, the most black, bleak, and bloody period in the history of Mecca and Hijaz started with the first Wahhabi occupation of the Land of Revelation from 1803 to 1813, followed over a century later by the second and most blasphemous occupation in 1925 by the desert brigand from Najd, Abdul-Aziz bin Saud, a British protégé, whose American-backed sons have continued to control the holy cities with even more sacrilegious means till this day, by destroying Islamic heritage and spilling the blood of Muslims.[43]

---

[41] https://www.chicagotribune.com/news/nationworld/ct-khashoggi-mbs-mohammad-bin-salman-20181204-story.html
[42] http://www.worldaffairsjournal.org/article/saudi-connection-wahhabism-and-global-jihad
[43] http://parstoday.com/en/radio/uncategorised-i25909-list_of_massacres_and_mishaps_at_mecca

iii—Jihadism

Saudi Arabia became "the only modern nation-state created by jihad," as the journalist Steve Coll once put it. At the beginning of the 20th century, and for most for most of the previous centuries of Arabian history, Saudi Arabia comprised three geographical units that were separate countries and, to some degree, cultures.

"It was the modern achievement of the House of Saud, through skilled and ruthless warfare, a highly refined gift for conciliation, and, most particularly, the potent glue of their Wahhabi mission, to pull those three areas together so that, by the end of the 20th century, the world's largest oil reserves were joined, sea to sea, to the largest center of annual religious pilgrimage in the world—and to their capital in the Wahhabi heartland of Riyadh," Robert Lacey wrote in his 2010 history of Saudi Arabia.

iv - The Most Famous Saudis in the World:

One is a murderer, the other is murdered by another Saudi

There is an enduring problem in Saudi Arabia that needs to be resolved by the Saudis themselves. They breed indigenous terrorists that go to war beyond their borders.

When Cuban mercenaries went to Angola, Saudi jihadists went to Afghanistan. Then when they came back, they went after the Americans. Nowadays, the regime is going after its own citizens. In extreme cases, the regime brutally and brazenly murders one of its citizens and then it tries to cover it up.

aa— Osama bin Laden

On one hand, Saudi terrorists attacked their best ally US, killing thousands of innocent citizens. The hijackers in the September 11 attacks were nineteen men affiliated with al-Qaeda. Fifteen of them were Saudi citizens. Osama Bin Laden was their leader. Some 2,750 people were killed in New York, 184 at the Pentagon, and forty in Pennsylvania.

The pattern of the 1920s, in which the Saudi rulers needed Wahhabi fundamentalists, then came into conflict with them over modernization, and ultimately co-opted that fundamentalism in order to neutralize it, has repeated throughout Saudi history. That pattern has shaped Saudi Arabia's severely oppressive rule at home and its support of jihadism abroad.

For the Saudi rulers, this foreign policy of jihad was at first a great success. It strengthened Saudi Arabia's effort to fund Afghan rebels, it positioned the often-lecherous Saudi monarchs as leaders of the Muslim world against the Soviet atheists, and, crucially, it distracted the Wahhabis from causing trouble at home.

But this strategy was destined to backfire, and disastrously. Those jihadists would inevitably turn their guns on the very Saudi government that had enabled their creation, just as the Ikhwan of the 1920s and the cultists of the 1970s had done. The most famous of those was Osama bin Laden.[44]

Bipolar world is no longer there. The US is the biggest producer of oil not depending on any country for its energy survival. So, what is to be done with Saudi Arabia and its problems, especially when current Saudi rulers continue to their own old ways, never visiting modernity.

bb— Jamal Khashoggi

As late as 2018, the crown prince of the country is implicated with the murder of one of its journalists in a consulate in Istanbul. Senator Lindsey Graham, one of Saudi Arabia's most vocal defenders in the US Congress, referring to Saudi journalist Jamal Khashoggi's murder, said Crown Prince Mohammed bin Salman, has "got to go" and vowed never to return to the country as long as the young leader remains in power. Graham also pledged to impose sanctions, saying:

"This guy is a wrecking ball. He had this guy murdered in a consulate in Turkey, and to expect me to ignore it—I feel used and abused."

As Saudi Arabia went on the defensive about Jamal Khashoggi's alleged murder, Ankara seized the chance to repair relations with Washington by releasing U.S. pastor Andrew Brunson. President Trump told reporters, expressing his hope:

"We feel much different about Turkey today than we did yesterday,"

"...having a very, very good relationship."

Turkish President Recep Tayyip Erdoğan has long wanted Turkey to supplant Saudi Arabia as the dominant power in the Middle East. The Khashoggi affair has presented a unique opportunity to undermine Saudi influence, potentially creating a regional power void for Turkey to fill.

The emergence of Turkey as a rival Middle East power traces back to the Arab Spring, when the Turks supported Egypt's Muslim Brotherhood government and the Saudis bitterly opposed it. Erdoğan is an Islamist; many like-minded political parties in the region look to him for leadership, and Saudi Crown Prince Mohammed bin Salman (MBS) has accused him of trying to "reinstate the Islamic Caliphate" of the Ottoman Empire.

---

44   https://www.vox.com/2015/1/26/7877619/saudi-arabia-questions

MBS spent the past year—and millions of dollars—positioning himself as a golden boy in Washington, just as Erdoğan and Trump came to blows over the jailed American pastor, resulting in crippling sanctions and a nadir in US-Turkey relations.

For Erdoğan, Khashoggi's death couldn't have happened at a better moment. The day after, Erdoğan gave a speech in which his ambition for regional leadership was on full display. The gruesome details of Khashoggi's murder trickled out, punctuating the claims of Turkish officials and their allies that the Saudi-Emirati-US alliance was morally bankrupt. The Trump administration's approach to the region has also fueled Turkey's rise, transforming the war against ISIS into a confrontation with regional rival Iran and blessing the Saudi-Emirati siege of U.S. ally Qatar. In response, Turkey sent troops to protect Qatar and is coordinating with Iran in the Syrian conflict, solidifying a new axis of influence. With Saudi Arabia on the ropes over Khashoggi, Erdoğan has more opportunities to ramp up his influence in Washington and the Arab world.[45]

b— A Democracy Under Siege

On November 10, 1945, American diplomats were brought in from their posts in the Middle East to urge President Harry Truman not to heed Zionist urgings. Truman had then bluntly explained his motivation: "I'm sorry, gentlemen, but I have to answer to hundreds of thousands who are anxious for the success of Zionism: I do not have hundreds of thousands of Arabs among my constituents."[46]

In 1948, when Israel was recognized by the US, it marked the beginning of the end of Britain's dominance in the Middle East.

i– The Idea of Partition

During the period of the British Mandate in Palestine, some experts tried to dress up the need for mutual Jewish-Arab recognition in geopolitical garb. This idea was known as "partition" and it mainly focused on two separate nation-states west of the Jordan. In 1948, when the Mandate came to an end and Israel was founded, the idea of partition was already more than ten years old. Now it is more than sev-

---

45 https://www.axios.com/after-khashoggis-death-turkey-sees-a-path-to-greater-influence-5a58595a-feae-47bd-a658-3c5e5fb63ccc.html

46 https://www.wrmea.org/1991-may-june/truman-adviser-recalls-may-141948-us-decision-to-recognize-israel.html

enty years old. "Does it still have a chance?" Asks Motti Golani, a professor at the University of Haifa.

ii— Globalist vs Nationalist Trends

According to Uri Ram of Ben Gurion University, geopolitically, Israel straddles the West (by being or being viewed as a protégée of the United States) and the Middle East (the heart of world Islamic resistance to the United States). Employing Benjamin Barber's colorful terms, Israel straddles "McWorld" and "Jihad." Meanwhile, within Israel itself there is a tension between the market and tribe. That is to say, the same two contending forces in the world at large are also present in Israel: a global, capitalist, civic trend on the one hand, and a local, national-religious, ethno-centric trend on the other.

c— A revolution in the making

Iranian border with modern Turkey was settled in 1514 after the Battle of Chaldiran between the Ottoman Sultan Selim and Safavid leader Shah Ismail. It stood the test of times for five hundred years.

It is a testament that Iran is safe from Western forces so long as there is Turkey because they settled on that border for good, reflecting the strength and balance of power between the two people of the region.[47]

Eight-year long Iraq-Iran war proved another point. Iran cannot be invaded from the south either. Iraq, with Western support, at the height of its power, could not do it. And, what about when the US decided to take control of Iran by toppling the regime there with a coup d'état in 1953. It was successful but was it a wise decision?

By 1979, Islamic revolution replaced the US installed regime and insulated itself and started to acquire nuclear power to prevent another attempt of sort or to be proactive and employ the first strike capability against its perceived enemies in the region. The problem is that the revolution is only forty years old, long way from maturation yet.

On top of that, Iran attempts to run an unconventional empire by exerting great influence on sub-state entities like Hamas (Palestinian territories); Hezbollah (Lebanon); the Mahdi movement (Iraq); and the Houthi insurgents (Yemen). In Afghanistan, Tehran's influence on some Shiite groups is such that thousands have volunteered to fight for Bashar al-Assad in Syria. Iran also provided arms to the

---

[47] http://www1.udel.edu/History-old/figal/Hist104/assets/pdf/readings/02selimismail.pdf

Taliban after it was ousted from power by a U.S.-led coalition and has long considered the Afghan city of Herat, near the Afghan–Iranian border, to be within its sphere of influence.[48]

In the second decade of the 21st century, one of the most pressing urgencies for the US is to prevent nuclearization of Iran when the rest of the world including the Western allies do not seem to be as worried much of anything. All the while, Iran, insulated with Russia in the north and Turkey in the east, cannot be influenced by outside forces. When toppling the regime in Iran seems to be the only alternative, not having close relationships with Russia and Turkey do not help.

Yet, the reality today is exactly that. Iran, Turkey and Russia—three very different countries with centuries long distrust and enmity are together and bonding like never before in history. Their sole reason for that has been the globalist Americans who have achieved the impossible! They started to bring them together with their policies since the Islamic revolution of Iran in 1979, and at a faster pace since the breakup of the Soviet Union in 1991. Donald J. Trump is now expected to entangle this big mess.

A globalist mess in the making for forty years on top of the Bermuda Triangle problem!

B. Coup d'états always fire back

If the Western strategies of the 20th century are to continue, the West will be in lot of trouble in the future. In fact, unless Western strategies are replaced in the 21st century, Muslim invasion of Europe will become a nightmare turned into a reality.

Throughout the 20th century, the US employed one tool, and repeatedly, only to see it blew in its face every time. The region is in total disarray after a very long Western hegemony that it ruled at will. But the world has changed as far as the old methods are concerned. They have no place anymore.

Turkey is a case in point. It is a much different world than what it was a century ago.

In the past two decades, it changed even more: it built more bridges, tunnels, dams, irrigation canals, highways, railroads, airports, seaports, stadiums, hospitals, recreation grounds, energy plants, military platforms, pipelines, walls on its borders, mosques, schools, universities, hotels, manufacturing plants, water and electricity infrastructure, and subway networks than ever before. Some of them are world's biggest marvels and there are many of them.

---

[48]   https://www.heritage.org/military-strength/assessing-the-global-operating-environment/middle-east\

Eighty-million are witness to the progress and most cherish it. Plus, there is another billion, some of which otherwise would be refugees, are closely watching it with admiration.

But in Turkey, the progress came only when there were no more coup d'états like in 1960, 1971, and 1980. They made Turkey go broke, penniless as one of its prime ministers once declared. Not having a coup d'état for thirty-six years in a row, one remaining a post-modern intervention in 1997 and the other totally failing in 2016 for the first time show how the tie turned. People power prevented the last coup d'état.

Turkey was tolerant and waited a whole century before reappearing as the old self. Turkey today will play a Zero-Sum game as a countermove on any attempts of old methods be it nation-building attempts or coup d'états. They are not limited with Turkey either. The fury of Muslim masses and their leaderships know very well that the bipolar world has long gone so does the methods and strategies of the past.

Since the end of World War II, there have been 225 successful coups in countries with populations greater than 500,000, according to the Center for Systemic Peace, which maintains extensive datasets on various forms of armed conflict and political violence. Most coups occurred during the height of the Cold War, from the 1960s through the 1980s.[49]

It is ironic that a prosperous Turkey today is savior of the West in the face of refugees which can also be leveraged as one of the countermoves if the West does not wake up fast. If only Eisenhower had seen how Turkey had saved Europe from refugee calamity twice since the Korean debacle, he would surely feel for Donald J. Trump what kind idiosyncrasies of the globalists he has to deal with in these modern times.

C. Nation building has even bigger repercussions

The globalists were in the nation-building business since 1980s. They successfully freed fifteen republics from the yoke of USSR in 1991.

After that, they also tried to create a Kurdish state in the Middle East, but they failed. They were doomed from the beginning. Their problem was that creating a Kurdish state had something to do with Ataturk's modern Republic of Turkey whose motto was "Peace at home. Peace in the world." It simply meant that there won't be an imposition by force to no one.

---

[49]   http://www.pewresearch.org/fact-tank/2017/11/17/
        egypts-coup-is-first-in-2013-as-takeovers-become-less-common-worldwide

ERBIL GUNASTI

Turkey proved Ataturk's ideals in the Korean war when it joined on the side of the US against an aggression from the north. It paid the price with the blood of more than seven-hundred martyrs and over two-thousand wounded soldiers. They came home as heroes and S. Korea free and intact.

Turkey has done it in a faraway land for a nation that it did not have much connection with until then. Turkey would surely do the same many times over in nearby countries like Iraq. That is why, solely because of the character of modern Republic of Turkey, nation-building in Iraq never worked and will never work by outsiders.

When Turkey says the territorial integrity of the countries is the number one priority in the region, it means that it will interfere to that end. Regimes in Iran, Iraq, and Syria will support Turkey even if they may be at odds on everything else with one another, including war.

Turkey did what it said it will do twice in Iraq. First, it stopped the forward progress in a decade long Western plan to create an autonomous Kurdish region in Iraq by early 1990s. In 2017, Turkey took away from Kurds, for good, with an additional military move, all the gains they had garnered towards autonomy in the past half century.

a— Failed 1980 plan

In the early 1980s, Turkey was cooperating with the US on Iraq policy. Turkey allowed for the US aircrafts, deployed at Incirlik air base, to enforce no-fly zone north of 36th parallel to protect the Kurds from Saddam Hussein's wrath. It lasted a decade. But in the early 1990s, Turkey realized the real intentions of the US agents and firmly stated that, autonomy meant only autonomy or self-governance, but never independence.

When Turkey was convinced that that no one was listening on the US end, it promptly ended the no-fly zone flights over northern Iraq. As quickly, Western plans to carve a chunk out of Iraq was over. The Kurdish independence dream died nascent.

After that, it is natural that Turkey would not allow the US forces to invade Iraq from its territory in 2003. Turkey knew that the US goal was still to create a Kurdish state there, using the pretext of removing Saddam Hussein. It is unbelievable how the Bush-43 administration will be so foolish that Turkey would not understand and allow the US forces waltz through its territory.

This episode also says a lot how the officials in the US administrations do not know or pay attention to history. Modern Republic of Turkey never forgets the betrayal during Cuban missile crisis or Johnson's letter or Carter's embargo. In

2003, they were still vivid memories in addition to the Kurdish nation-building dreams of the globalists.

One can also argue that it is the "American exceptionalism" that makes the US resort to such drives. That may be, but history also repeats itself and Turks are a by-product of history, too. Turks have been writing history in the region and beyond past 2,000 years. Maybe that is the Turkish version of the "exceptionalism" that says that the history has to be written by them in that region since they arrived there a thousand years ago.

Turks have always displayed their exceptionalism with their guts and lives. During the Korean war when the British and American forces were withdrawing, the Turks affixed their bayonet and moved forward to death or victory and victory was theirs at the end, according to the Western commander who witnessed it.

Turkey reminded one more time to all who needed to be reminded to who they were again in 2017.

b— Failed 2017 plan

In 2017, within days after a referendum for Kurdish independence was declared, it had to be aborted because Turkey mobilized its armed forces to invade northern Iraq as a retaliation, to end the charade. Iraq government joined the maneuvers on Turkish side, allying itself immediately with Turkey. Iran closed its borders to the Kurds from north.

The Kurds in the autonomous zone of Iraq were fooled again by the misguided US agents and their cohorts in EU. No globalist regime in the West had the political will to put up with Turkey. Nobody from the West came to help the revolting Kurds.

It is impossible to think that no globalist remembers the Dardanelles in 1915 or the defeat in Anatolia in 1922 or the Korean war in 1953 or the military operation to Cyprus in 1975. Turks will not let certain things to be changed against their will. They will simply not permit it.

It is also impossible how the West cannot understand a simple fact. Iran, Iraq, Turkey, and Syria will always unite against Kurds. They will never allow a Kurdish state. Carving a state from one would mean carving a similar portion from the other three. A simple logic and misguided British heritage coming back and hunting the globalists time and again. No nation-building can be allowed there when quarter of a billion people object it.

On the other hand, poor Kurds. When the Kurdish demands were quelled, they paid a heavy price. They lost most of the autonomy they had gained in Iraq since 1980s. They had to withdraw and leave Mosul and Kirkuk out of their jurisdiction. More importantly, they had to give up the oil fields and the right to export, independently.

It was a lot of work to bring autonomy to the Kurds in Iraq. Turkey was most instrumental in their accomplishment. Now Turkey was also feeling betrayed. In short, the autonomy that the Turks gave to Kurds in the 1980s took it back in 2016 when the Kurds went for statehood. Turkey simply showed once again who was ruling in the Middle East.

III. 21st century realities

In the Middle East today, there is only one player with capacity and political will.
Independent Turkey is back in the former Ottoman territories with force.
Plus, there is one issue that touches everybody.
Refugees are heading to Europe from Asia and Africa in massive numbers.
And then, there are two natural resources that could easily turn into casus bellis.
On one end, Euphrates and Tigris. On the other, eastern Mediterranean riches.
The US, the Russian Federation, and China are in play for the latter.
But they have to deal with Turkey. It is the main dealmaker and breaker.
President Putin joined forces with Turkey when Erdoğan shot down one of his aircrafts.
President Trump was smart enough to join forces with Turkey before China did.
Now the task is to save Crescent, peace in the Levant, and to let the Peninsula alone.
So that the balance of power over the continental shelves can be established.

1. Casus bellis

Refugee crisis is by far the biggest issue.
Scarce natural resources are the other.
The region is in dire shape. It is in ruins. Plight of the people is a powder box.
Iraq, Syria, Lebanon, Yemen, Libya, and Tunisia must be rebuilt and fast.
In the meanwhile, achieving security and then bringing modernity are in order.
But eastern Mediterranean balance of power must also be established fast.

A. Refugee crisis

Refugee crisis is the single biggest problem of the 21st century. Not having wars will prevent refugee explosions from the Middle East. Yet refugees will continue to trickle into the region from southeast Asia or Africa. They would like to continue to EU.

Better option is North America but only a small portion will be able to cross the ocean. Nonetheless, the likelihood of tens of millions of people will be at the gates of Western civilizations is a sure thing.

The prospects of refugee problem to challenge the Western civilization as we know it is very real. Building walls across the world, turning countries into city-states of the old, already seem to be the path for number of countries and regions.

In the US, it became a big issue when the Trump Administration wanted to build a wall between Mexico and the US. But Israel and Turkey are among numerous other countries with walls. They have already completed most of theirs. Hungary and Slovenia are doing the same between Croatia to stem the flow from the Balkans.

Year 2015 was a clear case in point. In 2018, 200,000 migrants landed in Europe, way down from the nearly two million in 2015, according to Frontex, the EU border agency. Hungary said the fences helped cut migrants on its borders by nearly 100 percent since 2015, along with a deal made by Turkey and the European Union to stem the flow of migrants reaching the continent.[50]

Walls in Europe means lots of refugees will look for alternatives. It is not surprising to see many refugees on the southern border of the US these days from non-American countries. They will come in increasing numbers both to Europe and North America.

They have no other places to go. And their numbers will grow as the world population will increase by another two billion within three decades.

In Africa alone, the EU soldiers are manning security check points in the middle of Mali and Niger in order to prevent refugees heading to the shores of Mediterranean. The way the refugees are overpowering the European territories in Morocco and elsewhere despite layers of walls, reflect how serious the problem is and how worse it will become over time.

Other than China and to a lesser extent, the investment from Turkey apart, Africa is an explosion waiting to happen. Asia is not lagging far behind.

B. Natural resources

Fast-rising world population brings other problems alongside refugees. "Water, oil and natural gas are projected to run out according to the current consumption and production records within the 21st century if no new sources are found.

Considering the world population is to grow more than two billion in the same period, the urgency of finding new resources and sources is vitally important."[51]

a— Access to water is the issue, not supply

For the water, it is more of an access question than supply. "It's a simple equation: As populations increase and incomes grow, so does water demand. The world's population, now at 7.5 billion, is projected to add 2.3 billion more people by 2050. How can the planet satisfy its thirst? Growing incomes also exacerbate the water problem, because of the water-intensive products—like meat and energy from fossil fuels—that richer populations demand."[52]

"Access to water is one of the pressing global issues of the 21st century. As the global population grows and becomes wealthier, the demand for water will greatly increase. We will need to find better ways to both manage our current use of fresh water and configure it for the future, to be able to serve our growing populations and preserve stocks for future generations."[53]

The quantity of fresh water is limited. Only 2.5 percent of the total amount of water on earth is fresh water, of which 69.4 percent is in the form of ice, snow, or permafrost and most of the remainder is ground water. Fresh water in lakes and rivers is only about 1 percent of fresh water available on earth.[54]

In the Middle East, water is a lifeline. Especially in the Fertile Crescent where Euphrates and Tigris flow for thousands of years. Yet, now there is not only Turkey at the fountain head, but it also has big dams and man-made lakes to regulate the water flow as much as it wishes. Access to water in the region is a real issue, an existential problem for sure. A benevolent Turkey is the only alternative.

b— Oil

For the oil and gas production, there is a limit to its availability so what is and where is the next source are the main questions and define the fight to getting it.

---

[51]   https://www.theguardian.com/environment/blog/2011/
oct/31/six-natural-resources-population.

[52]   https://www.wri.org/blog/2017/08/7-reasons-were-facing-global-water-crisis

[53]   https://ourworld.unu.edu/en/water-prospects-in-the-21st-century

[54]   https://www.ncbi.nlm.nih.gov/pubmed/12291371

"Oil and gas production in the North Sea is likely to sag in the coming years, but the industry won't go without a fight. By the early 2020s, production will start to drop off rapidly, falling to around 1.33m boe/d by 2023."[55]

"Saudi Arabia is the world's central bank of oil. Many in the oil industry, therefore, want to know how much oil there is in the Kingdom to calculate future risks. According to Wael Mahdi, who is an energy reporter specializing on OPEC and a co-author of OPEC in a Shale Oil World: 'There should not be any worry about Saudi supplies to meet demand for the next three decades at least.'"[56]

c— Eastern Mediterranean Riches

If oil were to run out in the Middle East, it is no problem. By the time it runs out, new energy sources are said to be recoverable from under the Mediterranean Sea.

One oil magazine quoted recently:

"The cradle of civilization, this corner of the world has always been characterized by instability. Now, thanks to energy, it could become a new focal point of development and unexpected opportunities...The eastern Mediterranean was the cradle of three great religions, bureaucracies, and market institutions. Alexander the Great was born there, the region was the center of the Roman Empire and its ocean was known as Roma's 'mare nostrum.' Centuries later, the countries bordering the eastern Mediterranean became the Byzantine Empire, and this is also the region where Islam reached its golden age. Cyprus, Greece, Lebanon, Syria, Israel, Turkey, and Egypt, the countries touched by this sea, were as alluring as they were unlucky."[57]

Turkey has the longest shoreline in this area of new contention and consequently the biggest share of the continental shelf. In addition, there is the Northern Turkish Republic of Cyprus, a self-declared, Turkey-recognized state that claims significant portion of the rights that emanate from the island of Cyprus's southern half (that is at odds with its other half).

Furthermore, there are complexities of international relationships and leverages over the other eastern Mediterranean countries. Major powers also seek a stake in the region with their advance technology and overwhelming resources. Their interests, coupled with their capital, create a very explosive powder mix.

---

[55] http://www.petroleum-economist.com/articles/upstream/
exploration-production/2018/extending-the-life-of-the-north-sea

[56] http://www.arabnews.com/node/1364846

[57] https://www.eniday.com/en/human_en/eastern-mediterranean-sea-of-gas/

Time will tell if the center of the world regarding oil and natural gas production will shift from the Arabian Peninsula and its vicinity to the eastern Mediterranean, but the issue of global security seems to have already shifted to the latter already.

2. What Needs to be Done

The Middle East needs security, rebuilding and modernity.

These must come in a new way and in that order.

It is not the 19th or the 20th centuries anymore.

Modernity will no longer come to the East through Western ways.

Rebuilding has to be made with China, the US and others altogether.

Security will come when nation-building or coup d'états are not the usual methods of operating.

A. Security

Turkey will be a critical partner in Alliance efforts to address security challenges on the European periphery, including risks associated with uncertain Russian futures. The United States will have an independent interest in security cooperation with Turkey for power projection in adjacent areas of critical interest—the Balkans, the Caucasus, and the Caspian, the Levant, and the Gulf. To the extent that NATO moves to become a more geographically expansive, power-projection alliance, this interest in Turkey's role will be more widely shared.[58]

The geopolitical significance of the Mediterranean Sea region is the result of three factors: its location at the junction of Europe, Asia, and Africa; its significant international sea routes and straits—Gibraltar, Bosporus, Dardanelles, Suez Canal; and its potential as a source of oil and natural gas. Recent gas discoveries in the Eastern Mediterranean have only reaffirmed this potential.[59]

The United States appears to be going through a unilateral moment. Visible tensions at the G-7 Summit in Charlevoix, Canada, the threat of trade sanctions on close U.S. allies, and the U.S. withdrawal from the Joint Comprehensive Plan of Action with Iran are all signs in the last month that traditional U.S. approaches to international relations are in transition. It is wrong to pin this all on President Donald Trump. In fact, he seems to have seized on a vein of popular discontent with the international order. After all, if Americans genuinely supported the insti-

---

[58] https://www.rand.org/content/dam/rand/pubs/monograph_
reports/MR1126/MR1126.chap4.pdf

[59] https://www.mepc.org/journal/energy-security-eastern-mediterranean

tutions and alliances he is challenging, there would be a wave of Republican opposition to these new strategies that contravene everything the party has represented for more than a half-century, and Democratic politicians would be wooing disgruntled Republicans to bolt the party. Nothing of the sort is happening.

And yet, many of the challenges that the United States faces in the world do not lend themselves to unilateral approaches. The necessity for multilateralism is well illustrated in the Eastern Mediterranean, where such an approach originated more than seventy years ago. While the structure of U.S. engagement in the region requires revision, the necessary U.S. response is not to engage less with allies, but rather to engage more comprehensively.

Despite dramatic changes on the ground and at sea, U.S. policy toward the Eastern Mediterranean region has become increasingly military and unilateral, even before the Trump administration. The diplomatic engagement, economic investment, and security presence of the United States, all hallmarks of U.S. policy since the 1940s, have dramatically receded. Especially in the last decade, other powers—primarily Russia, China, Turkey, and Iran—have increased their strategic footprint, weakening regional governments' ties with the United States and Europe.[60]

B. Rebuilding

No one yet is talking about the rebuilding. There is a reason for that. First Syria must be stabilized. Turkey and the US are doing it. In 2019, rebuilding can start and then they can move to Iraq.

Turkey will take the lead again with the US because no one else can. The West will not come to the region and risk loss of life and investment. The Arabs will not do because of two reasons. One, there is a division among them. No one can be trusted. Two, there are better alternatives.

But more importantly, there is no leadership in the Middle East other than the leadership Turkey can bring in conjunction with other powers. Moreover, if Turkey steps in, half of the Middle East will immediately welcome it. No other actor local or overseas can make the same claim.

C. Modernity

According to Britannica, modernity was associated with individual subjectivity, scientific explanation and rationalization, a decline in emphasis on religious world

---

[60]   https://www.csis.org/analysis/help-wanted-multilateralism-eastern-mediterranean

views, the emergence of bureaucracy, rapid urbanization, the rise of nation-states, and accelerated financial exchange and communication.

There is little consensus as to when modernity began. Histories of Western Europe suggest that a modern era arrived at the end of colonial invasion and global expansion, which date to the 18th and early 19th centuries.

In general, modernity was exemplified by the period subsequent to the onset of modern warfare, typified by two world wars and succeeded by postmodernism.

On the contrary, a radical view from the side of those who faced the modernity that was imposed on them by the Western Europeans would argue for example that there are three kinds of imperialism that sought to bring modernity to the weak states of Africa and the Middle East among others.

One was a case of colonialism, best exemplified, when French settled by force in Algeria and until they were thrown out with the bloodiest Algerian Revolution that liberated the country from the French yoke in early 1960s.

Another way the West tried to bring modernity to the Middle East was a case in point in Egypt when Egypt was invaded by the Western powers. It was also a way to wrestle another North African territory from the decaying Ottoman Empire.

Much like how the West imposed its will on Algeria and Egypt in the name of bringing modernity in the 8th and 19th centuries, the imposition of special administrative zone in Mount Lebanon became the third way to bring Western rule to former Ottoman territories in the name of modernity.

In short, the West used the excuse of modernity to dismember the Ottoman Empire of the Middle Ages in the modern times, as far as one side of the argument would go. The other side of the argument would be that there was no one specific way to bring modernity, except to try colonialism, conquest and imposition of special administrative zones.

a— The 19th and 20th centuries

There are many competing arguments how the modernity came or was attempted to be imposed in the 19th and 20th centuries in the old Ottoman territories.

One would argue that it came in stages "however the process was far from being a completely successful, irresistible and homogeneous movement. This modernization process was far from being a smooth process."

The other would argue that "modernization remained a rhetorical argument rather than a concrete political will, and the reality was closer to European's exploiting these territories' resources."

During these decaying years, the two successive phases or reforms launched by the Ottoman Empire between 1789 and 1876, [were] often described as "defensive developmentalism," namely as a response to the pressure of the Europeans' intrusive modernity.

In Egypt, at first, it was a "top-down modernization process under Muhammad Ali (1804-1849). Muhammad Ali's reforms significantly and deeply contributed to the construction of Modern Egypt." In 1882 with the British invasion of the country, a new version of the modernity experiment took place.

In Algeria, "modernization was implemented through imperialism which mainly took place when the French colonialized the country." Whereas at Mount Lebanon a special administrative mandate was imposed.

In the case of the Ottoman Empire, the Tanzimat was largely criticized by the Muslim population, who considered the Tanzimat as incompatible with Islam. Therefore, the reforms launched by the Ottoman Empire between 1876 and 1906 turned back the Tanzimat spirit.

It is also crucial to mention the role played by a genuine intelligentsia, in Turkey and in Iran, at the turn of the 20th century. In Istanbul, one of the most significant manifestations of this phenomenon is embedded in the Young Turks. Born on July 14, 1889, exactly one hundred years after the French Revolution, the Young Turks were a reformist political party, largely influenced by Europeans ideals, that seized power in 1908.

By contrast, in Iran, the reformist Persian movement gathered diverse secret societies called "anjumanha." These societies were particularly influenced by the Positivism of Auguste Comte. Moreover, at the end of the 19th century, the emergence of a European-influenced intellectual class in Iran finally led to the Constitutional Revolution of 1905-1906.

b— 21st century

In the 21st century, modernity seems to be catching up in countries like Saudi Arabia, Nigeria, Iran, Egypt, Pakistan, and Bangladesh because they will soon be some of the biggest economies of the world. They are projected to rank from number fifteen to twenty-eight and in that order. Economic growth will also bring them military might. More people will live in the newly built cities. They will taste the modernity.

The other two Muslim countries Indonesia and Turkey are projected to rank number four and five respectively. They are widely immersed into the modernity. But they will also have lot more resources to share with the rest. They will be a force to bring modernity to others.

Turkey is already sharing quite a lot with Indonesia and Pakistan, especially on security measures. Time would show how much Turkey will bring others on board, since it has lot to offer and share, and willing to work together on win-win scenarios.

Yet, when modernity comes, it does not mean that these countries will have less religion. On the contrary, they may embrace religion even more.

Many Muslim states would follow Turkish path. Secular state with political Islamist regime at the driver seat enjoying modernity is a viable example. On one hand, it lets the state govern. On the other hand, it lets the people live their lives and govern their conscious.

The West's definition of modernity may vary. The danger is if the West were to think that it could bring its own version of modernity. That means the West will continue with nation-building and coup d'états.

The attempt for the West to try to impose its will on the rest of the world is no longer possible. It is time for the rest of the world to live their way of life next to the Western values as we know it. The demographic numbers of the East will be many times of those that contend with the Western values. Minority trying to impose its own ways and means against majority will receive a reaction that can turn from unpleasant to catastrophic results.

Let modernity come its own way in the East. It is coming anyway. No one can stop it with technologies in place and widely available. It sure looks like it will be a melting pot soon everywhere. And they can do it without the False Prophets coming from the West or the East or within.

3. False Prophets

It is not fair to label Saudi Arabia or Egypt as "False Prophets" of the Middle East.

But Turkey and the US must appear together like the "White Nights" in the 21st century.

Presence of Turkey with its Ottoman and Seljuk past hinders Saudi Arabia or Egypt.

With powerful Turkey, they cannot claim leadership role among Muslims.

On top, most Muslims cherish the Ottoman heritage.

After all, they have been subjects of the Sultans for centuries.

Increasingly, they also see the ripple effects of the modern Republic of Turkey.

In the past two decades, under Erdoğan regime, Turkey built relationships.

Many Muslim countries, across Asia and Africa came in contact with modern Turkey.

Turkey approached them with a win-win strategy.

Having resources and political will power to deliver, also helped.

The Russian Federation and China clearly understand these factors.

But more importantly, president Trump gets it.

After all, there is only one superpower in the world.

Without its say, Turkey will limit itself or emphasis in the region.

It will focus on other priorities in the region with Russian Federation and China.

There are lot of areas to focus on or to develop in the region.

The US and Turkey can explore all of them in the lead.

In the Middle East, there is no room for False Prophets be it local or from outside.

A. Saudi Arabia

Saudi Arabia has never achieved a leadership role among Muslims of the world. It does not have endless oil wealth to share. Reportedly, natural resources are to run out or dwindle mid-century. Plus, the regime needs the potent Wahhabis, yet they adhere to a very strict rule of Islam. When Muslim masses around the world need tolerance, that is the last thing they look for. Moreover, there are alternatives to fill the vacuum the US left behind.

B. Egypt

Egypt has always been an African powerhouse. Without much physical leverage on the Middle East, it remains isolated. Gamal Abdel Nasser regime was a case in point when Egypt had joined forces with Syria. But it did not last long and was not effective.

In the past, Egypt was most powerful under the Ottoman suzerainty, controlling the whole region extending to Medina and Mecca. That was the only time, Egypt had a say in the region.

4. Independent Turkey

Turkey will determine the future of the Middle East together with the US.

It is important for the US to join Turkey before China does in larger role.

The Russian Federation has already covered lots of grounds with Turkey.

They are hard at work in the Black Sea, with pipelines to Europe and in Syria.

The US and Turkey must start a new journey in Syria.

After that, Iraq and Iran will come. Mediating in the Levant is thereafter.

A. Turkey will play a role in the Crescent

The Fertile Crescent has an independent Turkey nearby past two decades. As a benevolent power, it is raising its voice when necessary with strength. The US must support Turkey. Otherwise, Western plans in the region are a sure bet to fail.

In Iraq, neither the US invasion in 2003, nor the Kurdish uprising for independence in 2017 were successful when Turkey objected. In Syria, without Turkey on board, the US objectives against Iranian forces were not effective and president Trump wishes to exit from the Obama mess at the earliest. In Iran, the jury is out. Worse nightmares are still possible if nothing is coordinated with Turkey.

Iran, Iraq, and Syria are very important countries in the Middle East. International policies cannot be applied to them without impacting Turkey. Hence, Turkey will always fight to protect territorial integrity and independence of its neighbors. Plus, Turkey has the capacity and political will to make all four countries walk together to certain extend.

But with the US backing, Turkey will surely become even more stabilizing factor for the region. Considering the interest of China and India in the coming years to the region, the urgency for the US to act and achieve such a stability with Turkey is important.

Having said that, irrespective of what the US decides to do in this region in the coming decade, Turkey will further consolidate its standing in northern Iraq first and foremost. Securing a buffer zone in Syria will also come simultaneously. Iran will remain in the back burner as far as Turkey is concerned until Iraq and Syria fronts are taken care of. The US joining Turkey in this task will speed up the process and the Iranian nuclearization issue will be resolved promptly and effectively without resorting to violent measures, including military operations.

a— In Iraq

For Turkey, in Iraq, only the northern third of the country matters in the foreseeable future. It has also been the same in the 20th century when the region was forcefully yanked out of the modern Turkey proper. But it is more so in the 21st century and Turkey now has the capacity and will power to set its goals in the region.

The region has vitally important role for the future of Turkey. To that end, Turkey will always seek first to see peace and security are maintained in northern Iraq. The goal will be to bring modernity and prosperity to the region. Not until Erbil, Mosul, Suleymaniye, and Kerkuk prosper and become most modern cities in the world, the task in the north will not finish.

What Turkey would like to see to take place in northern Iraq actually serves the interest of the US. It is the only way nuclearization of Iran can be ended effectively but also peacefully.

As for the timeline, to join forces with Turkey? It is now or never. Turkey has already began the journey some time ago. It is a journey of no return. Whether it will be limited to northern third of the country or to the rest of Iraq will depend on the US.

i- The US must heed the sign from Turkey

In northern third of Iraq, the US must heed the message coming from Turkey.

In the 2020s, the US may still continue to believe keeping major military bases in this northern third of Iraq is vital for its national interest. If the need for these bases is to win Iraq back, then it is a mistake. If the need for these bases is to pressure Iran, it is a another mistake if Turkey is not on board. If the need for these bases is to keep Turkish advances over the PKK terrorists in check, it is even worse because Turkey already assumes the worst-case scenario in play in this region!

Hence, the US must heed the message coming from Turkey regarding northern Iraq and it must cooperate accordingly. One thing is for sure, Turkey will play a Zero-Sum game even against the US in northern Iraq. That is how important northern Iraq is for Turkey so the message must be heed no matter what.

ii- "Operation Claw" is the sign

It is the beginning of the end!

As of May 28th, 2019, Turkey already sent a message with the massive military operation, dubbed "Operation Claw." It is important to note the significance of this military incursion compare to others in the past. One, the Iraqi prime minister was in Ankara for an official visit in Turkey. Two, it was a massive operation on land and air. On May 29, Turkey even used for the first time its newly and indigenously developed 280 kilometer-long Bora ballistic missile on targets 160 kilometer-deep in Iraq with precision. Third, the US did not know about the operation until the Turks notified. On top of that, President Trump and First Lady were visiting the Imperial Palace in Tokyo, Japan.

Considering, the Qandil mountains, located roughly forty kilometers southeast of the Turkish border in Iraq's Erbil province, are being used as a headquarters by the PKK and its Iranian affiliate, the Kurdistan Free Life Party (PJAK), the scope of this military operation reflects the magnitude of the strategic initiative by Turkey. Operation Claw, reportedly, aims to establish permanent military authority in the region, unlike previous operations that only caused temporary damage to the PKK.

The other important aspect of the Operation Claw is that it is the third in a series of military operations by Turkey since 2016, and it is not the last. The first two took place on the western end of the Euphrates in Syria. Operation Euphrates Shield launched in August 2016. The other, Operation Olive Branch was in January 2018.

Some believe that the Operation Claw is still smaller in scale compare to what is to follow next. The official Turkish statement only talks about cleaning the PKK from the region. For the US, the Operation Claw must simply mean, it is the third and final message from Turkey. The US must either join forces in the next operation with Turkey or support Turkey indirectly, all the while turning its focus totally on China and the rest of eastern powers to establish a global balance of power which will also mean keeping Iran in check and maintenance of the Nuclear Proliferation Treaty.

b— In Iran

On that note, Iran can only come to the crosshair of the West after security is established in northern Iraq where Operation Claw is at work. Without Turkey firmly stabilizes the region in the north, the US will never have an opportunity or chance to influence Iran. Even then, the US must be in concert with Turkey to have a desired outcome.

Alternatively speaking, the US cannot play tit for tat game and win at the end against Iran. Seventy years after the US inspired coup, Iran is ahead and not looking back, and the US cannot do much about it. Today, if another tit for tat were to be initiated by the West: where would that go?

Soon, Iran will have more than a hundred million population. A mass of humanity that will have an influence over two-hundred million people when the rest of the brethren are considered in a region from Afghanistan to Iraq to Kuwait to Bahrain to Yemen.

i- Northern Iraq is key to have a leverage on Iran

There is no way to stop the proliferation of nuclear weapons in Iran until Iraq is stabilized. Stable Iraq will prevent, nuclearization of Iran for two reasons. One, Iran will no longer feel the wrath of threat coming from next door. Two, Turkey in the northern third of Iraq and possibly in the company of the US will present a real counterbalance.

ii- NPT must remain in effect

Letting Iran go nuclear will be the end of the Nuclear Proliferation Treaty (NPT). Nuclear Iran is not only a threat to Israel or Saudi Arabia, but it is also an existential threat to Turkey which has already begun the road with three nuclear power plant programs. The first to be operational in 2023 and followed by two others immediately. Saudi Arabia has not embarked on this road but UAE, its close ally has four reactors under construction.

According to NPT theory of domino effect, in the Middle East, all started with Israel. Iran's single biggest motivation is to counter Israel. That triggers Saudi Arabia and Turkey to go nuclear. Nuclear Turkey will push Greece to acquire it. That will give way to the rest of the Balkan nations to pursue the same.

Simply put, when the US closed its eyes to Israel acquiring nuclear weapons, NPT had no more chance to prevent nuclearization of the whole region and beyond.

On the other hand, could Israel have existed until now if it did not have the nuclear weapons? That is another valid argument in the face of never-ending hatred towards the Jewish state.

But before making plans what to do about NPT regime going into oblivion or for that matter rising Iran in the Fertile Crescent there is one urgency to note. There is a benevolent regional power Turkey that will take the lead, and consequently precautions it deems necessary no matter what, and it has the capacity and will power to do so.

c— In Syria

In the meanwhile, Turkey, first and most, has the urgency to return the Syrian refugees back. A stable Syria is vital for the chain effect to take place in the Fertile Crescent. When security and stability is achieved at least in the northern and eastern portions of Syria, northern Iraq will be totally isolated region where the security efforts can bring immediate results.

In Syria, security can only be possible after order is established by the Turkish forces. Turks will act alone to secure its border zone with Syria. But it will seek support from the US and Russian Federation (RF) in respective areas to enlarge the zone. Together they will accommodate the security priorities of the US as well as that of the Bashar Al Assad regime that the RF supports.

Until then, nearly four million Syrians will continue to live in Turkey. They have been there since 2012. Some of them are integrated to the Turkish society.

They will become a bridge for Syria to look West and modernity when Bashar al-Assad regime in Syria comes to terms with the rest.

Fast moving gas exploration ventures in the Eastern Mediterranean will eventually speed up the process of healing in Syria as well. Soon all countries with shoreline to the sea will get their fair share from the treasure throw. Interdependence of the countries to one another will become more apparent. Syria, with the shortest proximity to Yumurtalik in Turkey will have no better alternative to connect itself.

It is unbelievable how Obama could not understand or did not want to understand the realities in the making, when Erdogan approached him in 2012. Trump did not missed the opportunity when he had the phone call with Erdogan on December 2018. It was the same conversation for Erdogan, give or take!

i- What was Obama thinking?

As the Arab Spring was about to engulf Syria, what was Obama thinking in 2010?

When Erdogan offered a plan to work on Syria in 2012 why the US refused?

One thing is for sure. Obama never noticed the "New Turkey" rising.

Obama simply missed the boat. He was misled to say the least by wide ranging domestic and international players and interests. For example, he was taken for an ego trip so to speak like those who awarded him the Nobel Peace Prize. Why did Obama accept an award he did not enter into competition to win yet, worse when there was no competition to win in the first place? It should have been a hint to Obama that it is the European intrigue in play. Unfortunately, he never noticed it. Nor the ensuing ploys in the Middle East when the Arab Spring began or initiated by certain forces.

The results are before the whole world to see. First of all, seven million Syrian refugees and another seven million displaced people in the country later, the world is back to square one in Syria. Second, the Eastern Mediterranean finds will be contested primarily with a naval warfare, not on land, if it comes to that. But the prize or the incentive, the leverage or peace will come through pipelines that will be shipped through Yumurtalik, Turkey.

By the way, it is curious to note that the first discovery of the Eastern Mediterranean riches was in 2009, exactly a year before the Arab Spring began or initiated? It is also curious to note how miracles and mysteries waited to take place until Obama came to power? Conspiracy theories aside, what a difference Trump makes!

ii- How Trump sees what Obama misses

Turkey will also provide for Syria, direct access not only to Iran and the Caucuses and Russia but also to Europe. It will simply become part of the New Silk Road between Beijing and London. Syria will benefit from road and railroad networks and pipelines carrying energy in Turkey.

Did Trump immediately notice what Turkey brings to the table from the beginning?

In the 2020s, Syria will be free of all militias, including the Iran militia! A decade after the Arab Spring started or what was imposed on the unsuspecting Arabs, however one may see it, Turkey already put a dent to the ongoing humanitarian and political problem with two military operations in its border region. In 2019, a massive incursion to the eastern portion of the country will effectively clear two fifths of the country from rouge elements. More Kurds, Turkmens, Arabs, Yazidis and others will be able to go back home.

Turkey will bring amnesty to those captured or surrendered in due process. It will help stabilize the region, but it will also give relief to refugees already in other countries. International system will feel the relief.

Is this what Trump talked about when he called Erdogan on December 14, 2018?

Whatever transpired between two leaders and continues to transpire with each encounter they have, one thing is becoming more and more apparent: Turkey has an international role to play and Trump knows that better than anyone else.

B. International structure requires "New Turkey" to play a role

The Western hegemony and bipolar world ruled the day in the Middle East throughout the 20th century. But not anymore.

Yet today, the West, led by the US and Russia continue to have stakes in the Middle East. They will always seek their interest. But now, there are new players to contend with as well. China and India are two of the most prominent with resources and wide-ranging interests, mainly due to the size of their economy. Turkey is the other because it is there with its fast-rising economy and massive military presence, no other country can compete in the region.

The West lost its hegemony in the region because it did not ally with Turkey in the region. Russia is back in Syria for the next fifty years, primarily because of its relationship with Turkey since the end of 2015. That is also the year when on 15 July, the West supported coup d'etat against Erdogan failed when people power for the first time in the history of the modern Republic of Turkey said that the times have change and there is now "New Turkey" reckon with.

a— New Turkey working with the US can resolve many issues

Clearly, at the turn of the Millennium, Turkey has a role to play in the Middle. That role will also contribute to the balance of power between the East and the West.

Stabilizing Iraq and Syria and taking care of life in Bagdad and Damascus will allow Beirut to return its heydays. Only then, Israel will benefit tremendously. Turkey is the only country with significant weight to enforce such a change. No other local country or outside force has the capacity Turkey has.

The prosperity to the Middle East and benefits to the West will come only if Iran is also brought into the mix. To resolve outstanding issues with Iran, the US and Turkey will have to work together.

The world does not need NPT domino effect to get out of control. Without Iran, there is no alternative. It is in the interest of everybody that this problem is resolved. Turkey, Iran and the US working together can make progress when other attempts are failing and will fail.

Turkey will make a comprehensive difference when it works with the US in the region. Otherwise, Turkey will limit itself to its border regions and let the remainder be resolved other times and other ways and in due course.

It is in the interest of the US to work with Turkey. The consequences are unimaginable from nuclear Iran to terrorism and refugees heading Europe and elsewhere.

b— New Turkey will also work with Russia

In the 1950s, not until Turkey abandoned Middle East and joined the West, the Soviet Socialist Union of Republics (USSR) filled the vacuum. Since it was Cold War, the bipolar world deteriorated the fabric in the region. At the end, neither the US nor the USSR were able to stay in the region anymore.

The Russian Federation (RF) replaced the USSR. It is back in Syria. Since then, it is working with Turkey. They have mutual interests in the Black Sea Basin, Caucuses, and Central Asia. European Union (EU), RF and Turkey are also interdependent on transshipment of oil and natural resources.

When Erdoğan regime called Obama Administration to work together in 2012, the latter missed the opportunity. RF arrived at Syria three years later in its place. Now it is to stay there for the next fifty years.

When Erdoğan regime called Trump Administration to work together in 2018, the latter agreed and now together they will control eastern and northern half of Syria and leave the rest to the Russians and Iranians. In the 21st century, it is win-win for Russia and Turkey in the Middle East when they work together. Idlip in Syria is a good example.

After that they should be cooperating in the Eastern Mediterranean riches where natural gas to be explored. Finally, there is the rest of the Middle East to build, to bring modernity and to provide security. Together and with local partners win-win can easily become win-win-win.

President Trump seems to have already figured it out before anybody else in the US. He jumped on board in Syria by the end of 2018 with a twit to make it win-win-win-win.

With the cards Obama and the other globalists left to him, it is a great return so far, instead of losing the whole thing in a no-win situation.

IV. A new western strategy

The US has to decide on a new strategy before China and India focus on the region.

It must join Turkey and welcome the milestones together in the Middle East.

It must primarily abandon Saudi Arabia and embrace anew, urgently.

All the while, the rest of the Arabian Peninsula must be left alone so it can prosper.

1. Join forces with Turkey

The Middle East cannot be lost.

If Middle East goes, Africa goes next.

When Africa is gone so will the Western Europe.

Without Western Europe, where will the North America be?

It sounds far-fetched.

Yet a hundred years is not a long time to end up with a catastrophe.

Looking back at past 200-years and how the Western plans foiled, the time is now.

Turkey is the only one that still stands tall in the region after a thousand years.

The US has to decide fast and must act before China and India make inroads.

The Middle East must be won, and now, by the West, that means by the US.

Only then the West can establish the right balance of power with the East.

The task can only be achieved together with Turkey.

A. *What We Have to Avoid with Turkey*

The West once had a hegemony. It employed methods and strategies. This hegemony is now long gone. Methods and strategies backfired. Nation-building will now never work in the Middle East for a long time to come. Coup d'états are also a thing of the past and must no longer be resorted to.

Coup d'états are nowadays more likely to come back and haunt the agitators, not in the regions themselves but back home, just like 9/11 did. A decade or two or for that matter a century or two are a short time for the Middle East. They are even shorter for Turks who will soon celebrate six-hundred year and a thousand year anniversaries, respectively in 2053 and 2071.

Mind you, they will celebrate these events like a lifetime-anniversaries and no can tell that these are not well ingrained dates in the minds of the Muslims and Christians alike, when the time comes and when the Muslims appear at the gates of the Western civilization in larger numbers.

a— Don't resort to nation-building

When the US became the master of the Middle East in the 20th century, it could have elected different route. Unfortunately, nation-building became the choice of the globalists at the end. Trying to break up the Middle East into smaller nation-states was even worse idea. And using the Kurds, repeatedly, to that end to prove a point was inhumane.

Like Ataturk has said it clearly: "Sovereignty is not given, it is taken." Kurds could have built a state of their own in the past, but they have not. The world order was established in the aftermath of the WWI and then again in the aftermath of the WWII in the 20th century. Since then nearly a hundred new nation-states were formed or reclaimed their independence.

Saudi Arabia and Israel are two good examples of how sovereignties are taken. House of Saud created its kingdom in the aftermath of WWI by pure determination and brute force. Israel too after WWII created a state, totally built with its own effort after hard fought wars. In both cases, they fought and declared their state. Turkey rightly is the first state that recognized both states in 1032 and 1048, respectively, the day they were founded.

That is the only way to create a new state, with blood and tears, like the US was created after a revolution, like the modern Republic of Turkey was created after long war against seven different foreign powers.

b— Don't resort to coup d'état

Coup d'états in the 20th century became a by-product of the bi-polar, reaching their peak years between 1950s and 1980s. They became the will of superpowers, replacing the will of people.

In the 21st century, in the absence of a bi-polar world, the coup d'états lost their legitimacy altogether. In the US, as late as mid-1970s, Bill-12333 outlawed assassinations of foreign leaders.

Unfortunately, as late as 2016, the globalists in the West were still dreaming that a coup d'état can reverse the results of the 2013 electoral process in Turkey that extended Erdoğan regime's stay in power.

As a result, Turkey no longer has much trust in its relationship with the West. Coup d'états are also the reason why the US has lost Iran for good and why the West does not have a hold in the Middle East anymore.

What is worse is that, the West does not understand or accept the fact that the times have changed. Time to employ a coup d'état without impunity is long gone.

9/11 atrocities were committed by the US trained jihadists, once fought alongside of the Western forces against communism they hated. But nowadays, there is no communism to hate. There is still the West to go after for those who look for an excuse for their misfortune. A coup d'état these days presents lots of justification for lots of disenfranchised.

And that is the least of the problems in the age of numerous countries with intercontinental ballistic missile technologies in the making.

B. What can be done with Turkey

In the Middle East, the most urgent is the fact that the US must act in Syria and after that against Iraq. But it must take the initiatives with turkey. Moreover, it must not only allow Turkey but also encourage Turkey to take the lead.

In view of the newly brewing issue of the Eastern Mediterranean Sea continental shelves and hydrocarbon riches that needs to be explored and then shared by the bordering countries and others, Turkish leadership is all the more important. Turkey controls practically half of the Eastern Mediterranean as the country with longest shoreline. Equitable partition of what comes out of this sea cannot be handled without Turkey having a greater say. Otherwise, nothing could be done there without a war that ends all wars when Turkey looks at its interest in the Eastern Mediterranean Seas as nothing but a Zero-Sum game. If the international regimes in place are violated, that is.

a— In Syria

It is in the interest of the US to work with Turkey in Syria. In addition, the locals prefer to work with Turkey more than with any other power within the region or beyond, including the Bashar Al Assad regime.

i— The Best Alternative for the US

The working relationship between Turkey and the US is already underway. US forces will not stay in Syria forever. On the other hand, Turkey has been in the region for the past thousand years and figures to stay there for yet another thousand. But what is different in the last one hundred years is that Turkey no longer wants to stay disinterested. Rather, Erdoğan regime choses to engage more and more with what transpires beyond its borders nearby and in far ranging distances.

President Trump already diagnosed what moves Turkey and Erdoğan within a year into his presidency. His numerous predecessors came and left but never understood what should have been so easy to grasp. Turkey is nowadays is a "New Turkey" that plans to become "greater" Turkey that takes responsibility over larger and more numerous masses in the region and beyond.

Trump also understood that there is a bigger problem in Syria than fighting against DAESH/ISIS. Lebanon attack that killed the US marines decades ago is one example. Stationing the US forces in an area consisting of no man's land in the western Iraq and eastern Syria, surrounded with rouge elements and the explosive dynamics of local populations is a calamity waiting to happen.

ii— Turks have the capability to control eastern Syria

All the while, the Turkish forces nearby never have such problems because they are deployed all along the Syrian and Iraqi borders with massive land and air forces within striking distance deep into the region. Turks with their 280 kilometer-long missile batteries and 200 kilometer-long air to ground precision missiles can strike any target in the region with precision. Not to mention, hundreds of tanks or military vehicles can advance within days beyond the bases where the US forces are stationed.

Turks have already demonstrated their ability and effectiveness with two military incursions in their border regions. They also indicated clearly that with the US logistical support they can advance far deeper into these troublesome areas to help the Western interests as well.

iii— Locals prefer to work with the Turks

The fact that in Syria there are Sunni Arabs, Turkmens, and Kurds that prefer to be in alliance with Turkey is crucial. They have been together for centuries in the same region. They lived together. Turkey brings them modernity and security from north. Cross border trade is very profitable. These inhabitants of the region know it all too well that Turkey will establish peace after it cleans the rogue elements from the region.

They also know that; Turkey have other incentives to offer to the Syrians. Turkey can easily extend visa free walking rights to the Syrians like it did with number of other countries in the region. That in itself brings Syria closer to Europe and modernity that it can enjoy.

Not until Lebanon develops further and Israel establishes relationship with Syria, Jordan, and Iraq are the only other alternatives for Syria to turn towards. But none offers what Turkey has. Vibrant cities, highway and high-speed train networks to Europe are the least of them. Turkey has incentives that would ensure Syrians to incorporate to the modern West than stay behind in the East.

iv— The West doesn't have viable alternative anyway

It is also no brainer that Turkey has an overwhelming leverage over any Western force to offer Syrians. While Turkey continued to develop, and rapidly since the early 2000s, the West was busy making enemies in the Middle East with wars and destructions. Decades long lose-lose Western policies in the region never realized Turkey's win-win strategies to finally bear results that will make Turkey the dominant regional power over locals and outsiders.

At this stage, in Syria there is no better alternative for the US to join forces with Turkey to end the Obama-weaponized Syria problem once and for all.

b— In Iran

Once, the US were to work in harmony in Syria with Turkey, why would not the US and Turkey cooperate the same way against Iran? The answer is: they can, and they will so long as Iran is included into the mix on equal grounds.

When Turkey and the US are on the same page, Iran would surely be on the same page with them too. Turkey is an "interlocutor valable" for both Iran and the US. Turkey has a leverage on Iran. It exports Iranian oil to the West via Turkish land-bridge. Turkey can also allow its territory for the US to attack Iran in worst case scenario. The US has no better alternative than Turkey for pressuring Iran to come to the table and reach an agreement.

The ongoing and growing relationship between Turkey and Russia will also bring a leverage to such a gathering. Iran is at home with Russia and Turkey in Syria. It will expect Turkey to be fair as its role in the middle. Plus, communication channels between Russia, Iran, and Turkey will ensure that the US also communicates effectively with all parties to the agreement.

Simply put, with Turkey on board, the US will have all the leverage it needs against Iran, irrespective of where Russia stands. Much to the surprise of many in the states and in Europe, president Trump already figured out these dynamics of the Iranian problem. Now it is time to deal with the details and to figure the road to get there with Erdoğan.

With Turkey in the lead, Iran will no longer present an existential threat to the likes of Saudi Arabia and Israel. Turkey will pursue towards this end voluntarily. It will primarily seek to keep the Nuclear Proliferation Treaty intact. That is in addition to having its eastern neighbors become part of modern society with increased trade and tourism. It is a win-win-win-win strategy, including Iran, Turkey, and the West but also the eternal adversaries of the Iran (according to some): Saudi Arabia and Israel.

On that note, the US must act on Saudi Arabia at the same time it is to embark on a policy against Iran together with Turkey. That will further guarantee the success of the policy towards Iran.

2. Abandon Saudi Arabia

It is time for the US to abandon the Saudi Arabia of the past and embrace anew.

House of Saud must make the transition and until then the US must give it a space.

The urgency is to replace the old with anew before centennial celebrations.

Saudi Arabia will have two of them in 2032 and 2037.

The former is when the kingdom was founded.

The latter is the date Aramco, the US—Saudi oil company was created.

But there are two more dates that are even more consequential for Saudi Arabia. They are 2023 and 2024. They involve modern Turkey.

One created the secular republic of Turkey. The other abolished the Caliphate.

Both dates have big significances on Saudi Arabia.

They are the *raison d'etre* for the Kingdom to exist.

Especially the latter because it involves Muslims, hundreds of millions of them.

1937 is the day in infamy for having Mecca and Medina taken away from them.

Lots of Muslims have a very emotional view about that date and change of authority. Some will try to exploit it. Most others would like to see a peaceful transition.

Yet, for radical combatants fifty years or a century is never a distant memory.

Only fifty years ago Saudi jihadists were fighting against the USSR in Afghanistan.

Thirty years later they reappeared in the US as 9/11 terrorists against their brethren-in-war.

In the Muslim Middle East, there will always be rogue elements that will hate the West. They are the Voltaires of the East. They must be tamed. But with the right leadership.

There must be one in Saudi Arabia but also the for the whole region.

Senator Graham said it right when Saudi regime must find the right people to lead them. He was referring to the crown prince in particular in the aftermath of Khashoggi murder.

But Saudi Arabia has more than a leadership issue to deal with.

There are Wahhabis, too, in Saudi Arabia. They have rights and aspirations, too. Saudis and Wahhabis don't need to be one and all.

They can both look to the future proudly with their own identity.

A. Let Saudis resolve their domestic matters

Saudi Arabia will celebrate its centennial in 2032. Only eight years after the centennial of the abolishment of the Caliphate by Turkey. Year 2024 has a direct bearing on Saudi Arabia because the Muslim ummah in 1037, reacted with disbelief when Saudi Arabia assumed the role of protectorate for Mecca and Medina.

The ummah never accepted the imposition. In short, Saudi Arabia will go through changes between 2024 and 2037, and find its rightful place in history, after the Wahhabis also can freely call themselves Wahhabis proudly and not hide behind the Muslim veil.

a— Absolute monarchy must evolve

The West must abandon Saudi Arabia and embrace anew. There is a change in Saudi Arabia, but more change is still to come. For example, public is yearning to see women driving cars. But the change must also come at the top.

It will take some time until the transformation will be completed. Until then, it is best to keep a distance and allow the domestic forces reconcile.

In an extraordinary power play by the heir to the throne, Crown Prince Mohammed bin Salman (MBS), hundreds of Saudi royals, billionaires, and senior government officials were detained. The move was described, by Saudi authorities, as a crackdown on rampant corruption. "This was a shakedown operation and a power consolidation operation," said one former senior U.S. official who was in office at the time.

Some of those targeted included royals or officials linked to the late King Abdullah, who died in 2015. His relatives and associates are distrusted by the circle around King Salman, who now holds the throne.

A year later, the event has taken on even more importance in the wake of the death of the Saudi writer Jamal Khashoggi, who was murdered after entering the Saudi consulate in Istanbul on October 2. Bin Salman is suspected of ordering Khashoggi's death and is struggling to defuse the crisis that has put the country's international standing in jeopardy.[61]

In reality, that is the least of the problems MBS is facing in Saudi Arabia.

King Salman bin Abd al-Aziz's accession to the throne in 2015 led to the rise of Prince Mohammed. The crown prince's public denunciations of extremist ideas and promises to promote moderate Islam have been interpreted as a renewed desire to break with Wahhabism. A closer reading shows that Prince Mohammed primarily condemns the Muslim Brotherhood and jihadists and exonerates Wahhabism.[62]

b— Wahhabis must find their rightful place in history

In Saudi Arabia today they don't say: "We are Wahhabis." They say, "We are just Muslims."

But they follow the teachings of Muhammed bin Abd al-Wahhab. He is the one who paved the road for Abdul Aziz ibn Saud, the patriarch of the family, to conquer the rest of the [Arabian] Peninsula and to rule. Anyone who's subscribing to someone else is not very much welcomed. So, there is very great cohesiveness between the two.[63]

The Wahhabi Islamic thought is more fundamentalist, much more conservative. The religious curriculum in Saudi Arabia teaches that people are split in two: Salafis [Wahhabis], who are the winners, the chosen ones, who will go to heaven. And the rest: Muslims, Christians, Jews and others.

Maybe it is time for the world to recognize the Wahhabis equally as they deserve. So that the rest of the Saudis can continue their modernity as they wish.

---

61   https://www.nbcnews.com/news/mideast/how-saudi-royal-crushed-his-rivals-shakedown-ritz-carlton-n930396

62   https://www.nytimes.com/2018/07/03/opinion/saudi-arabia-monarchy-wahhabism.html

63   https://www.pbs.org/wgbh/pages/frontline/shows/saudi/analyses/wahhabism.html

There is room for everybody to express themselves and live their life so long as the West and the rest does not have to experience their hatred or frustration for no reason.

This is also true for the Muslim world when some Muslims cherish the Wahhabi ways strict rule of Islam, others look for tolerance like the Ottomans or the modern Republic of Turkey favors, like the Saudis may favor.

Wahhabis aside, the Muslim ummah has its own issue to settle with the House of Saud led Saudi Arabian Kingdom.

B. Muslim ummah can no longer be ignored

In 1924, the Muslim ummah was without a Caliph. Mustafa Kemal Ataturk, the leader of the modern Turkish Republic had just abolished the Caliphate, reportedly due to pressure from Britain. Muslims were clinging to Mecca and Medina, the birthplace of the Islamic religion, not knowing what the future hold for them like a headless mass of humanity. They were in sorrow for having lost their great Islamic empire, the Ottomans, as their leader for centuries.

2024 is the centennial. Saudis founded their state in1932. In 1937, they garnered the US endorsement and incorporated the holly Muslim sites Mecca and Medina under their protectorate. They never asked the ummah if that was what they wished. Naturally, the ummah revolted. Today, they still look at it as a betrayal. Their pain is still vividly ingrained in their mind. They are waiting for an opportunity for the day of reckoning.

Time would tell what will happen in 2024, if anything. The West has to sit and wait, but the West actually would do better for its own sake, if it were to leave all the states in the region alone to let them be for a while. Let the Muslim reckon with their past in their own way among themselves. Let the pieces of history find their place without the influence of the West.

3. Leave all states in the region alone

Let them be
　　If the countries in the Middle East were left alone, they will be better off.
　　It happened in Europe.
　　Why not there?
　　The West tried it for a whole century and could not tame the Muslim masses.
　　They became the worst enemy of the West instead.
　　Now, if they are let alone for a while maybe they will do a useful soul searching.
　　Oh! If the Western intention was to divide and conquer the Muslims.

Then, the results speak for itself. They are divided but not really conquered. Rather, they are getting up with a renewed vengeance nobody wants to see.

No matter what was the strategy in the 20th century, the results do not bode well.

The idea to try something altogether new sounds like the better choice.

No one can justify to go the same tried path and face the worse as a result.

A. Arabs are wealthy they can handle their own

21st century is the time to let the Arabs be. They all have enough riches to welcome modernity in their own way and at their own speed. Qatar is a great example. UAE is another. So is Kuwait. Oman also.

The 2022 World Cup will take place in Qatar. A little country that can do what lot bigger countries could not. It is a big feat to get to host the FIFA World Cup, the football tournament when more than a billion people will be glued to their TV sets for a whole month. It is a testament how modernity comes to the Middle East or how the Arabs bring it to their domain beating out the best of the best in the world.

Dubai and Abu Dhabi are also the reflection of modernity in the Middle East. More people recognize these capitals like they do Paris or London. That is the sign of modernity already arrived.

Kuwait was invaded by Saddam Hussein in the late 1990s because it had all the riches of the world and it was liberated a year later by the US forces for the same reason. It had all the riches in the world to pay for the expenses. Today, life is good in the Kuwait City for many years. They know modernity and they have been enjoying it for a long time.

B. Nothing to protect from, except from themselves

As for the question of security. The US continues to be the sole policeman of the world. It has overwhelming economic and military superiority. It has a threat power to prevent aggression.

Turkey as a benevolent regional power with capacity and political will, but more importantly as a staunch ally of the US will want nothing more than prosperity of the countries in the region and beyond.

China and Russia in particular have no interest other than to see prosperous economies because that is the best way for them to remain as great powers themselves and further grow as economic powers.

It sounds like win-win-win for everybody, unless of course the Arabs start warring among themselves. So long as it has nothing to do with the West.

4. Abide by the international regimes in place in the Eastern Mediterranean

The discovery of large hydrocarbon reserves in the Eastern Mediterranean brought to surface some old problems, alongside opportunities in the Middle East. All the neighboring countries in the region: Turkey, the Turkish Republic of Northern Cyprus (TRNC), Egypt, Greece, Lebanon, Syria, Libya, Israel, and the Cyprus Republic (CR) naturally jumped into fray. The U.S., Russia, the U.K., France and Italy also immediately positioned themselves to maintain influence in the region.

The more the merrier, right?

So long as the equitable division of the riches in the region is decided according to the international regimes in place, regarding continental shelves, this should work out for the good of everybody involved.

Not so fast! There is another saying: "Too many cooks spoil the stew!"

At the end, the latter may end up becoming what would be the appropriate one for the Eastern Mediterranean. And one would think it would quickly turn into the "World Wrestling" type melee where everyone is pitted against one another.

No! Not necessarily… When there is Turkey or a Turk in the ring melee takes a life of its own. Suddenly, all wrestlers would gang up against the Turkish wrestler.

Well, that is what happened in the Eastern Mediterranean in July 2019 as soon as Turkey introduced the second drilling ship Yavuz to start its work on the eastern end of Cyprus. The world unanimously joined to confront Turkey against the move.

What about the international regimes in place?

Ah! That depends on the interpretation of the international regimes themselves!

The West can always come up with the right interpretation. No problem! Might is right!!!

A. So how does the West defends its aggressive behavior

The Republic of Cyprus (RC) took the lead, encouraged by Greece and then the European Union itself, the US and its cohorts Egypt and Israel not far behind, but also Russia, as a surprise new comer on the side of the majority against the lonely Turkey and its protegee the Turkish Republic of Norther Cyprus (TRNC).

The embolden RC unilaterally declared a region composed of thirteen parcels and started negotiations to assign them to Western suitors. Turkey in turn gradually increased its voice and presence in the Eastern Mediterranean Sea like never before in history.

Turkey, together with the TRNC, immediately claimed on all but tenth and eleventh parcels of the thirteen parcels for two reasons. One, Turkish continental shelf extends into parcels four, five, six, and seven according to the well-established international regimes. Two, the TRNC make the same claims over parcels one, two, three, eight, nine, twelve, and thirteen like the Cyprus Republic is making.

a- First argument

The first, of two Western arguments, is pretty forward.

Since the Turkish Republic of Northern Cyprus (TRNC) is not recognized as a nation-state by any other country except Turkey, the Turkish community in the north will not have any right on anything on the island and beyond in the international community.

Yes, but what about the Green Line, currently being patrolled by the United Nations Peacekeeping Force (UNFICYP) past forty-five years? Apparently, the international community recognizes the "green" border between two countries.

It sounds hypocritical, does it not?

b- Second argument

Well, at this stage, there is no second argument on the table coming from the West, regarding Turkey making claims on the parcels four, five, six, and seven!

B. Turks have formidable arguments and a lot more

On the first point, Turkey does not feel the need to enter into a debate so long as the West comes in unanimity and with intimidating show of force with nearly two-hundred warships and fully stacked energy companies in tow, and with total disregard to the established premises of the international regimes in place.

The West and its cohorts leave clear impression that there is no room for negotiations or give and take with the Turks in principle. As a result, Turkey increases the ante by starting to drill with its two ships in the Cyprus waters with a license granted by the Turkish Republic of Northern Cyprus (TRNC), while at the same, employing its naval superiority, to prevent anyone drilling in most of the exclusive economic zone in the south.

But on the second point, Turkey counters with precedents and long-established regimes in place.

First, there are clear precedents, between Libya and Malta and between Germany and Dutch and Danish islands, when the International Court in La Hay decided on the side of countries over islands when there were continental shelf disputes.

Second, in the TRNC's case, since there are two communities on the island, international regimes in place say that no unilateral declaration can be made by either community. Apparently, non-recognition of the TRNC as a nation-state, as the UNFICYP in placed proves, is nothing but an anemic excuse. Knowing that, Turkey is adamant that the international regimes in place must be observed.

C- Consequences of this bickering

Yet, this bickering cannot go on forever. It will come to an end sooner or later and there are two likelihood how it may end.

On one hand, cool heads will prevail. Sides will start negotiating and respecting on other's grievances and split the spoil of the riches equitably and fairly.

Of course, no one should expect resolving the division of Cyprus. That is a whole different emotional matter for both side that will not heal for a long time to come. Meanwhile, the Green Line is there past forty-five years and stood the test of time. It is able to keep two communities apart from one another without fighting.

On the other hand, the sides will continue with the melee and attack Turkey and the TRNC in unison which will surely force Turkey to resort to a large or even full-scale mobilization of its armed forces on land, air, and sea.

There is no reason to go into probable war scenarios. In that case, suffice it to say, Turkey will pursue a Zero-Sum game at all fronts.

On that note, Turkey already started to demonstrate to the rest of the world its political will and military capacity with massive naval maneuvers, unprecedented political moves, and military build up that will take any military flare up in the Mediterranean Sea to additional theaters.

i- Naval maneuvers

Turkey conducted two naval maneuvers in 2019. Each one was unprecedented. In March, 103 Turkish warships participated and conducted live fire wargames in all three surrounding seas. It was a massive display. Two months later, Turkey did another of the same called "Sea Wolf." This time, there was 150 Turkish warships in action.

Turkey simply declared about 500,000 square kilometers as its own, and called it "Mavi Vatan," meaning exclusive maritime economic zone belonging to Turkey. This included practically half of Black Sea, significant portion of Aegean Sea and close to half of Eastern Mediterranean including much of the waters around islands Cyprus and Crete, not to mention hundreds of islands and islets in the Aegean.

Considering the total number of warships belonging to the rest of the countries in the Eastern Mediterranean Sea is reportedly around two-hundred, Turkish naval power presents a formidable threat. It must not be forgotten that two dozen or so warships among these two-hundred belongs to the Russian Federation. The fact that Russia and Turkey have common interest in the Middle East, over pipelines carrying Russian energy to Western Europe, ever-increasing trade and tourism and transfer of military and nuclear technology exchange between two old enemies turned into transactional best of friends, the West is in even a more vulnerable position against Turkey in the region.

That is of course before even considering the other divisions that exist among the Western alliance partners and their cohorts. For example, Western European intention to create PESCO despite NATO objections is still ongoing even though it may be in the backburner for the moment. Then there is the fragile and tentative tie between countries like Israel, Egypt, and Greece. When war conditions exacerbate it is likely that each country will first consider how to best survive. History has many examples, how lot changes after initial salvos are fired!

ii- Political move no one was expecting

Turkey and the Erdogan regime at helm on the other hand do not wait for the first salvos. They embark on political moves never before seen in the past half a century. The Western presence with warships and energy companies ready to drill are enough reasons for Turkey to take extraordinary steps.

First, the Turkish Republic of Northern Cyprus (TRNC) decides to reopen disputed Varosha to tourism after a forty-five year seclusion since the invasion of Northern Cyprus in the 1970s. Nothing happens in the TRNC without the blessing of Turkey of course. Two, Turkey raises its voice with brute force. Erdogan in Osaka, Japan firmly made his point publicly before a large audience what he told France's Emmanuel Macron on the sidelines of the G-20 Summit on Sunday. "I told him: 'You cannot speak about Cyprus. I can speak, Greece can speak, the UK can speak, and the EU can speak, but you cannot speak.'"

This is not the first time that Erdogan sternly warned Macron, but it may also be the last time! Turkey would surely revert to Zero Sum game if Macron decides to increase the ante or not get the message.

It is the last thing the US would like to see Turkey is going after France with more than a diplomatic or political move of no return. Turkey did it before against Russia when it shot down one of its aircrafts in Syria. Russia is militarily lot stronger than France. Considering the fact that France cannot match Turkey militarily not in the sea or in the air, the intentions of Macron regime becomes all the more confusing.

After all, there is some truth in what George Friedman famously said regarding the state of Western European military powers nowadays if they face an escalation: "Turkey could beat Germans in an afternoon, French in an hour."

iii- Military build up

Unfortunately, Emanuel Macron is the leading globalist in Western Europe, now that Angela Merkel has announced her pending retirement. The globalists somehow never noticed how the world has changed in the East in the past two decades. Today, Turkey has an insurmountable military power against Western European states.

But more so than that, Turkey acts with realism. One, Turkey no longer trusts the West. Two, any statement on the island of Cyprus is taken at a face value. Hence, when France started to negotiate with the Republic of Cyprus for a naval base and Britain announced that it will deploy more than a hundred F-35s in its bases there, Turkey countered them immediately with military moves of its own.

To that end, Turkey reportedly decided and put it in motion to build the biggest navy base of the region in the Iskele, Cyprus, and a massive land forces base next to it. Coupled with the deployment of the S-400 defensive missile batteries from Russia, Turkey will be ready to challenge the Western ploys with a strength they did not plan.

All these preparations are to ensure that the Turkish Cypriots have equal rights with the Greek Cypriots and receive their fair share from the hydrocarbon exploits. Turkey, on the other hand, argues nothing more nothing less on its part in its continental shelves. To that effect, it has already underlined that it would not allow any party to conduct research and production operations in the areas colliding with Turkey's sea realm of authority.

iv- Drilling with Fatih and Yavuz

In the meantime, Turkey's drilling ship Fatih (Conqueror) actively carries out research and drilling activities in the A, B, C, D, E, F, and G areas which were licensed by the TRNC. They are the TRNC declared "exclusive economic zones" in the north, like the Republic of Cyprus announced in the south.

Turkey's second drilling vessel, Yavuz, is expected to be operational in the region, in Cyprus waters, by July 2019.

No sooner, the Greek media came up with hysterical headlines, calling the positioning of Barbaros Hayreddin Pasa seismic vessel, together with the drilling ships Fatih and Yavuz around Cyprus, in the form of a Crescent, thousands of years old Turkish military prepositioning for an attack!

Nonetheless, they have reasons to be hysterical because Erdogan regime at the helm already stated clearly that it will protect all its interests in the exclusive economic zones at all cost. That in turn means that Turkey will not limit its fight to the waters around Cyprus, rather it will enlarge it across the whole Eastern Mediterranean and beyond, as necessary.

v- East-Med pipeline project anyone?

For example, the East-Med pipeline project that aims to transfer Mediterranean gas to Europe through Israel, southern Cyprus, and Greece comes into play.

Recent political and military developments in Libya clearly indicate how Turkey is adamant in getting its fair share from the Eastern Mediterranean. Reportedly, Turkey supplied nearly a hundred of its newly developed, formidable, and heavily armed Kirpi vehicles to the United Nations recognized regime in Tripoli to fend off Khalife Hafter led rebel forces trying to take over Libya. Hafter not only was rebuffed but also lost the most strategic city Garyan to the Tripoli regime.

In the meantime, in light of the geological fragility of the region and length of this project, featured pipeline is not viewed as feasible from technical and economic angles. On top of this, this project—which is also supported by the European Union—goes through Turkey's territorial waters. In order to be able to operate on a legal basis, the actors in the controversial region must act taking Turkey into account.[64]

In summary, in the Middle East but also in the Eastern Mediterranean all roads do not lead to Rome but to Turkey. The West must be the first to understand and adjust itself accordingly.

---

[64] https://www.albawaba.com/business/overview-energy-resources-eastern-mediterranean-1291470

CHAPTER SIX

THE WEST

In 1923, the West was forced to make a choice between two bad options: to keep secular Turkey close to the Western civilization or let it remain in the East.

It decided on the former and anchored it tightly to the Western European community.

Turkey grew as a land force but was also kept weak economically for the next eighty years.

It worked for the West until 2003 when Turkey started to slide into Islam and Turkism.

No one noticed it first, but it was quickly getting stronger economically and militarily.

Rising eastern powers jumped and embraced Turkey as one of their own.

By then, it was already too late for the West. Turkey was long gone.

It was Anchors Aweigh!

When the West truly realized what transpired, it was even worse.

Turkey was independent and had an account to settle.

* * *

In 2016, it was not pure luck why Trump revolution took place in the US.

Besides the domestic problems, Americans knew the Middle East was a lost cause.

Trump revolution gave a pose for the world to see if there was a new US to watch out.

Erdoğan regime in Turkey too wanted to see a new US after ninety-year yoke.

Come 2019, Turkey and the US are on a fork on the road.

They can take the same road and face formidable China together or they can go their separate ways and face China alone on their own.

Either way will work for Turkey, but it will be better if there is an alliance with the US.

But for the US, it is a Zero-Sum game. Without Turkey, it is big mistake.

I. Catch-22

Since 1923, the West elected to play Catch-22 to keep Turkey anchored nearby.
It was a successful strategy throughout the 20th century.
But two decades into the 21st century, Turkey suddenly said: "Anchors Aweigh!"
No one knows if Catch-22 will now give way to a chicken or a Zero-Sum game.
The reality is that the West nowadays cannot afford to play a Zero-Sum game.
Turkey on the other hand will not play anything but that.

1. Keeping Turkey anchored to the West

Turkey became a viable country, the day it was founded in 1923.
That was not good news for the West.
It had to be kept shackled and firmly, subservient.
It worked very nicely until 1991.
After that, it worked for another eleven years.
But in 2003, all bets were off.
Yet, the West never realized it until 2007.
By then, Turkey was long gone, and it was making the rules.
Genghis Khan
Genghis khan had a rough childhood.
But he made a name for himself after he broke his chains.
From an early age,
Genghis was forced to contend with the brutality of life.
Rivals poisoned his father.
His own tribe expelled his family,
and left his mother to raise her seven children alone.
Rivals abducted both he and his young wife.
He spent time as a slave before making a daring escape.
By his early 20s,
he amassed an army of supporters,
began forging alliances,
consolidated confederations under his banner,
and turned his attention to outside conquests.
He is said to have killed forty-million people.

According to Huge Pope, a journalist who lived in Turkey longtime, the greatest pure Mongol leader, Genghis Khan is not included in the official Turkish pantheon.

But one of modern Turkey's most popular early rock groups is called "The Mongols" and what does it tell when many Turkish mothers chase after little boys calling them Cengiz (Genghis Khan), Timur (Tamerlane) or Atilla (the Hun)?

A. Subservient Turkey (1923 to 1991)

In 1923, for the West, the immediate goal was to keep modern Turkey out of former Ottoman territories. The Middle East, the Balkans, and Africa were now the primary economic zones for the Western European powers to grow. Turkey at best had to be anchored to the West.

Throughout the 20th century, Turkey remained subservient to the West. It was in proximity to Europe, but that was both a blessing and a curse. It was growing faster than most of the Muslim countries but not enough to pose a challenge to anybody. That is exactly what the West wanted.

The Western Europeans had never thought to include Turkey into their mix in the first place anyway. There could have been no room for a thousand-year-old enemy.

The Soviet Union in the north was also handy. The Cold War was keeping Turkey away from the Balkans, the Caucasus, and the Central Asia. On top of that, under the pretext of bulwark against Soviet expansionism, Turkey was assigned the role to protect the southern flank of NATO.

In the meanwhile, the US hegemony in the Middle East was keeping Turkey away from the Arabs and North Africans. The West was getting the oil from Iran, Libya, Iraq, Saudi Arabia, and Kuwait. Nothing could be better!

The problems for the West started in 1979, with the Iranian revolution. Loss of Kuwait was next. Loss of that much oil production and quagmire with the Saddam Hussein regime forced the West to look elsewhere for alternatives.

The dismemberment of the Soviet Union was it. Oil fields in the Central Asian republics and Azerbaijan were the answer. Ronald Reagan started the process in 1980. By 1991, it was done.

The Soviet Union was no more. It was a great relief, but it also brought new problems.

Turkey was one of the big beneficiaries. It was now the end of a seventy-year journey with Turkey.

B. Unfettered Turkey (1991 to 2003)

In 1991, the disintegration of the Soviet Union freed the Balkan states from the yoke of the empire in the north. Also, five new Turkic states in Central Asia were now independent republics.

Turkey suddenly had room to grow. It started to make overtures and then inroads in the Balkans and Central Asia. But the attempts had limitations. The Balkans were explosive. There was war. Turkish influence could have made difference. Yet, no one was willing to open arms to the old Ottomans.

In Central Asia, too. Turkey reached out to brethren Turkic states. But it was limited. Having "Turanism," union of five new Turkic states with Turkey was the last thing the world needed. The Russians were against it. So were the West.

It was time for EU to make its next move to keep Turkey in check. In 1995, Greece, Portugal, Spain, Austria, Finland, and Sweden admitted to membership. New boundaries were set. Same year, EU signed "customs union" agreement with Turkey. Short of full membership, Turkey was now firmly anchored to the West again at least for the foreseeable future.

But the West had other problems and Turkey was making progress elsewhere. The oil pipeline from Azerbaijan had no alternative but to pass through Turkey to Yumurtalik in the Mediterranean port. No one could have thought but that was the beginning of the end. Turkey was about to break-lose from the grip of the West altogether. Like a daring escape, Turkey never looked back.

By 2003, when the US invaded Iraq. Turkey was long-gone. It was roaming free in Central Asia, the Balkans, and Africa. The West never realized it for another four years. By then it would be too late to do anything about it.

2. Keeping up with Turkey and the Erdoğan regime (Since 2002)

Brinkmanship became the Turkish norm

Erdoğan regime changed the rules of engagement when it came to power in 2002.

European Union had a dilemma: Catch-22 was no longer a viable game against Turkey.

By 2018, EU was talking about giving visa-free walking rights to Turks.

To play hard ball with Turkey was a thing in the past.

Turkey was now making bold moves in the Middle East, Africa, and the Caucasus.

Moreover, now technology transfer from the US and Germany was also on the table.

A. To admit Turkey to the European Union or not

EU and Turkey reached maturation together since they were found thirty years apart. Over the decades, they became more dependent on one another. They basically learned to live together, replacing their thousand-year past of wars and hatred. It lasted until the end of the 20th century.

By 2002, EU and Turkey were integral part of one another yet never fully formally integrated. Erdoğan regime in power was now demanding without further delay admission of Turkey to the union as a full and equal member. The goal was to correct the historical process and to move along with times.

The dilemma was a big problem for the union. Turkey was no longer the fledgling republic of the old century and was now holding most of the cards.

a— On one hand, EU cannot do without Turkey

Turkey is a NATO ally and has customs union with the European Union. It is anchored to the West both militarily and economically as the only member of either organization with a Muslim majority population. Yet, it is not a full member of EU.

Turkey is a geo-strategic country. It protected the southern flank of NATO during the Cold War. Since the breakup of the USSR, it has been a stabilizing force in the Balkans. Lately, it filters refugees coming from the Middle East and Africa, acting as a gatekeeper for Europe.

The country straddles two continents, neighboring with the likes of Iran, Iraq, and Syria in the Middle East. Their only land route to Europe, mainly for their oil and gas but also refugees. In the north, there are Caucuses. More oil and gas come from there through pipelines and go to Europe. Beijing to London Belt and Road Initiative also passes through Turkey. Without Turkey, there will not be and cannot be Europe as we know it.

b— On the other hand, EU cannot do with Turkey

Turkey wants to become a full member of the EU which is essentially a Christian club. Turkey is about 98 percent Muslim majority country. Although most of its citizens are Westernized with many years of exposure to the Europeans, there are cultural differences. Large portions of its population have never integrated fully with the Europeans. Integration problems of guest-arbiters and their extended families are ongoing.

Plus, there is already a fast-growing and sizable Muslim population in Europe. Full member Turkey will have a direct impact on them. Activism and intransigence to integration of Muslims in Europe will increase. Their numbers will continue to swell rapidly.

Including Turkey as a full member will also make a difference economically. Europe will face a stiff competition from the Turkish agricultural production. Further problems will arise when the EU-US trade on agriculture is affected.

Competition makes both economies grow stronger, yet can EU handle the stress factor? Turkish economy is projected to reach parity with major European economies, including Germany. A decade ago, German economy was four times bigger than the Turkish economy.

The other EU members are facing even worse prospects. Turkey will soon have bigger economy than each one of them. In a sense, EU countries will need access to the Turkish market more so than otherwise.

c— Visa-free walking rights

It was reported as early as in March 2018, the eventuality that "Brussels is likely to open the door for visa-free travel to Europe for Turkish citizens, even if Ankara doesn't fulfill all the conditions imposed."[65]

Since then, within six months, a lot has changed in favor of Turkey. Referendum and ensuing elections allowed Turkey to have a presidential system and gave Erdoğan more powers and a new term of five years to be renewed with another five in 2023.

In 2018, it was all clear to EU. A new era had started with Turkey. Erdoğan regime was there to stay until 2028. It was no longer business as usual with Turkey. Visa-free walking rights for Turkish citizens in EU short of full membership looked like, clearly the least of two evils.

To play hardball with Turkey or not

2002 was also the year when playing hardball with Turkey became a thing of the past. In the 1970s, Turkey started to invest on its indigenous defense industry. In a quarter of century, it built the infrastructure strong enough to go into mass production for domestic procurements.

---

[65] http://www.spiegel.de/international/europe/europe-at-pains-over-visa-free-travel-for-turks-a-1090040.html

Recently, it also became number eight biggest exporter in military hardware and software in the world. That also meant the genie was out of the bottle. Turkey was now independent.

Since then, the West does not have much option against Turkey. Rather, the US and EU need Turkey even more so than Turkey needs them. But the West still cannot believe that the times have changed and that the Catch-22 will had to be replaced with "chicken" games.

In the past, when Turkey had nothing and was dependent on the West, and there was a belligerent Soviet threat in the north, the West still could not play hardball against Turkey. "Chicken" games never worked then, when Turkey decided for example before taking over one third of Cyprus outright with a military operation.

What is worse in 2019, Turkey is tinkering with is nothing short of countering Western attempts with Zero-Sum games, when the West resorts to nation-building or conspires in coup d'états.

a— With EU Catch-22 quickly is becoming a Chicken game

In the past, the game between the West and Turkey has always been a Catch-22. But since 2002, "chicken" simply replaced it. But the West did not want to admit it until 2007. By then, the West started to realize that there was no way to win this game when played against Turkey, especially when Erdoğan like regime was in power.

In Europe, the games against Turkey are basically played under the leadership of Germany, the most populous country and the biggest economic power of the EU. The others did not have the leverage or status to play games against Turkey, except too much lesser extent on mundane matters by France or UK. But nowadays in Europe, none other than Germany can play any game against Turkey because there is practically an economic and military parity with them.

In 2019, Germany still has much bigger economy and more technology to put up a stiff competition against Turkey. Yet, it also has the most to lose because it has the biggest contingent of Turkish guest-arbiters entrenched in its society in the millions. Using them as a leverage and other Muslims in Europe, Turkey has an even further growing influence and leverage.

In view of these facts, Germany has no choice but to prevent Turkey's admission to EU first and foremost. Having Turkey as a full member will swell their numbers and make governing even more difficult. In the meanwhile, Germany has to work with fringe elements in its domestic politics, among radical right or left to counter Turkish moves.

But eventually, Germany will face insurmountable amount of pressure from both end and will have to make unpleasant choices. That is when Germany will be forced into a "chicken" game that it can never win on either front. In short, Germany, since the 2005, put itself in a box where on one end domestic radicals and Turkey on the other end will continuously be exacting demands with consequences for the regimes in power to handle from the point of weakness.

i— Turkey Demands an Answer from the EU

Since the turn of the century, Turkey has started demanding immediate and full membership in the European Union as if EU's days were numbered. It was clear that Turkey was no longer willing to play Catch-22. It was forcing EU into a "chicken" game. Erdoğan has been demanding a definite answer.

By 2019, Erdoğan is openly expecting for the EU to say no to Turkish membership in the union. In the meantime, an indecisive EU does not even want to think about the repercussions of losing Turkey. Yet, in some circles, it is also clear that the day of reckoning is at the door.

This is not the only area where Turkey is geared to play a new game against Germany but in view of dominant radical factors and entrenched domestic politics, Turkey can easily punch its way until it gets what it wants before a helpless Germany.

ii— Radicalization in Western Europe

The EU is a twenty-eight-member union. It represents wide-ranging agendas. Germany is its leader with both the biggest population and the biggest economy.

Germany has also the biggest dilemma to deal with. Over the years, under globalist regimes it opened arms to radicals from the Middle East. These days, when these radical elements in the Middle East cannot confront Turkey to their liking with their own means, they come to lobby against it at the European Union.

Germany has no option but to listen to their demands which automatically means a reactionary policy towards Turkey that in turn strains the relationship between two countries. As the number of the radicals in Germany swelled over the years, Germany finds itself more cornered.

The more Turkey becomes active in the region, the likelihood of radical voices to increase in the West becomes greater. Naturally, the trend leaves Germany in a lose-lose path of no return.

Nowadays, Turkey basically demands full membership to the union and technology transfer from Germany that it cannot grant. The results are double whammy for Germany. One it has to deal with domestic discontent and outright objection to Turkey. Two, the consequences of not selling Turkey what it seeks when Turkey procures elsewhere and then takes away German markets as a result in the long run.

Yet, downward spiral for Germany is not limited with loss of markets. In the last decade alone, Germany had to redeploy its military aircraft from Turkey to Jordan when Turkey gave ultimatum that Germany could not comply.

In short, from 2019 on, the Germany must avoid entering into "chicken" games with Turkey, knowing all too well how domestic radical elements in the country undermines Germany. On top of that, Turkey with Erdoğan regime in charge is selective when to push the ante against EU or Germany. When it does, it means that it decided to play the Zero-Sum game because "chicken" games were in play between 2002 and 2018.

With 2019, Turkey and Erdoğan can even entertain playing Zero-Sum game against Western Europe as well. No one knows what would happen when more Muslims will side with Turkey within and outside EU in the coming years. They will surely give more leverage to Turkey and Erdoğan. How Turkey and Erdoğan, gamechangers will use them will also determine the nature and timing of the game they will play.

b— Hardball never worked against Turkey

Simply put, the 2002-2018 cycle proved that hardball does no longer work against Turkey.

Bush-43 faced rebuke from Turkey in 2003 when the US forces were not permitted to invade Iraq from north. Obama administration never dealt with Turkey to the detriment of the US interests in the region. On top, it elected to weaponize Syria to make life ever more difficult to the incoming Trump administration.

By 2007, both side of the Atlantic wanted to see Erdoğan regime disappear from the face of the earth. Yet, they had no choice but to tolerate it with disdain until 2013 general elections in Turkey. They expected a new regime to come to power which will be much more in line with Western alliance partners like before.

In 2013, when Erdoğan won again, they tacitly supported a Western inspired coup d'état on 15 July 2016. People in Turkey rose up unlike never before in the modern Turkish history. They stopped the coup d'état achieving its objectives. More than two-hundred people died, including innocent soldiers, policemen alike.

Erdoğan regime steadily from there on increased the ante. Every encounter with the Union was now a Zero-Sum game. EU foolishly still thought that it can continue business as usual with Turkey. Without Turkish indulgence to stop them, one million Syrian refugees ending up in Western Europe in 2015 never crossed their mind.

By 2018, when Idlip crisis in Syria was about to erupt, Erdoğan communicated the predicament that the Union was in. Thank God, the EU realized it was helpless. It finally came to its senses that Erdoğan was holding all the cards. The idea to rely on "chicken" games was suicide. The next game with Turkey was meant solely a Zero-Sum game that the EU had no means to match or stomach to play.

In retrospect, hard ball never worked against Turkey either. Even when Turkey was much weaker. Lyndon Johnson and Jimmy Carter administrations threatened Turkey in the 1960s and 1970s, respectively, to no effect. Turkey, then, countered them brazenly, when it invaded northern third of Cyprus. In its aftermath, when the EU, the US, and Soviet Union further threatened Turkey in concert, Turkey still went ahead and proclaimed the Turkish Republic of Northern Cyprus few years later.

What did not work against much weaker Turkey, will never work in the 21st century. Nowadays, the Russian Federation (RF) yearns for an increasing integration in economic activity and military cooperation with Turkey. Western European powers are on the verge of parity with fast-rising Turkish economic and military power. Moreover, EU, RF, and Turkey have practically established a three-way balance of power when they have become interdependent to one another like never before.

Victory of the nationalist Trump administration in 2016 presidential elections also took away the chances for the globalist leftovers in Europe to resort to hardball for the foreseeable future.

i— Iraq

The globalist Bush-43 tried to play hardball against Turkey in 2003. Fully loaded US warships arrived eastern Mediterranean with a plan to enter into Iraq from north via Turkey. Turkey simply objected and did not permit the use of its territory from north. It forced the fleet to go through Suez Canal. The US forces invaded Iraq from south.

ii— Kurds

In September 2017, Kurds tried to play hardball in northern Iraq with a nod from globalists in Europe and the US. They declared a referendum date for independence. Turkey warned the Kurdish leadership of consequences, but the globalist West was adamant to challenge Turkey.

Turkey simply quelled Kurdish effort to hold a referendum effectively and promptly. Iraq complied fully with demands from Turkey and took away oil fields and border posts from Kurds. Iran joined forces with Turkey during rebellion not allowing radical Kurds finding refuge in its territory.

The Western globalists never came to the help of the Kurds. They forced the Kurds into something they would not have sought and then they left them on their own when a counter threat from Turkey was too much for them to handle. Kurds lost the semi-autonomous status they had gained in the past forty years in Iraq.

Turkey has never gave in to the demands of Kurdish tribes that were manipulated over the decades by international agents. When Kurds first revolted in 1925, after Turkey abolished Caliphate, Turkey showed its resolve firmly. Then again twice in the 1930s, Turkey suppressed revolts brutally.

iii— Syria

In Syria, in 2017, Turkey countered a similar Western backed Kurdish militia challenge. It dislodged Kurdish militia from their strong hold in Afrin within two months with a military incursion.

In Syria, a desperate globalist Obama administration left a very unfair hand to the incoming Trump administration to play against Turkey. As if its accumulated mistakes since 2011 were not enough to hurt the image of the superpower in the region, it sought a political hit job. The goal was to weaponize Syria against Trump. The result was predictable.

In 2018, when the US forces did not clear the Manbij region in Syria from Kurdish YPG forces, Erdoğan informed Trump that the Turkish forces will organize a full-scale invasion of east of Euphrates in 2019.

What Erdoğan communicated to Trump was not an ultimatum. He simply stated the facts in the field. Turkish armed forces had the ability to pinpoint Kurdish militia throughout the region with precision bombings. In other words, the US forces were going to be sitting ducks while Turkey were to conduct a military operation all around dozen or so US bases in the field.

What is tragic in Syria is not that the globalist cannot bully Turkey. Rather the fact that an outgoing US administration, at the expense of domestic political gains, will jeopardize so much US prestige and status in the region.

C. Technology transfer to Turkey or not

The root of the problem between the West and Turkey has always been the transfer of technology. The West was afraid of an industrialized Turkey in the early 1950s. Fifty years later, Turkey did not miss the new technology boat, like the West made sure, it did on the industrialization.

Having learned its lesson Turkey was ready for the next phase of life. As early as mid-1970s, Turkey embarked on electronics, computers, sensors, and other technologies of the future. By 2000, it had the necessary infrastructure and brain power to embark on a great push.

Between 2003 and 2013, Turkey made an enormous leap forward when the US was bogged down by the globalist Bush-43 regime in Iraq. In 2005, Germany too was busy bringing to power its own globalist Angela Merkel. Together they ignored Turkey and allowed it, practically, to leave the alliance. They never noticed it.

By 2013, desperate globalist regimes on both side of the Atlantic kept their fingers crossed that Erdoğan would not win the general elections in Turkey. That was their only hope to continue keeping Turkey anchored to the West like it was throughout the 20th century. But Erdoğan won the elections. That is why the globalists became desperate. They tacitly supported the 15 July 2016 coup d'état against the Erdoğan regime. When that too failed, the game was over for the globalist West.

In short, when the world media was writing about Erdoğan becoming a dictator, the West was trying to hide the big failure of the globalist regimes. They blundered big time and now they were facing the consequences. There, Turkey was standing tall and was ready to negotiate with the West, the US, and Germany alike from the point of strength.

Turkey was demanding the latest military platforms. Intercontinental ballistic missile technology, 5th generation aircraft and latest generation tanks. Turkey was producing the rest already. It had already found alternatives to the US and German products from the rest of the Western alliance members like Italy, Spain, S. Korea, or Japan. It was now demanding the rest. The primary alternatives were Russia or China but also others like Ukraine with tank engines.

a— Turkey works less with US and Germany more with Russia

In 1950s, Turkey started industrialization process. It sought a billion-dollar investment and technology transfer from the US and Germany. They rejected it. Turkey turned to, then, the Soviet Union. They built together Iskenderun Iron and Steel complex with a 1.5 billion-dollar investment and know-how.

In the 1960s, the US came back and gave Turkey 1.5 billion dollars but still refused transfer of technology. That did not win many friends in Turkey and Turkey turned its attention elsewhere instead what it could do without Western technology. Turkey started to build dams over the Euphrates and Tigris rivers. Hoover types and many of them!

By 1975, Turkey knocked on the door of the West again. This time it was asking basic military instruments like radars and walkie talkies. When the West refused, Turkey finally understood it was time to move away from the West.

In the last two decades, Turkey no longer relies on technology transfer or most of the major military platforms the US or Germany have like tanks or helicopters. Turkey builds them better, faster and cheaper with technology transfer from other countries and takes away Western markets.

i— Arms embargo was costly for the US

Every time the US imposed an arms embargo on Turkey, it lost leverage, but it also lost markets because Turkey cultivated technologically advanced products at competitive prices.

Turkey first created Aselsan in 1975 when the US imposed arms embargo on Turkey because of Cyprus crisis. In 2018, Aselsan is one of top one-hundred global defense companies in the world. Turkey is the eighth biggest exporter of arms and rising fast. Other Turkish companies are making great strides. Three others are in the top one hundred and more expected to make the list soon. Seven companies operate on land and air vehicles, four on sea vehicles, seven on rocket-missile fields, fifteen on electronic military software, and seven on IT. Some of them have one of a kind technologies NATO and the US forces rely on.

A recent development is another case in point when the US is always late in trying to recover from its earlier mistakes of rejecting to work with Turkey. When Turkey could not buy Sikorsky helicopters from US in the 2000s, it developed an attack helicopter with Italian license. Turkey now has close to a hundred of them operational. Plus, it exports them to Pakistan and Philippines as well. In June 2016, Sikorsky changed plans. It agreed to build with Turkey in a joint project 109 Sikorsky-70 helicopters. In the meanwhile, a Turkish indigenous utility helicopter also made its maiden flight in September 2018. It is 100 percent Turkish made, other than the engine which is expected to be operational within few years.

ii— Arms embargo was also costly to Germany

With Germany, it was the heavy industry products like tanks, warships and engines.

In 1999, reportedly, Turkey bought 976 million Euro worth of armament from Germany. This number fell to 440 million Euro in 2003 and to 44 million Euro in 2008. Since then, the volume is even lower. Turkey bought seventy-one Leopard-1 tanks from Germany in the 1980s and 320 more in the 1990s. In 2000s, it bought 354 Leopard-2A4 thanks. When Germany declined to sell the third version of the

Leopards, Turkey built its Altay prototypes. It is now ready for mass manufacture 250 of them in the first batch.

When Germany also refused to provide engines for these thanks, Turkey decided to develop them on its own. They are projected to be ready when the first tanks are delivered by late 2019. Turkey built the tank with S. Korean license and is in the process of mass-producing various engine types with Ukraine and others. Germany did not make the same mistake in submarines. Together with Turkey, Germany is building six submarines for Turkish navy and an additional set for Indonesia in a joint venture.

iii— Russia started to fill the void

When the US rejected technology transfer, involving Patriot missiles, Russia moved in with S-400 batteries. Turkey will receive them starting in 2019.

In the past, Turkey repeatedly inquired nuclear power plants from the US, but it never materialized. Russia is building a nuclear power plant in Turkey and it will be operational in 2023.

b— Trump was smart and fast to stop the damage

By the time Trump came to power, Turkey had long achieved 65% indigenous defense industry and was increasing the percentage fast. Plus, the utopian nation-building goals of the Western globalist regimes in the Middle East had already alienated Turkey from the alliance. Turkey was getting licenses from other providers for similar platforms.

President Trump wanted to correct the mistakes of the past US administrations and moved fast both on the sale of the Patriots missile systems and the delivery of the F-35 joint strike fighter aircrafts to Turkey.

In a sense, by 2018, Trump knew well what most everybody else in the US had not yet realized. It was long clear to him that Chicken game was no longer possible to play against Turkey. The only realistic game was a Zero-Sum game.

Trump had four-star US generals on record that were against any kind of game against Turks. These generals knew all too well that the Turks would die but never back down when motherland or religion was at stake.

The danger for the US was the ignorance of the facts by the globalists, thinking that Chicken game aside, even Catch-22 was still a viable game against Turkey. Trump had no such illusions but by the end of 2018, he was also in minority as the president of the US.

Maybe that is why to emphasize the complexity of the impasse, he stated publicly in Osaka, Japan during G-20 meetings, that it was Obama's miscalculations that put the US and the world into this quagmire regarding Patriots and S-400s, concurrently F-35s when he told Erdogan that it was not his doing. It was Obama that had refused to deliver Patriots to Turkey when Erdogan first asked for them.

i— American missile defense systems

In the US, forces that are not willing to share military technology with Turkey never lost their fervor. Irrespective of who the president was, they continue to be against it for their own reasons.

They are still in majority two years after the Trump revolution swept them off their feet. They are still opposing to give Patriot surface-to-air missile systems to Turkey even though the technology was already shared with others in the alliance for more than a decade. Furthermore, Turkey as a staunch and prominent ally believes it should be a priority for the US to share it with Turkey sooner than later.

Yet, during the Obama administration, the US went even further on the wrong direction and threatened Turkey not to acquire Russian or Chinese technologies for similar long-range ballistic missiles. In the end, Turkey moved away from China because it was not willing to share the technology either. But Russia agreed to sell S-400 missile system and it also agreed to technology transfer. By the time, Trump came to power it was a done deal.

When President Trump came to power, he put an end to this charade. It was already clear to him that Turkey had already moved away from the West during the globalist regimes like Bush-43 and Obama. He started to support the sale of the Patriots to Turkey at the end of 2018 and release the delivery of F-35 aircrafts.

ii— The Joint Strike Fighter

There are a dozen Turkish defense industry companies that contribute to the F-35 project. "If Turkey is excluded from the JSF program, it would in turn cease providing components to the *F-35 Joint Strike Fighter* production line."

That's why Secretary of Defense James Mattis opposed the proposal, arguing in a letter to Congress that, "If the Turkish supply chain was disrupted today, it would result in an aircraft production break, delaying delivery of 50–75 F-35s, and would take approximately 18–24 months to re-source parts and recover," Marcus Hellyer wrote.[66]

---

[66] http://www.atimes.com/article/the-consequences-of-cutting-turkey-out-of-f-35-program/

In the US it may sound like there is a healthy debate on the matter. But among countries with leading military technologies, it is viewed as an opportunity to take away markets from the US. Especially, when such domestic debates in the US come after backstabbing, betrayals, brushing asides, arms embargos like Turkey faced from the US, the client states lose interest even faster and competitors capitalize effectively.

Turkey was no different with the F-35 project by late 2018. Turkey took precautions and started its indigenous fifth generation aircraft project. Prototypes are to be readied by 2023. Half a dozen countries are working with Turkey in the development. Mass production is projected by 2030.

But it is more than that. Turkey is also the producer of the SOM, a cruise missile that can be launched from air, sea, and land. It is specially produced by Tubitak SAGE, a leading Turkish defense industry contractor. It is the most sophisticated and competitive in its class. Turkey has produced SOM-J for F-35. The alternative would be for Turkey to use them on its indigenous 5th generation TFX aircraft it is developing. That also means SOM-J may also be available for other fighter planes if it is not exclusive for the US brand fighter crafts.

II. The Trump Revolution

Donald J. Trump took the world by surprise.

He was a Yankee and a Nationalist.

A double whammy for the US and the world to stomach.

On top of that, he came right after Bush-43/Obama calamity in the Middle East.

Bush was a disaster for the region. Obama was even worse.

In the Middle East, the misery index was like a downward vortex no one had answers.

In Turkey, nationalist and Islamist Recep Tayyip Erdoğan was in power long time.

It took two full years for Erdoğan and Trump to connect once in for all.

That was in Argentina, when they met at G-20 meeting in 2018.

It was the meeting of minds.

They followed it up on December 14 with a phone call.

They understood that it was time to revisit the relationship and open a new chapter.

It was time for the US and Turkey to act on equal footing in the region.

Turkey needed the US logistic support to extend its military reach in Syria.

The US needed Turkey to cooperate in Syria and Iraq towards a greater goal.

Trump knew well that the US needed Turkey on its side to resolve the Iranian problem.

But it was also clear that what was important for Turkey had to be resolved before that.

Northern Iraq and Syria had to be in Turkish control.

1. Within two years Erdoğan and Trump were suddenly on the same boat

Late 2018, Trump and Erdoğan agreed on the basic tenants of an understanding.

They are both homeland-first.
They are also against nation-building.
They know that they are both for trade.
One says that it should be free and fair trade.
The other is simply saying that it should always be win-win.

A. Homeland is their starting point

Trump is trying to right the ship in the US. Globalist policies of Clinton, Bush and Obama administrations had taken their toll in twenty-four years.

The US was in twenty trillion-dollar debt when he came to power. The destiny was no longer in the hands of the US and the superpower was in free fall. Closest allies Canada and Mexico were taking big bites away from the mothership in North America. Allies on the other side of Atlantic were no different. Even Japan and S. Korea were still taking advantage of the grand old USA after many decades of recovery.

In the meantime, for Erdoğan the main problem was border security. The terrorists, mainly as pawns of the Western interests, were inflicting heavy toll on the country since 1970s. Erdoğan was determined to end it.

But when Trump came to power, he found himself with a weaponized Syria, a gift of Obama. Two-hundred or so US soldiers were deployed there in a hurry solely to complicate Trump's relationship with Erdoğan. Erdoğan knew it. Trump did not. When he realized at the end of 2018, he immediately announced that he is withdrawing troops from Syria much to the surprise of everybody in the West.

With that move, Trump had already moved a step ahead of all advocates of the issues at hand in that corner of the region. He summarized it. There was no need to confront Turkey in Syria. Turkey had overwhelming power to resolve the outstanding military challenges. Plus, border security was vitally important for its national security. No one was going to stop Turkey going in and clearing a buffer zone to its liking. At the end, Turkey was adamant to send some of the four million refugees, if not all, back to their homeland. It was a win-win-win for Turkey, refugees, and the Western interest even though some in the latter was stubborn for ideological differences never to notice or appreciate it.

For Turks, the issue was terrorism. There were all kinds of it in the region and no sovereign had the right to legitimate any of them for any reason. Unless all of the terrorists are eliminated, close to four million refugees had no chance to return to back to their homeland. Together, the goal was to tackle a bounty of vitally important global challenges from competition over the eastern Mediterranean riches to the expansion of China in Central Asia, Indian Ocean and beyond.

Turkey had to provide security to its homeland first before working on mutual interest with others. It was no different than "America First." It was easy for nationalist Trump to understand nationalist Erdoğan.

B. Against nation-building

Nation-building has been the single biggest problem both the US and Turkey. They faced the burden and ill effects for many decades. Even though Trump and Erdoğan were on the opposite side of the process, they were still on the same page.

For Trump, wasting lives and money for utopian causes were not acceptable. They were un-American. What Bush-43 did was not forgivable. Trump had always loudly objected the invasion of Iraq since the beginning. He had attacked Hillary Clinton during presidential election campaign for having supported Bush-43. To replace a regime with force was the gravest mistake. To Trump, this was not the "American Exceptionalism" that he was proud of. This was Bush-43's personal vendetta that was in sync with the globalist agenda of the Clintons and Obamas.

Erdoğan could not have agreed more. Now it was mere meeting of minds between Erdoğan and Trump. It was time to put nation-building aside. It was time to bring order so that modernity and security could follow in the region that the globalists left in shambles. All they had to do first was to pacify northern and eastern regions of Syria. After that, northern third of Iraq where other rouge elements were still present was to be settled. For Turkey, they were the PKK terrorists. For the US, they were Iranian supported militia, DAES, ISIS and the likes.

Short of nation-building, for Turkey it was enough to clean terrorists from border zone and to keep it under control so that refugees can return and live in safe environment. For the US, it was important that Turkey went deep into Syria and controlled one third of eastern Syria, bordering Iraq. Ultimate goal was to cut off the link between Iran and the militia in Syria.

By 2019, Turkey had amassed massive amount of military hardware and personnel to move beyond the buffer zone to take over the entire region and relieve the US forces from the task so long as Trump provided the logistical support Erdoğan sought. Such cooperation would turn large portion of Syria into secure zone where life can be rebuilt by locals and returning refugees. It will also set an example to move forward with the next step of recovery in the region.

C. More trade is the way out

Both Trump and Erdoğan knew very well without order in the Middle East, nothing will move forward. Terrorism had to be eradicated. Nation-building hypocrisy also had to be taken off the table. They were the root of the problems.

Trade in the Middle East was important for Turkey but not a priority for the US. Yet, reconstruction and increased trade activity in the region was the best way to keep order. More importantly, it was clear that it was the only way to keep refugees at home and prevent next phase of migration.

Of all leaders in the West, Trump knew well the migration problem. Immigration reform was his priority. The realities in the southern border posts of the US was indicative. There were more and more migrants from overseas. It was sure indication that the current problems of the Middle East are also the problems of the US, not only Europe's.

Vibrant economic activity followed by increased international trade were the ways out of many problems. Like Kennedy said, "when economy was bad nothing was right." was so true. On top of that, since Erdoğan had his own plan in action across the world with a Win-Win strategy and Trump with Fair and Free Trade the goal was half done.

a— Erdoğan's Win-Win

For Erdoğan, in the name of freeing people from bondage in an age of competitive world, creating new states were something in the past. Erdoğan believed the 21st century was the turn of Muslim countries to achieve greatness and they were going to do it mainly with increased trade.

Erdoğan was acting as their leader. He was at the beginning of a long road for Turkey to achieve economic growth and maturity. He was appealing and approaching to many new and potential markets with a simple Win-Win strategy, starting with Africa.

"We want to improve our relations, built on mutual respect,
in all areas on the basis of win-win and equal partnership.
Since we took office, we have been working in this spirit
in order to strengthen our cooperation with the whole of Africa
without any discrimination."

According to Yeni Safak Turkish daily, during his tenure in the past fifteen years, Turkey expanded trade volume with African countries six-fold increase to 17.5 billion dollars. In this period, Turkey completed forty-five commercial and economic cooperation agreement with the African countries. It has increased the number of agreements for the reciprocal protection of investments, from six to twenty-six.

While Turkish direct investment in Africa was a hundred million dollars in 2003, it approached 6.5 billion dollars in 2017. Turkish entrepreneurs employed seventy-eight thousand people across the continent, the volume of projects carried out by Turkish contracting companies exceeded fifty-five billion dollars.

The number of embassies in the continent rose to forty-one in 2017 when it was twelve in 2003, when the African expansion began. Turkish Airlines increased its destinations to fifty-five in thirty-five countries in the continent.

b— Trump's free and fair trade

For Trump, Turkey was setting a great example how free and fair trade should have been. Yet, the hands of the US were tied with multinational agreements that were all written against the interest of the US like in NAFTA.

WTO was not fair for the US. When the US economy was half of the world's economy, it was all right to help other economies but not when they have reached parity. The rules had to change for the trade to become win-win for the US as well, like Erdoğan was arguing.

Yet, in the US, Trump is hardly the first president to complain about trade deals. Barack Obama criticized the North American Free-Trade Agreement (NAFTA) during his campaign to be president, then negotiated an upgrade while in office, the doomed Trans-Pacific Partnership. Trump's plans for a huge renegotiation of NAFTA are arguably an escalation rather than an absolute departure. The depth of his suspicions of the World Trade Organization (WTO) looks like a fundamental shift.[67]

---

[67]   https://www.economist.com/briefing/2017/05/13/
what-donald-trump-means-by-fair-trade

Furthermore, Donald Trump does not espouse the formula to which Woodrow Wilson, Franklin Roosevelt, and their successors subscribed to—namely that international trade fosters the growth of democracies which in turn leads to enhanced prospects for world peace. There may be number of reasons for that.

First and foremost, the current administration has announced that it intends to redress the imbalanced trade relationships with other countries. This, the primary announced goal of current U.S. trade policy, clearly resonates with a not inconsiderable number of American voters. These supporters of the President, concerned with their own failure to participate in the benefits of globalization, are likely to believe that America has done enough for the world trading system. More pointedly, in the view of some, it is time for America to be paid back for the investments it made for the global public good.

Second, there is little belief at present, in American policy circles, that movement in the direction of free markets, at least in the foreseeable future, is accompanied by movement toward democracy. The progress toward greater political freedom does not appear to be linked to rising standards of living and greater market orientation. A third may be that it is felt the post war reconstruction has accomplished all that it could accomplish through trade.

A fourth may be that the U.S. does not have much more to give in terms of lowering trade barriers in an era where industrial tariffs are on average very low for all developed countries. (26) The world of trade has become multi-polar. The U.S. is no longer the largest trading country, and adding in the European Union as a whole, it is only the third largest trader.[68]

2. Erdoğan and Trump have more reasons to work together

In 2019, Turkey is a domineering economic and military regional power.
Turkey can do more in Syria, Iraq, and Iran with the US logistic support.
But Turkey has also leverages and means to deliver beyond region as well.
The US can make greater use of Turkish leverages and resources globally.

A. Turkey is a domineering regional power

In 2019, Turkey is a domineering regional power in the Middle East. It is the only country that can make and is making military incursions in northern Syria and

---

[68] https://www.wto.org/english/news_e/news18_e/ddgra_09feb18_e.htm

Iraq at will. It is also the only country that can have and is having influence over Iran without resorting into military means.

Between 2016-2018, the US set up more than dozen military posts in Syria, cleared a large swathes of eastern end of the country from DAES/ISIS and positioned itself to confront state sponsored militia. But brinkmanship of the Turkish forces nearby undermined the US force projection and continues in an increasing fashion over time.

Basically, the disarray in Syria and Iraq obliged Turkey to take military initiatives in its border regions to create buffer zones: free of DAES/ISIS to PKK/YPG/PYD. Incursions by the Turkish armed forces were efficient and effective. Zones were cleared from all militia. Refugees returned home.

Yet, Turkey is also aware of the fact that nuclear Iran is a priority over refugee crisis Europe has so far faced and will continue to be facing in the future. Iran is not a Middle Eastern problem. It is not a Western problem. Ending Nuclear Proliferation Treaty (NPT) formally is the problem. Turkey as a domineering regional power cannot allow NPT to come to an end.

The US has to join Turkey to bring an equitable resolution to the Iranian nuclearization. Turkey does not act as a domineering regional power when it comes to dealing with Iran, nor in its relationship with the United States. Rather it is an "interlocutor valuable" with weight that has threat power and incentives. One, Turkey has the power to prevent either the US or Iran to enforce their will defying the rest of the world. Two, Turkey has the capacity and political will to offer what no other country in the world can offer both to Iran and the United States in the region.

Turkey cannot let Iran acquire nuclear weapons nor it can allow the US to go after Iran by force to prevent acquisition of nuclear weapons. Since Turkey is projected to become top five economic and military power in the world in the coming decades, Turkey will continue to become a domineering regional power that can impose its will. On that note, it means that Iran will not acquire nuclear weapons and there won't be another colossal war in the Middle East involving the US.

a— In Syria

The main priority for Turkey is to clear the northern and eastern sections of Syria out of rouge militia so that the refugees can return home safely. Turkey will be satisfied when it establishes a buffer zone in the northern most border regions. The US has interest that Turkey goes in across the eastern portion of Syria as well, beyond Raqqa. For that, the US has to provide Turkey logistic support.

The status of the Turkish and the American forces in Syria and Iraq make all the difference. Turkey conducts military incursions lasting months. The US deploys troops permanently and sets up bases. When Turkish armed forces pull out of the countries, they leave behind legitimate local forces to establish order. When the US pulls out, who they leave behind dissipates and replaced with another anti-Western militia.

b— In Iraq

Turkey will work with the US in Iraq only after two conditions are materialized. One, Turkey must be in total control of the eastern Syria with the US help. Two, the US foreign policy objectives must totally and formally be walking away from working with rouge Kurdish-terrorist elements anywhere in the region.

The US needs Turkey in Iraq to have any leverage on Iran. On the other hand, Turkey does not need the US in Iraq. Over there, Turkey has two paths. One is to establish a terrorist free zone. Turkey, in the last decade of the millennia, cleared a zone of thirty kilometers inside northern Iraq with Turkish bases.

Two decades later, the terrorist elements largely supported by radical elements and politicians of EU countries have established new bases approximately sixty kilometers inside Iraq from Turkish border. Turkey now is in the process of clearing an eighty kilometer zone inside Iraq to get rid of terrorist bases from Kandil and Sincar mountains.

The other path for Turkey is to work with the US to bring Iran to the negotiating table on nuclear weapons. It is in the mutual interest of both parties that there is no nuclear Iran. But the US has to acknowledge like Turkey does, unless they work together, Iran will go nuclear and so will Turkey, as a domino effect.

c— In Iran

Today, the US has a soon to be nuclear Iran problem that is its own doing. The US is also the only country that can prevent this eventuality. The vacillation of the US foreign policy objectives must end in order to achieve the desirable result.

The non-nuclear Iran can only be possible if Turkey is in the mix of a solution which has to be a negotiated settlement between Iran, Turkey, and the US. Russian input is also crucial for the best result.

Otherwise, if Iran goes nuclear, Turkey will go nuclear no matter what. Then Saudi Arabia will want to go nuclear. Then there goes the NPT because of the domino effect. When the US does not have good working relationship with neither Russia or Turkey or Iraq, the eventuality of Iran going nuclear is a sure bet.

Iran, thanks to Bush-43 and Obama regimes, has great influence at least over the one third of Iraq because of its ethnic and religious ties. Turkey filled the vacuum in the norther third of Iraq since 2014 and further consolidated its status since the 2017 Kurdish referendum fiasco.

Neither Turkey nor Iran will relinquish their hold in Iraq until there are no more outside threat to their region of influence. Considering Western inspired coup d'états both Iran and Turkey in the 20th century and the presence of globalists still on the mend with their nation-building agenda, there is no likelihood for Turkey to cooperate with the US, or Iran to come to an agreement with the West.

d— In the Mediterranean Sea

In the meantime, Turkey already declared through many platforms its stand over the Mediterranean riches. But it must be noted that the US attitude in Syria and Iraq in the third decade of the millennia will influence Turkey how much to cooperate with the US elsewhere.

Meanwhile, irrespective of what happens on land in the region, Turkey will continue to protect its continental shelf rights in the Eastern Mediterranean Sea. Turkey will coordinate its efforts there with the US where applies, but more so if there are harmonious relations in establishing at the least a secure border zones along Syria and Iraq borders.

i- Turkey is the biggest stake holder

Turkey is the biggest stake holder on the continental shelf. Egypt, Israel, Lebanon, Syria, the Republic of Cyprus, and the Turkish Republic of Northern Cyprus have much less say. Other players will also join the fray. Western Europeans behind PESCO, Pentagon led NATO, Syria based Russia are the other major players next to Turkey.

The other local countries with stake in the sea will have to take their sides with these powers until there will be an equitable distribution of the sea among countries bordering the region. For that to happen, balance of power must be established between the US, Russia, PESCO, and Turkey in the region.

ii- There are balance of powers in place to weigh in

There is already two balance of power dynamics in place in the region involving Russia and Turkey. One is in the Black Sea basin. The continental shelf is equitably divided among all countries with border to the sea. Russia and Turkey established the line with smaller countries in agreement.

The other is between EU, Russia, and Turkey. It involves Turkish land-bridge. Turkey allows oil pipelines from east to go west and acts as a floodgate for refugees heading EU from the east. Russia is committed to provide 30 percent of Europe's energy need via Turkish pipelines while EU is expected to give visa-free walking rights to Turkish citizens to return the favor.

The arrangement should go in effect in full by 2020. It can also then present a working formula for the Eastern Mediterranean riches with the addition of the US to the equation.

In short, never mind the fact that the West has to work with Turkey in Syria and Iraq, the West needs Turkey in the Mediterranean Sea. Only then, the West will be able to benefit having Turkey on board. So that the West, and the Muslims in tow, will give the Western alliance a leverage against rising China in establishing global balance of power.

B. Turkey has leverages beyond the region

Turkey has major cards to play in Europe, over the balance of power between the West and the East and the fast-rising Muslim world. They are global problems. They involve economic, military and religious factors. They require universal resolves.

a— Saving Europe

In Europe, the root of the problems lies in the past century. The exploits in the Middle East and North Africa nowadays produce different problems and opportunities.

A century after the Ottoman yoke, the Middle East is worse off than it has ever been. The wars, destructions, and loss of life the people in the Middle East have endured under Western hegemony are catastrophic from Algeria to Iraq to Yemen.

Europe now has to compete in these markets against many other challengers. In the meantime, Europe also has to deal with the seven Muslim countries that are replacing their Western counterparts among top twenty economies. The Muslim countries have rapidly growing markets but also technology, resources, and alliances that give them further edge. Most importantly, they are no longer subservient but actual competitors.

Plus, Europe has to face the brunt of the refugee influx from these fast-growing Muslim countries. Without Turkey, they are helpless. In other words, Europe is in defense, unlike in the past century when it was roaming free at will. It is in a sense, reaping what it sowed.

Some in the West would argue that the Muslims are ungrateful. Others among the Muslims will argue that nothing good came from the West in the past century.

In short, Europe has to settle an account not only with Turkey but with other rising Muslim countries over time. In view of these apparent problems, for European leaders like Angela Merkel and Emmanuel Macron to have a spat with Trump only weakens their hands further across the board. Building PESCO to counter NATO on top of that is simply an act of desperation that is sure to blow in the face of EU when the West has to show a unified front.

On the other hand, Turkey and the US are still the best options for Europe to ally with. It is in the interest of both sides of Atlantic to join forces with Turkey to establish the balance of power between the East and the West. But all three must be on equal footing. Independent Turkey with projected economic size and military proves will have significant say that must be taken on face value.

The destiny of Europe aside, Turkey has resources and the political will to change the balance of power in a large portion of the world. Turkey has direct say in North Africa, Middle East, Caucasus, the Balkans, and the Black and the Mediterranean seas. The Horn of Africa, Red Sea, the Gulf, and the Indian Ocean are not spared either. Overseas Turkish military bases and navy and sophisticated indigenous defense technology make the difference.

Turkey will leverage the balancing act alone between the East and the West by joining forces with Russia and China. With Russia: in Syria and bringing energy to Europe via pipelines. With China: by building the main line of the Belt and Road initiative via Turkey. With Trump administration in power, Turkey has more room to cooperate with the US. They will work in NATO, in the Eastern Mediterranean and in countries with explosive populations in Africa and Asia. The plight of the Rangoon Muslims is a case in point when the US joined Turkey with repeated and supportive statements.

The changing realities in the world with economic developments are bringing unlikely countries together. Recently in South Africa, Turkey was the guest of the BRICS. The member countries voiced expansion of their organization by bringing on board countries like Turkey and Indonesia. BRICS is growing in size and might because its member countries like China and India are projected to become number one and two economies in the world in the decades to come.[69]

The union of most powerful countries in the world under one international organization is not an exclusion of Western powers. The fair and balanced representation of the world's soon to be most powerful economies as a group will create a realistic forum that will correct what is wrong at the United Nations Security

---

69   https://www.yahoo.com/news/china-stays-track-brics-countries-103237057.html

Council as well. Currently, Japan and Germany are not represented there. Neither the most powerful Muslim countries when the world will be a Muslim majority world soon.

Erdoğan regularly louds the common sentiment saying, "the world is bigger than five," referring to China, Russia, UK, France, and the US, acting as the Permanent Members of the United Nations Security Council when no Muslim country has a seat.

Having a nuclear weapon is not a valid argument anymore. First, there is a half a dozen countries with known nuclear weapons and delivery systems that are not formally recognized as nuclear powers. Two, there is another half a dozen country that can produce a nuclear weapon or has certain technologies that give them lethal means equal to nuclear weapons. From electromagnetic rail guns to submarines that can stay under water for longer periods of time without nuclear plants, but in capacity, effectiveness and applicability. For example, Turkey as a Muslim country has these technologies and soon will enter into mass production.

c— Bringing Muslims with the rest

Turkey has numerous cards to play and Erdoğan translates them into a Muslim card. He makes it easy to understand for the West so long as the West is not in a delusional state. There is a reality out there regarding the Muslims.

Erdoğan argues that today the Muslims must have a proportionally equal say in the world affairs. When the world population reaches 9.5 billion people by 2050, 2.7 billion will be Muslims. By the end of the 21st century, when the world population reaches eleven billion people, 35 percent will consist of Muslim, 34 percent of Christians. Chinese will follow with around 10 percent and Indians with around 14 percent.

Secular Turkey with political Islamist regimes in power will surely be in a position of influence or directly control large portion of the 35 percent Muslims. No other Muslim country is in Turkey's stature or leverage to achieve or to meet the same feat.

Turkey with enlarged responsibility in the region and around the world will be more effective when it acts with the US for a common good of all concerned. It is also in the interest of Europe to do the same, considering how most Muslims will be heading to Europe first as their population swell and migration continues.

In the past century, Turkey, as a fledgling country, was poor. It was a liability. It could have brought the standard of life down at the European Union because of its sheer size. Nowadays, there is 11 percent unemployment in Italy. The chances are more Italians would move to Turkey than Turks to Italy for many reasons.

If Turkey is now blocked from the Union when visa-free walking rights are not granted, short of full membership, more Turks will want to venture to EU, like a "forbidden fruit." Turkey, that is kept out of EU, will be less interested in who goes into the Union illegally.

In the Indian Ocean, Turkey forms another major dynamic with Pakistan and Indonesia. When the population of Bangladesh and Muslims in India are considered, more than a billion, surrounding the ocean where Turkish navy will be one of the biggest in the coming century.

Coupled with Turkic presence in the Central Asian Turkic republics, Turkey has a significant role to play in Asia. The US can only benefit from such presence if it allies tightly and on equal footing with Turkey. Together, the US and Turkey can counterbalance China which will become the primary challenge for the West if not already.

3. Could there be a unified front with Turkey: US vision for the future?

Trump revolution took place because 20th century plans of the West went bunkers.

There is a rising China and independent Turkey and the West in free-fall.

The Western dominance has ended and need to be saved before trampled.

Two world wars and five other major wars summarize the rise and fall of the West.

The US became a superpower after WWI, WWII, and the Korean war.

The US faces China as a superpower after losses in Vietnam, Iraq, and Afghanistan.

War of attrition against Turkey was also to the detriment of the West's superiority.

Turkey grew bigger, stronger, together with the fast-rising Muslim nation-states.

Can the West afford letting Turkey go independent and away from the West?

China must be the focus of the world including the US.

Turkey should be siding with the West when China is kept in Western crosshair.

How could there be balance of power with China without the US and Turkey coming together first?

A. 20th century was a big lesson that should not repeat

For Trump, Bush-43 war in Iraq and continued US military presence in Afghanistan and Syria are the problems lingering from the 20th century. Trump came to power to put an end to such nation-building adventures.

For example, there was no reason to put the US forces into harm's way like they were put in Lebanon in 1983. Terrorist bombing killed 241 US marines, together with fifty-eight French peacekeepers and six civilians.

When Obama administration deployed approximately 200 US soldiers in Syria, a similar risk was taken. Trump immediately increased the numbers of the troops, almost by tenfold to prevent another tragedy. Better result was to pull them out and he indicated his intention to do it from the point of strength after resolving outstanding matters in the region.

Bigger mistake was in Afghanistan. Soviet invasion of Afghanistan in the 1970s should have been another big lesson for the West. In its aftermath, Saudi Arabian allies of the US came back to commit 9/11 atrocities against their American brethren, displaying their eternal hatred.

The US should have learned great lessons from WWI, WWII, Korean, and Vietnam wars and avoided new, deadly, destructive adventures. The Algerian revolution against the colonialist French forces in 1962 should have been another big lesson when more than a million people were savagely killed next door to Europe.

Maybe it is understandable that the West had to go through a series of trials and tribulations out of desperation after double defeat against Turks first in the Dardanelles in 1915 and again during the war of liberation in the early 1920s when the modern Republic of Turkey was founded.

B. Turkey must not be lost

The relationship with Turkey over a century covered a lots of ground. There are two pertinent questions to answer. One, is it worth losing Turkey after all that investment and maturation in the relationship? Two, can the West lose Turkey and survive in the 21st century?

The West lost Iran in 1979, the world has never been the same ever since. The prospect of nuclear Iran is number one worry of the West together with prospect of having nuclear North Korea with intercontinental missiles.

Anti-Western Turkey can easily play the refugee card or pose nuclear threat with intercontinental missiles. It is not wise to discount cyber or space wars either overtime.

On the other hand, Turkey at best will remain as a benevolent but domineering regional power acting independently. At worst, it can be vicious like in the Korean war or swift and decisive like in Cyprus but at larger scales.

No need to revisit the glorious history of the Turks. Most recent examples should be enough. Nothing changed with the Turks. They are benevolent until they are poked.

Today, like Turkey, some of the most Westernized Muslims would like to be integrated further into the Western world. There is no need to lose them and face them as an arch and formidable enemy from the past with nightmarish memories.

All the while, the West has still China to worry about around the corner.

C. What about the rise of China?

In the immediate future, China is the main problem of the West. China's rise is unstoppable. It will grow bigger in Asia, but also in Europe. Its rise will follow the Belt and Road Initiative, one stop at a time coming from Beijing to London.

Central Asian republics are first in line on the Western thrust. Pakistan and Afghanistan come next. China alone can dominate the region and take under its influence like Soviet Union did in the 20th century.

Independent Turkic states have a stake to join forces with Turkey. Together they can have a balance of power against China. But they will need more support. Pakistan, Afghanistan, Bangladesh, Indonesia may bring leverage as other major Muslim states nearby, but they are far too spread to play a significant role in the Asian mass.

The US has to come into play for its own sake. In order to create a balance of power with China, the US must have a strong footing in the Middle East and in Central Asia. There is one common denominator in both places that has the capacity and political will that is worthwhile for the US. That is Turkey. Together they can counterbalance China power for decades to come.

III. New beginning

Turkey would love to have the US on board from the West as an ally.

The benefits from such a union are mutual.

NATO was the fabric that was holding the US, Western Europe, and Turkey together. Almost forty years later, without Soviet threat, they practically have nothing in common.

The Reagan Administration won the war against the Soviet empire with NATO.

By 2016, the globalists in Europe were already building PESCO instead.

Russia became best of allies with Turkey.

Russia alone was no longer a threat to Europe but with Turkey, they became lethal.

Russia and Turkey also demonstrated their unified power in Syria against the West.

By 2018, Turkey was the only hope of the US or the EU in Syria.

President Trump moved fast and capitalized on the opportunity before it was too late. He announced the withdrawal of the US troops from Syria to win Erdoğan.

The same Erdoğan that Obama had lost in 2012.

The EU too made a 180 degree turn since 2015 and embraced Erdoğan by 2018.

EU finally realized the dilemma it was in.

Without Erdoğan, EU was destined to have the same fate as the USSR or NATO.

It was about to be disintegrated and PESCO was a dream too far.

It was time for the Turkey to sort the future of Europe with Trump.

It was time for them to save the Western civilization.

1. Need for new US plans in the Middle East

In concert with the Tandem

President Trump understood Middle East well after two years in office.

He then moved swiftly in December 2018.

Bush-43 aside Obama was a big blow for the US to lose Middle East altogether.

Obama not only lost Iraq altogether but also gave Syria to Iran and Russia.

Obama also caused irreparable problems in Iran together with EU globalists.

Trump could not come to power in time, the Middle East was long lost by 2016.

A. Obama's kiss of death to the US policies in the Middle East

Obama administration was fast and effective. Originally Carter had lost Iran in 1979. It began end of the US hegemony in the Middle East. Obama said I can do better. I can lose Iraq and Syria all at once in a very speedy fashion that no incoming administration can save the US foreign policy objectives in the region again. He was successful.

In 2016, Obama had dealt a hand to Trump, full of holes in the Middle East. He had signed a nuclear deal with Iran in 2015. He had weaponized Syria by deploying 200 US soldiers in his last days in office, knowing all too well they had no role but to cause problem to the incoming Trump Administration in 2016.

In 2014, Obama had already withdrawn the US forces from Iraq, with a special heads up to the likes of ISIS and DAES. They, in turn, had promptly took the invitation and declared their Caliphate in their capital city Raqqa, occupying practically half of Iraq and Syria.

As president of the only superpower in the world, Trump had also noticed that the secular Turkey under Erdoğan regime was domineering the Middle East. He could not have believed how ignorant the globalists could have been. He had always believed, rightly so, the Bush-43 war was the demise of the US in the region. But what Obama had done to the US in the region was nothing less than a betrayal of the homeland. His inexperience actually was the case in point. His wise grandma said it to his face in Kenya.

Pulling the US forces from Iraq prematurely, signing the nuclear deal with Iran and not working with Erdoğan regime in Syria were fatal mistakes. They were strikes one, two, and three, and out. Nuclear Iran was surely going to make Turkey go nuclear as a domino effect. Pulling out of Iraq, was the right choice yet, considering the hole that the Bush-43 put the US is in there, it could have been handled better if it was done in concert with Turkey. It was pure ignorance and inexperience not to take Erdoğan's offer in 2012. The US could have had a free Syria today: Free of Russia and Iranian militia.

For Trump, 2019 was to have a new page in the Middle East. By working with Erdoğan's Turkey, the goal would be to stabilize Iraq and Syria with locals taking control of their future in respective countries. Only then Iran could have been contained. Benevolent but powerful Turkey was the best choice to work with.

Independent Turkey was not in the plans of anybody, especially not many in EU but it was a fact by 2018. President Trump had already understood it very clearly. He had also understood the new destiny of the Arabs: It was about to change hands and the US had to be in a position to be readmitted to the region with a welcome instead of through imposition, like employing nation-building as a tool. The folly of the globalists came back to haunt them and cause the US loss of prestige that is sure to hunt its interests elsewhere across the globe.

B. The West did not need a Syria problem going global

Second fiddle to Iraq

In Syria, it is no surprise that Trump announced pull-out from the country right before Christmas-2018. Having captured Raqqa and cleared most of the region from ISIS/DAES, the US had entered in a period of losing war with allied nation-states in the region.

Working with non-state YPG elements no longer had any good use, on the contrary they were becoming an untenable new and bigger problem. It was another globalist problem that Trump had inherited and it was time to end it.

The staunch US ally Turkey had long before already declared at the beginning of the year with a statement form Erdoğan. "We will 'strangle' U.S.-backed force in Syria 'before it's even born.'"[70]

---

[70] https://www.reuters.com/article/us-mideast-crisis-syria/Erdoğan-we-will-strangle-u-s-backed-force-in-syria-before-its-even-born-idUSKBN1F41HJ

The reference was for the remaining YPG forces in Manbij and the rest of Syria, east of Euphrates river that was enjoying umbrella protection from the US forces deployed there against the ISIS/DAES in Raqqa and beyond.

In 2017, Turkey had already cleared YPG from Afrin, on the western end of its border with Syria. The operation "Olive Branch" lasted less than two months before a Turkish flag was hoisted in the city center.

In 2016, "Operation Euphrates Shield" cleared in an attempt to push Islamic State militants from a sixty mile stretch of the border. The Turkish armed forces and Turkish backed Syrian rebels have captured several towns, including Jarablus, finally moving south to the strategic town of al-Bab. The Turkish operation was also aimed at preventing the Kurdish Popular Protection Units (YPG) from gaining more ground in northern Syria. The YPG is regarded by Turkey as a terrorist organization and an extension of the PKK.[71]

By December 2018, it was clear. Turkey was about to enter the rest of Syria with or without its traditional allies in tow. It was no brainer for the US other than for the globalists to understand to pull out the US forces from the region.

Trump and Erdoğan talked on the phone on December 14 It was a done deal.

a— An Obama problem: an administration with no clue

'Red line' fiasco gave half of Syria to Russia

Syria was, all along, a president Obama problem in 2012 before he drew his infamous "red line." He could have resolved it then, when Turkey had offered help. Instead, Obama ignored and limited himself to lip services. In 2016, he weaponized Syria, by deploying 200 US troops during his last days in office.

The urgency for Turkey, then, was to prevent the displacement of Syrians. Turkey, in the past, had hosted refugees from Afghanistan, Iran, and Iraq. Muslims knew Turkey was the only place to go when they faced wars at home. The country is most developed, but also tolerant among Muslims, and the last stop on route to Europe.

Turkey knew all along Syria crisis was no different. More than three million migrated to Turkey, as predicted. The West did not understand the enormity of the crisis until one million additional Syrians ended up at their doorsteps in 2015. By then it was already too late.

That is how Iran and Russia came into play in Syria in October 2015. They were the last alternatives for Turkey to work with to resolve the refugee problem, becoming even bigger. It worked.

---

[71] https://www.bbc.com/news/world-middle-east-39439593

As a result of close relationships with Russia and Iran, Turkey had a say in northern Syria like no other power with weight by 2018. The US had increased its presence with the coming of the Trump administration, but it was not in a position of strength thanks to idiocrasies of the Obama administration.

When Idlip crisis erupted towards the end of the year. Turkey saved the West single handedly, one more time!

TD: One would ask what the Obama Admin. was doing in the meantime.

BO: He had other plans.

TD (in awe): Like creating a Kurdish state perhaps!

BO: Oh, Yes! Oh, yes! Why didn't I think of that!?

TD: Fighting against or finishing off ISIS/DAES!?

BO: Sorry, I was not paying attention. What did you say?

TD: Terrorists!?!

BO: No, that was not a priority for the Obama Administration. Otherwise it could have sent lot more than 200 soldiers. And not the last day in his office. You get it right?

TD: Trip, a delicate surrogate for Trump

BO: Ben, a confident for Obama

Nation-building

Refugees were never an urgent global problem, until they became an issue at the gates of Europe. The latest most vivid example was the 1 million Syrians walking through Europe. Their misery became a reality TV show for the world to watch.

A similar show was to repeat in 2018 when another crisis was about to erupt in Syria. But it never made it to TV like the earlier one. The only reason for that crisis not making the prime time was because the refugee crisis was prevented appearing at the gates of Europe.

In 2018, Turkey prevented it single handedly, again. It eliminated the conditions for the civilians to become refugees again from the same origin nearby. If Idlip had developed into another refugee crisis, would there be a Europe today as we know it? Bigger question, where was the US Administration at the time?

TD: Where was the Obama Administration when Turkey was at work?

BO: It was there but it had another more urgent agenda.

TD: Oh, Yeah!?

BO: It was working on the foundation of a Kurdish state in Syria.

TD: Kurdish state!?

BO: Yeah! Clinton and Bush Administrations were working on it in Iraq

TD: In Iraq!? Clinton? Bush?

BO: Yeah! These dam Turks. They spoiled it there.

TD: And…

BO: Obama thought he had a brilliant plan: we can do it in Syria instead.

TD: So?

BO: Like I said. He was working on a plan. These god dam Turks…

TD: Trip, a delicate surrogate for Trump

BO: Ben, a confident for Obama

In Syria Obama was in charge when refugee crisis exploded, and nothing was done. The priority in Syria for the US Administrations was to create a Kurdish state in northern Syria. It was to start from Iraq border and end in the eastern Mediterranean shores. It was supposed to have extended all along the border with Turkey.

The globalists were at work in the Fertile Crescent since 1980 to create a Kurdish state. They had already failed miserably in northern Iraq by 2017 when Turkey put an end to their attempt. By the time the 2016 elections were underway in the US, the Obama Administration was hard at work desperately trying to create another one in northern Syria instead.

By 2018, Turkey had put an end to that scenario as well. The same way it did in northern Iraq.

c— Realist Trump

He noticed rising Turkey like no one else did.

In December 2018, Turkey said enough is enough. In 2012, it had warned the Obama Administration about Syria. In January 2018, it had warned the final time, the Trump Administration. Now it was time to talk the talk and walk the walk.

Two leaders had a meeting in Argentina during the G-20 meeting. When the US media was asking who Trump would meet there, the answer was Recep Tayyip Erdoğan. When asked about other leaders. He was the one that was standing out. Yet, among other issues involving Russia and China, Turkey never seemed to be as important to anybody. It was simply not a prime-time material!

In the meantime, two leaders had their talk there quietly, and they followed up over the phone.

RTE: Here is the plan.

DJT: I see.

RTE: I had given the other, the full version, to Obama in 2012.

DJT: Interesting.

RTE: We were to take Damascus and meet with our friends from Tel Aviv there.

DJT: He did not get it.

RTE: What do you think? Red line. And lip service.

DJT: Don't I know it. All talk. No action.

RTE: Right. We go in and cut it from the middle. That is, it.

DJT: When?

RTE: My gift for you in the new year. Don't mention it.

DJT: Merry Christmas.

RTE: Yeah. Have a happy one. Stop by sometimes.

DJT: Good idea.

RTE: Recep Tayyip Erdoğan, President of Turkey

DJT: Donald J. Trump, President of the United States of America

Trump knew all too well how Turkey had already cleaned the YPG terrorists from Afrin with "Olive Branch," military operation within two months. No one had expected it. It had also cleaned ISIS/DAES from its eastern borders with Syria with its "Euphrates Shield" military incursion a year earlier in record time. ISIS/DAES were in full strength at the time. Their caliphate was in full force.

At the time, the Trump Administration was new in office. Turkey was offering to work together to clean the rest of the terrorists from Syria. But Trump was stuck with the Obama cards left on the table. It had to take Raqqa to show progress, before leaving the rest to longtime ally Turkey was the right thing to do. Surely, he was in touch with Erdoğan all along. They both knew 2019 was the year to begin: cleaning the mess of the globalists in the making past forty years was not easy.

C. Independent Turkey was not in the plans

Neither the US nor the Western Europeans expected an independent Turkey to emerge.

By 2018, Turkey was still part of the Western alliance and member of NATO. Yet it was anything, but in the alliance. Turkey was on a path of independence since the 1990s, but it did not act on it, not until Erdoğan regime came to power in 2002.

a— Planning for independence

Erdoğan set the course for the independence at the end of 2007. He was prime minister by then for five years. Tenth president of the republic A. Nejdet Sezer had just finished his term and was replaced with Abdullah Gul, an Islamist like himself.

He knew Turkey always made great leap forward when the president and the prime minister were from the same party. Turkey grew bigger and faster during Ataturk (23-38) and Menderes (50-60) regimes. Also, during Ozal (83-93) regime, which benefited having a strong and then popular Kenan Evren as president. Ozal extended his regime when he became president in the next elections and continued to be a strong president like his predecessor until his passing in 1993, never completing his seven-year term.

b— Time to exploit Obama

Soon after Erdogan set the course for independence in Turkey, in the US, Barack H. Obama became president. He was a young and inexperienced senator. Even his grandmother Mamma Sarah had told him "to stay little longer as senator" when he had told her a year earlier that he was planning to run for president. Inexperienced president coupled with the changing global balance of power was a deadly mix.

In 2008, the world was moving inexorably from the G8 to the G20, where Europe's influence will be diluted by major new players like China and India. The Europeans were becoming a little sensitive as the president is seen to cozy up to the new players.[72]

c— Time to break chains for Turkey

That was also the time when Turkey was at the beginning of a pace to attract 180 billion dollars of international investment until 2017.

In 2008, Erdoğan first set out to free the country from the IMF. Having announced that Turkey would no longer be taking a loan from the international organization controlled by the West, Turkey paid off its 23.5 billion-dollar debt in 2013 and free itself from the shackles so to speak, according to the Erdogan regime supporters.

"Do you know what happened after that?
They asked us for a loan of 5 billion euros."
Erdoğan said afterwards, referring to the IMF and the Western powers.

d— Time to declare independence

When Donald Trump became president in 2016, Turkey was already independent. The Europe was in stagnation to no end in sight, while Obama had driven the

---

[72]   http://www.cnn.com/2009/POLITICS/12/09/obama.europe/index.html

US economy to ground, having increased the US debt during his eight years by an additional 8.5 trillion dollars. All the while, China and India were fast rising as economic powers.

Turkey was everywhere. On one hand, Russia was working with Turkey, getting ready to supply 30 percent energy of the EU and managing the war in Syria. On the other hand, Turkey was preventing Saudi-Egypt-UAE from aggression against Qatar. When Trump moved the US embassy from Tel Aviv to Jerusalem, Turkey was leading the majority at the United Nations General Assembly against the US initiative.

Trump was no Obama. Brinkmanship was Trump's game, yet he also knew how to avoid falling into a "chicken" game with Turkey unnecessarily which he knew naturally would lead to a "Zero Sum" game.

When he had the opportunity to see how powerful Turkey was and how determined Erdoğan was during two military incursions into Syria, he moved fast and announced that he was pulling the US forces out of Syria before the third probable Turkish incursion began.

He knew there was no need to play a Zero-Sum game with a long-time staunch ally. Turkey was a domineering power in the region in size, resources, capabilities, and political will. It was better to work with Turkey and get all the benefits easily then confront. It was that simple and smart for him to understand unlike many others. Turkey was long independent role player anyway in the world not to mention in the Middle East.

D. Arab destiny to change hands again

Trump also understood that the Erdoğan-Turkey tandem was sure to play a role in the future of Arabs. Arabs were in disarray and they did not trust the West.

Nobody had a choice but to turn to the domineering and benevolent Turkey. Secular Westernized Turkish state and Islamist regime with a charismatic pious leader was too good to be true manageable mix to fill the vacuum.

As for the method, no one was talking about colonialism, conquest or imposition of administrative zones like it was tried by the Western powers since the 18th century or the regimes like the Ottoman Empire of the past had.

a— Arab mess cannot be fixed in fifty years

Trump knew all too well that the US alone cannot resolve the Bush-Obama mess in one term as a US president. What they destroyed in sixteen years will need decades to repair. In Iraq and Syria, the fabric of a nation-state is no longer there. They have to be rebuilt and they will be rebuilt by the locals.

It took Turkey eighty years to go over the bumps on the road to be ready to propel itself into stardom. Algeria is another example. It has been more than half a century since it won independence from France in 1962. It still has a long way to break all the chains to save itself. Iraq and Syria went through equally horrendous devastations since 1980 and 2011, respectively. Half a century more is a sure bet to see any noticeable improvement in these countries.

b— New beginning for the Middle East only comes with Turkey

For those who are in the belief that the modernity and security come to the Middle East solely via Fertile Crescent, this is a sobering news. Bagdad and Damascus have always been the center of the region. Unless they are as vibrant as they have always been, the Middle East will not reach its potential. The Arabs are at a crossroad.

Yet, the route to the West goes through Anatolia. They need Turkey and Erdoğan to get there. Plus, Turkey will never let these countries be divided into pieces: it will protect their territorial integrity.

Maybe it is time for a new experiment in the Middle East. Eastern Mediterranean is the focal point of all major powers positioning themselves for the riches of the continental shelves. The Middle East has to be rebuilt. And there are many more players than just the Westerners in the region.

China is there with the Belt and Road initiative (BRI) and investments. Turkey is there with its growing economy. The US with the Trump administration can build everything bigger, faster, and greater.

It is not nation-building. It is the physical building. Nation-building is for the locals. The rest can be done together with the contribution of the international community. Turkey in the lead it will be achieved. The new nationalist regime that came to power with the Trump revolution in the US would support it because the US does not need a soft belly in the Middle East when it is set out to establish the balance of power at a global scale with the rising East.

2. New US plans in Europe

No plan without Turkey and Erdoğan

But first, the US must have plans for Europe, taking into account the EU and Russia.

Otherwise, Europe will remain the second soft belly that the superpower cannot afford.

Turkey & Erdogan must be part of the next US plans for Europe.

Turkey is integral part of it when it comes to the EU and Russia anyway, simply because Turkey has leverage both over the EU and the Russia Federation.

The best plan for the US would be to ensure that this balance of power endures, so that the US can focus on the rising eastern economic giants China and India.

That is of course, as soon as the domestic squabbles in the US also come to an end.

Yet when all said and done, with Trump, the US can always handle the EU alone.

But that is not the case when Russia and Turkey are so much united as one.

Dealing with Russia is one thing but having messy relationship with Turkey is too much.

When Russia problem remains regional, new Turkish problem sure to become global.

Russia knowing these dynamics well will not let Turkey lose its independent standing.

Russia will use Turkish cause both against the EU and the US for a long time to come.

A. Russia to work with Turkey

Russia will work with Turkey for the foreseeable future. Not until at least 2030, no one should expect Russia to walk out from its close relationship with Turkey.

That is ironically both good news and bad news for the US. It is good because the balance of power in Europe will be sustained. It is not good news at all when the US and others in the West would like to prevent Russia expanding at the expense of its neighbors like it did in Georgia or Ukraine.

But that is not all of it. When Russia works with Turkey, there are other ill effects coming from the Turkish end. Turkey ends up buying military and nuclear technology from Russia when the US and the Europeans among others in the Middle East would not want Turkey to acquire them.

Well something has to give! How important for the US to have a balance of power in Europe so that it can focus on China? That is the primary question. The needs and worries of the rest of the world become secondary, including little pawns in the Middle East and around the Eastern Mediterranean Sea.

Russia on the other hand benefits tremendously from working with Turkey. In reality, Russia needs Turkey. Yet, no one can tell for sure if Turkey needs Russia as much.

But it does not matter. Thanks to Obama Administration, they did not have to haggle. They suddenly and naturally found themselves as best of friends, plus strategic and transactional partners because of Obama. It is a good bet Obama and his cohorts who advised him throughout his eight years still do not understand how they hurt the US interest by brining Russia and Turkey together like that. No one could have pulled it of better even if they tried! It surely turned out to become a great gift to the world from a very naive US Administration.

a— Russia benefits from Turkey

With great help from Obama Administration, Russia suddenly gained a great friend in Turkey. Strategic and transactional partnerships increased at all fronts and in full speed. It became a win-win for bought countries every step of the way, at the expense of the US. Even the EU started to notice ever increasing benefits from their partnership.

Currently, Russia supplies one third of the energy needs of European Union. Pipelines from Russia cross Black Sea to Turkey. After Turkey takes what it needs for domestic consumption, the rest is transshipped to Europe. Ukraine was the previous route for the Russian pipelines. Now Turkey is doing the job.

Strategic relationship with Turkey is equally important for Russia. It is the single biggest reason why Russia settled in Syria for good for the next fifty years. So long as Russia maintains its close partnership with Turkey for another decade, it will be very difficult to force Russia out of the region altogether.

The Soviet Union never had as much influence in the Middle East when Turkey was the bulwark that constituted the southern flank of the NATO during the Cold War. Access to warm waters in the Mediterranean through Turkish straits were in the hands of Turkey. Plus, the Turkish navy was a menace for the Soviet navy in the Black Sea, keeping up the pressure for the NATO.

Friendship that came as a result of these strategic and transactional relationships between these two old enemies, also translated into personal touch between Vladimir Putin and Recep Tayyip Erdogan which established the trust factor. Hence, when Turkish F-16 shot down Russian aircraft over Syrian border region, and a year later when the Russian ambassador to Turkey was murdered brazenly by a vogue Turkish policeman, two presidents did not fall into conspiracy theories, thought to be at first the making of the Western forces to break their relationship. Rather, both leaders focused on more areas of cooperation in trade, tourism, developments and technology transfers.

b- Turkey also gained a lot from this relationship

Primary need of Turkey has always been transfer of technology and financing from the West. And now Russia was delivering it both on two different fronts.

First, Russia agreed not only sell the S-400 batteries but also co-production of these best defensive missile systems in the world, together with transfer of technology. Something, the US, and then China, had rejected to give to Turkey over the years.

Next was the nuclear power plant. Russia agreed to build the Akkuyu Nuclear Power Plant in Turkey. Turkey was in the market for a number of them for decades. No one was willing to sell them from the West, mainly because of the forces in the US.

Russia knew what it was doing. It was simply providing Turkey two of the most lethal and last instruments that would make Turkey fully independent of the West. The question is why Russia would go to this end and make its eternal enemy gain two unique technology that Turkey has no way of getting from anywhere else in the world to elevate itself to another league against the West but also against Russia in the long run?

The answer was exactly that. Russia's primary goal was to undermine the West. A Turkey with a threat power against the rest and defensive mechanism that could protect it from a counterpunch was something the West did not need Turkey to have. For Russia, a Turkish menace with offensive and defensive capabilities, making it in par with the most powerful states in the world was a sure bet to keep the West meddling into the regional affairs of the Russian Federation in the foreseeable future.

In short, Russia needed time to bolster its economy and military in order to recapture parity against the sole superpower and rest of the rising powers of the East. For that it needed Turkey as a temporary bulwark. Hence Turkey became the beneficiary for everything from Russia that it would not be able to get otherwise from elsewhere.

c— *Obama's inexperience became Russia's gain*

Unfortunately, it was Obama that did it to the US! He was not in the same league with the likes of Putin and Erdogan. And he came to power when Turkey and Russia needed him the most. The two countries mended the bridges during his administration.

Obama simply thought better policies for the region, or missed the boat, however one may put it, when the Arab Spring began in 2010. Since then, he did mistake after mistake to bolster Turkey and Russia's standings in the region. One of the most famous was his "Red Line" on sand that crumbled as soon as Bashar Al Assad challenged it. At the end, he left the US out of the equation in Syria with that in sense out of the Middle East in the long run. When Trump came to power, neither Turkey nor Russia needed the US there anymore.

The US always needed numerous leverages against Russia in order to prevent what happened in Crimea and earlier in Northern Ossetia where Turkey ordinarily would have lots of leverages that the US and the West could have used if they knew. It is a simple fact that the US will always need Turkey when it comes to the Black Sea and Mediterranean Sea where Russia constantly reinforces its pressure points. There is no alternative to Turkey against Russia in these waters, as the Cold War era proved it.

Unfortunately, it was Obama that lost Crimea in 2014. It would be very naïve for anyone to think that Russia did not test the Obama Administration and notice how weak it is in handling the Georgian invasion, earlier when Russia pushed its forces forward?

Oh yes, Georgia invasion took place few months before Obama came to power in August 2008, but it was Obama policies that assured Russia that there are other moves that it could make that Obama would not know how to best counter. So came the Crimea disaster! That is how the international system works. Alas Obama and his advisers had no clue. The results speak for themselves.

d- Obama's mistakes gave Turkey a "Carte Blanche"

But even worse mistake of Obama was to lose Turkey, a long time and staunch ally of the US. Everybody in the West always knew it very well: Losing Turkey has never been an option for the West!

Turkey, soon, within a year or so, but for sure before 2023, will be considered as a fully independent country from the Western Alliance, but also from the yoke of the US. Turkey has been on its way becoming independent from the Western yoke for decades anyway. But it will not be fully independent and strong enough to confront the US threat power until it acquires the S-400s, further develops its indigenous Siper missile defense system that is in its last phase of development and mass production and all three nuclear plants under construction coming to fruition, first starting by 2023.

Obama contributed greatly for Erdogan regime to make headways on all military fronts. It is commonly known in Turkey that the Obama presidency was the starting point for Turkey to set its course towards full independence from the US. Unfortunately, Obama never understood what was transpiring.

Messing up the trillions of dollars' worth F-35 JSF project was perhaps the biggest Obama dagger that the US did not need. The project was supposed to have kept the sole superpower of the world in control of its "flock" by keeping the data coming back home to the US manufacturing company from each aircraft sold and operated by a client state. Hence, in theory, no one was supposed to have been able to fly and make use of these most lethal technological wanders against the will of the US.

Obama apparently never knew how to play chess either. Even a novice would know that not giving Patriots to Turkey would trigger for Turkey to buy S-400s from Russia. That in turn would force the US hands not to give F-35s to Turkey which is what Turkey wanted all along since 2009.

By then, Turkey had already realized that relying heavily on F-35s was ironically going to keep the country subservient to the US for another decade if not more when Turkey had started its great push forward for independence in the early 2000s.

So, Turkey positioned itself well for the 2016 presidential elections. And when the Trump Administration came to power, it smartly turned Obama's grave mistakes into a "Carte Blanche" to pursue its independence at full speed.

B. Europe to work with Turkey

At least on the EU front, Obama was not as destructive against the US interests so far as eye can see! Actually, Obama was lucky because there were other globalists there that were doing the colossal damage on behalf of the Western interests and well-being of the Western civilization. Russia's advances against other European countries were exceptions of course. Crimea, for example, fell prey to Putin solely because of Obama.

None the less, when Trump came to power, the US was benefiting from Turkey leveraging the EU and Russia. Turkey was delivering was a land-bridge for goods and as a floodgate against refugees, Turkey was an assurance to keep the EU remain intact, secure, and prosperous.

a- The weaknesses of the West is apparent

As for the arguments that Trump supported Brexit and recommended to the French president Macron to leave EU and the fact that he labeled Germany's trade practices worse than China's, they do not mean a policy change. In fact, according to NATO General Secretary Stoltenberg under the Trump administration, the US commitment to NATO increased.

The disunity among the Western alliance members on Iran nuclear program aside, there is still one very real and sad fact. The European countries are no longer the military and economic powers of the past century. So, they don't have leverage that they used to have around the world to contribute to the US to achieve a global balance of power.

b- The luck of the EU is Trump

On the contrary, the left-over globalist regimes of the EU still believe that the PESCO is a way out to set an independent course from the US. Even though knowing full well that the PESCO without Turkey will go nowhere. Ironically, they are still under the illusion that Turkey will still be under their control too. If it was not for Trump presidency, they were in the process of putting this folly in effect more and more to their own detriment further each time.

3. New US plans in Asia

Trump understands well the importance of Turkey in Central Asia.

That is why his policy to pull the US troops from there has been paramount.

Afghanistan is a case in point: Did not the US go there together with Turkey?

Turkey, in the 21st century, has even bigger role to play in Central Asia with US.

Turkey has strong ties with the Turkic republics there sharing race and religion.

Turkey has also additional ties with Georgian and Azerbaijan republics in the Caucasus.

S. East Asian states, Indonesia, Malesia, and China are part of Turkish domain as well.

So are Bangladesh, India, and Pakistan because of a billion Muslim living there.

For that, Turkey and US have to coordinate their long-term plans in the region together.

A. Working with the Turkic republics

Turkey and five Turkic republics of former Soviet Union have a common destiny. They are to integrate more and more, and throughout, in the coming decades. They share common history, culture, language. It is their century to unite and interact further with one another or cohesively as a group. It is their century to try a cohesion.

Their union may not be a welcome news for Russia or China or for that matter for the West because as a union they will become a formidable block, in addition to the Muslim block they will naturally be siding with. Nonetheless, it is a reality waiting to happen. Nothing less can be expected since they are all independent states and can basically integrate one another geographically as well.

B. Leveraging S. East Asians and Indonesia

The US needs Turkish leverage over one billion Muslims in this area. Without Turkey, the US does not have a chance. No other power alone can replace what Turkey brings to table.

Indonesia and Pakistan independently are a force to reckon with in the region. But together with Turkey they become part of global balance of power. Their total population is to hit one billion people, coupled with Bangladesh. They make a formidable presence. Considering there is another three-hundred million Muslims in India, the region is overwhelmingly Muslim with Arabian Peninsula completing the circle with Afghanistan and Iran in the western end.

Turkey has strong bilateral relations with Indonesia, Pakistan, Malesia, and Bangladesh. Turkish navy anchoring in Somalia, Qatar, and Suakin Island, Sudan, in Red Sea is in proximity to complement the presence of this overwhelming Muslim union in the Indian Ocean must be noted.

Turkey also has strong bilateral relations with India, Iran, Oman, and Yemen on the eastern tip of the Arabian Peninsula. There is a significant role for Turkey to play with its new ocean-going navy.

C. Dealing with China

All the while, even China depends on Turkey. The Belt and Road Initiative (BRI) passes through Turkey but it also passes through Central Asian Turkic Republics and Azerbaijan. Turkey will work in cohesion with these Turkic states more and more and will balance China's influence in the region so that a harmonious growth in modernity and security can be achieved.

The role of the US in this mix is important. The balance of power China and the US will establish in this region together with other Turkic states will stabilize the world at large greatly.

Afghanistan will also be part of this equation as well as Tajikistan that is closer to Iran than to Turkey, but they are important countries, complementing the Turkic republics and China's sphere of influence. This way the US will be in a position to rebuild its standing in these countries.

The US has no choice but to involve in this region in concert with China and Turkey. They are the two countries that will make difference in the global balance of power because of their role in the Central Asia.

CHAPTER SEVEN

LOSING TURKEY NOT AN OPTION

When the West loses Turkey
The East gains, gains, and gains

I. Big time loss

Losing Turkey is not an option for the Western Alliance.

It will become a loss that the West cannot recover from.

Losing Turkey is a lot worse than losing Iran that is soon to become a nuclear nemesis.

Losing Turkey simply means numerous losses, each more catastrophic than the other.

First, access to a staunch ally, vital seas/air space, and natural resources will be lost.

Then, most of the Muslims will not be with the West. Their good-will will also disappear.

Finally, the gatekeeper will be gone. The land-bridge will not be there.

1. Losing access

Losing Turkey means losing access to sea lanes and air space.

It means losing a vital ally and natural resources.

It also means losing a big portion of Muslims.

A. Sea lanes and air space

Turkish air space and sea lanes extend from Russia to the middle of the Mediterranean Sea. It simply means commercial airlines will have to fly over African shores when crossing the region, if Russia also closes air space.

a— Loss of Black Sea

NATO warships will not be able to venture to the Black Sea at will, and never during times of crisis and war.

b— Loss of Aegean Sea

Navies in the Aegean Sea will be sitting ducks.

c— Loss of eastern Mediterranean

Eastern Mediterranean Sea depends on four factors to be an open sea: Suez Canal, Cyprus, Crete, Aegean Sea. Losing any one of them means it is no longer an open sea. Losing Crete and Cyprus makes Black, Aegean, and Mediterranean seas lakes of the adversary. Without Turkey in the Western alliance, no current regime will be the same.

B. Pillar for NATO, PESCO, and MUOS

Without Turkey, NATO will lose a precious ally in the region. But at a time when the EU is in the process of creating PESCO, losing Turkey on top of that does not make sense. For the US, it is important to keep NATO to project its power beyond Europe. So, Turkey is still vitally important to have on board.

Plus, in the age of cyber world and space age, the US is in the process of developing new global communication system called MUOS. Turkey provides a strategic alternative for MUOS. Turkey, in fact, is an alternative for the US against the EU when it comes to the US foreign policy objectives.

a— NATO

NATO will lose its southern flank without Turkey. Since there is no more Soviet Union to worry about that should not be a problem, but Russia is still there. More importantly, not having Turkey on board will make it difficult for the US navy to roam in the Mediterranean and Black seas. A soft belly in the region does not help the US building a balance of power against the East.

b— PESCO

PESCO will not have Turkey to count on in the Mediterranean or Black seas when Western European powers come to the region in search of natural resources. It is not in the interest of NATO and the US, a PESCO that pesters in the region when a unity is the only thing that will counter ever growing China presence in the Middle East and Europe.

c— MUOS

Developed for the U.S. Navy by Lockheed Martin, the Mobile User Objective System (MUOS) is revolutionizing secure ultra-high frequency (UHF) satellite communications (SATCOM) for mobile forces. The MUOS network is sustained by an initial configuration of four orbiting satellites (MUOS 1-4) and four relay ground stations.

Izmir, Turkey is the only location outside EU for one of the four ground stations in the region. Currently, Wahiawa, Hawaii; Chesapeake, Virginia; Niscemi, Italy; and Geraldton, Australia are slated as relay stations.

C. No way to access natural resources

Turkey has become the transshipment point of natural resources from half a dozen countries in the east, supplying the West. Without Turkey alternative routes are not viable.

Even Israel makes a good example. Israel today sells its newly found natural riches from the Mediterranean only to Egypt. It is not able to sell them to Europe. The only viable alternative is via Turkey land-bridge and connecting to the existing pipelines. Only then, what it found will be competitively priced to make profit.

As for the reports pointing at Greece, Italy, and Cyprus having reached an agreement with Israel to lay a pipeline connecting the Jewish state's gas reserves to the three countries, in a major project estimated at costing over seven billion dollars that will supply gas from the eastern Mediterranean to Europe, as the continent seeks to diversify its energy supply, the problems abound.

The fact that the European Union agreed to invest a hundred million dollars in a feasibility study for the project before the agreement was reached over the laying of the longest and deepest underwater gas pipeline in the world says it all. The deepest version is the only way to avoid the continental shelf disputes that are making this project costing more and a technological challenge.

Without political resolve, nothing will become viable.

2. Losing Muslims means losing one third of the world

Eighty million in Turkey will no longer be part of the Western alliance. Plus, others among Turkic states and Muslims of the world will switch sides in due process.

A. Anti-Western alliance will become a lot bigger

Independent Turkey will enter into new alliances. It will seek alliances with China, India, and Russia. They are also the three major powers with soft Muslim bellies when Turkey will assume larger and more active role among Muslims around the world.

B. Floodgates will open

Byzantine was a gatekeeper for Europe for the first thousand years. Turks are doing a good job with refugees past twenty years. Europe will always need a gatekeeper at the floodgates against refugees in the foreseeable future. Without Turkey doing the job happily, refugees will overwhelm Europe.

3. Losing Turkey

Turks used to be great horsemen warriors. They are still warriors after two thousand years but now they have mastered new weapons and technics.

A. Ignoring history never a good sign

Turks built the biggest empires that terminated Christian rule in Asia among other civilizations. Yet, they no longer conquer. They already settled next door at the European gate. There is no need to aggravate them to open the old wounds.

a— Seljuks and Ottomans

The Seljuks and the Ottomans were the two latest empires of the Turks before they founded the modern Turkey. One lasted three centuries, the other seven. The first took Asia Minor from the Christian West. The other took Constantinople from Byzantines.

Modern Turkey will celebrate its centennial in 2023. It is a Westernized and secular republic led by a political Islamist regime growing fast economically and militarily despite numerous domestic and international attempts trying to derail its progress. It has been friendly to the Christian West throughout.

B. Ignoring recent history even worse

Modern Turkish republic became independent in action and spirit from the Western alliance. It is in a wait and see period for the West to make its next move for a final decision to continue together or go another way.

II. Wining Turkey

Losing Turkey is not an option for the Western Alliance or for the US.

Yet, the telltale signs point at hard economic and military realities in place.

Turkey is already back in the old Ottoman territories but also in lot other countries.

Plus, it is at hard at work with Russia and China, on military and nuclear platforms.

At this moment, the West must accept that the West has already lost Turkey.

The globalists did lot of damage in the past three decades to the relationship.

They basically did everything to sever political ties and turn Turkey into a powerhouse.

Obama was worse. He simply paved the way for Turkey to seek full independence.

Now, only new policies and strategies by new players can win Turkey back.

Only "America First," a nationalist Trump administration can make a difference.

Avoiding old methods and strategies of the 20th century against Turkey is a must.

Also, employing viable policies and actions towards Turkey are vitally important.

This way, at least, the US can keep Turkey in NATO.

And with that, access to the Incirlik and Kurecik bases would be ensured.

Otherwise, even the future for Israel may be put in jeopardy.

Who in the US Congress is familiar with the issue, one wonders, sometimes!

1. Employ viable policies and actions towards Turkey

Trade and diplomacy are the only way to win Turkey.

A. Trade wins Turkey

EU has one of a kind relationship with Turkey. Trade with EU is half of Turkey's international trade volume. It accordingly brings leverages to employ.

Trade with the US is ridiculously minimal. If there was a big trade volume, the US foreign policy objectives would have gained lots of pull power over Turkey.

Trade with Russia, India, China give Turkey great leverages. Also vice a versa. They gain great leverages in reaching the European markets easily and cheaper and many ways with Turkey.

Turkey is one of the biggest players in Africa in the past two decades and growing faster. Trade is the number one reason for that. Cooperating with Turkey in the continent naturally would open more markets and opportunities for Western companies that have lost their trust.

B. Diplomatic approach wins Turkey

Between the US and Turkey, it all started when the US did not recognize the modern Republic of Turkey until 1927. Four years delay in recognition is significant. For Turkish culture it is an important negative symbolism. Turks pays much attention to such minute details.

Turkey also does not forget that the agreement with EEC in 1963. Nowadays, it is commonly known as the European Union. In 2023, it will be sixty years since Turkey first applied for EU membership. It is a diplomatic bad blood that will never go away.

If one day Voltaire can ever change his heart and mind towards Turks and Muslims and forget his hatred, Turkey may also eventually say "what is in the past is in the past."

But must there be a price to pay for the Western Europeans for making Turks wait at the gates of Europe for more than sixty years!? Time will tell. Modern Turks are modern. They will move on like the modern Westerners will.

2. Avoid old methods and strategies

Resorting to nation-building policies is not a viable practice any more in the region.

Turkey is adamant to spoil these attempts with new pro-active counter strategies.

Yet, on the other hand, nothing is off the table, including military action to stop them.

Ongoing military incursions in Syria are cases in point.

Qatar crisis and Turkish reaction was an example how far Turkey may and can go.

Prompt and stern reaction of Turkey against many states at once in Libya is another.

There is no telling how Turkey would react to an old method if the West resorts again.

Sultan Abdülhamid in the 1800s did an impeccable job even when his hands were tied.

In the 21st century, modern Republic of Turkey is not the "Sick Man of Europe" anymore.

Rather, it is a period when Turks believe mythological "Red Apple" is within their reach.

Union of Turks is one thing, nothing to look forward to for adversaries if they poke.

Coupled with awakening Muslims make life for the rest on earth even more complicated.

A. Not resorting to coups wins Turkey

The seeds of the 1950 elections in Turkey were planted by the US in 1947 when the US signed Economic and Technical Cooperation agreement with Turkey. For the People's Republican Party (PPP), the regime that founded the modern Republic of Turkey and led as a single party until 1950 considered it as an American inspired coup.

The reaction of Turkey was a domestic repercussion. In 1960, Prime Minister Adnan Menderes was hanged. Later on, it would reveal that reportedly it was another foreign agents inspired coup. In 1980, it was time to end the "democratic" experiment in Turkey. The US inspired agents, reportedly were in action, reporting back saying "our boys did it."

The Turks accepted the 1980 coup d'état, as the coup to end all coups. It was also non-violent. Ensuing 1997 military memorandum, 2003 and 2007 military warnings with an email no less, reflecting the maturation process underway, military and civilian establishments were addressing their disagreements without resorting to troops in the barracks.

2016 failed coup d'état reflects the mood in Turkey when the establishment immediately turned against perceived foreign sources of the coup. Not resorting to coups will win Turkey because Turkey will start going beyond its borders to look for culprits. That is never a good sign, but Turkey now has the resources and capabilities.

B. Not threatening wins

Betrayal during the Cuban missile crisis followed by the Johnson's letter were the other one-two punch by the US in the 1960s. They were perceived as outright threats. The public opinion, then, turned delirious against the US. More and more Turks started to doubt the loyalty of the US towards their country.

1974 arms embargo following the invasion of Cyprus by Turkey, in the eyes of most of the Turks marked the time when Turkey started to move away from the US. The embargo was a final blow. It was a point of no return.

Cyprus war also marked the worldwide division lines between Christians and Muslims.

Turkey for the first time in its modern history of the republic witnessed the support of Muslim masses beyond its borders. It was their first awakening since 1924 when the Caliphate was abolished.

In the US, recently, when there is a talk that Turkey is no longer a staunch ally, the reference is made in regard to 2003 when Turkey did not permit the US forces to invade Iraq from north. It is not true. Turkey stopped working with the US in 1975. Turkey also turned to Islamist alternatives soon after that with the 1980 coup d'état.

Not threatening wins Turkey because when Turkey is threatened, Turkey continues on the same path unwaveringly. Worse, when it turns the fight into a Zero-Sum game.

3. Having someone compatible and competent at the helm was important

Thank God. The West made the right choice in 2016 when Donald J. Trump became the 45th president of the United States. He immediately brought to the table what Clinton, Bush-43, and Obama, together could not offer against or could deal with rising Turkey and the East.

First of all, Trump not only understands who Erdogan is but also what Turkey as a country stands for. Plus, he has the character, personality, and experience that present a perfect match against a long-time staunch ally and a formidable counterpart Turkey and Erdogan tandem represents.

The fact that Donald J. Trump and Recep Tayyip Erdoğan come from the same neighborhoods is also a blessing. They are in a sense both "Kasimpasali." That also means they are both street smart and nationalists. Finally, that means they have mutual adversaries like the globalists who live on the other side of the town, far away from "Kasimpasa," which is a neighborhood in Istanbul like the old East End in New York City.

Simply put, they have a lot in common. They understand each other like no one else would. Yet, not until Erdoğan and Trump learned that they came from similar neighborhoods, they had a rough first two years. They went for tit of tat all throughout.

By 2019, they both already realized that they are on the same page and it was time to bury the hatchet and adjust to one another. They suddenly discovered the root of their problem. It was Barack Hussein Obama, the 44th outgoing president of the US. He was the worst of all three globalists that had severed the relationship between two old and staunch allies.

A. First two years was not a good amen

Unfortunately, due to big mess Trump took over from his globalist predecessors, he could not connect well with a range of leaders. Erdogan of Turkey was one of them.

When Trump was expected to be conciliatory, for example, he showed aggressive behavior against Turkey from day-one in order not to look weak in the international arena. Obama had left him a weaponized Middle East among others. His sole purpose was to undermine the next president of the US instead of protecting the standing of the US worldwide in the eyes of the international community.

Despite that Turkey continued waiting patiently for an overture from the US to set everything right. Past two US Administrations had brought Turkey to the brink of breaking most relations with the US. Hence Erdogan, like many other leaders in the world, was hoping that the US finally would pick a leader that one can look eye to eye and deal with bilateral and multilateral problems of the world.

Unfortunately, during the first two years, nothing of that sort took place. On the contrary, the Trump Administration was beyond a disappointment for the Erdoğan regime. The US deployed thousands of trucks and plains loads of armament to Syria. After that it distributed good portion of these weapons to Kurdish militia that Turkey considers terrorists because they organize attacks, killing and injuring civilians in eastern provinces and major cities.

It is in these two crucial years that Erdogan finally gave up and ordered from Russia S-400 missiles. During Obama Administration Turkey had sought to purchase the US versions of the same commonly known as Patriots. Obama's repeated refusal had made Erdogan wait for the next US president as a last resort. That is exactly the reason why in Osaka Japan, Trump told Erdogan "it is Obama's fault." It was clear to him only two years later when it was too late why Turkey was buying these missiles. It was clear how Turks were patient with the US all along.

B. Turkey is open to cooperation not for tit for tat

In the interim, Trump had to go toe-to-toe against Erdogan.

First, the US made a friendly overture to Turkey and asked for an American priest to be released from Turkish jail. Turkey could not believe the brashness of the US. When Turkey snubbed and did not release him, insisting that he was in bed with the separatist/terrorist Kurds for the past two years and the judicial system was to decide on his fate, the Trump Administration raised the ante, believing Turkey can still be bullied on the release. Turkey showed resilience and boldness in return.

At the next stage, the Trump Administration set itself on a further collision course of no return against Turkey instead of resolving the outstanding issues diplomatically through negotiations. Resorting to tit for tat was the next series of actions on both sides. Turkey started to reciprocate every step the US took be it sanctions against cabinet members of Turkey versus secretaries of the US or trade related tariffs.

After tariffs, when the US interfered to devalue Turkish Lira, Turkey responded to lower its positions in dollar denominations and decided to issue bonds in Yuan while Lira started to stabilize. For Erdoğan, tit for tat is played with blood in the Middle East. For Trump, tit for tat was only negotiation steps.

When Erdoğan and Trump finally realized that they were both Kasimpasali minded, suddenly it was all clear to both. That is when Trump referred to Erdoğan: "He is a tough man." They had already understood that both were. What is important is that they finally found out about each other's origin and what the "tit for tat" meant to the other.

Now they were on the same page!

If only, somebody had told them little earlier!

C. If someone had also told them that it was Obama all along!

In Osaka Japan, Trump said, according to widely reported news that the United States had a "complicated" situation in how to respond to Turkey's deal to procure Russia's S-400 missile defense system. Trump also expressed sympathy with his Turkish counterpart, Tayyip Erdogan, blaming former U.S. President Barack Obama's administration for placing conditions on Turkey's purchase of Patriot missiles.

Actually, blaming Obama at G-20 in Osaka is telling. Seven months earlier in Buenos Aires, Argentina, when Trump decided to pull the US troops out from Syria after his meeting with Erdogan at another G-20, he did not blame what was apparent. It was Obama that had weaponized Syria with 200 US troops in his last days as a political hit job against the incoming Republican president. It was offensive to no end to Turkey for the US to deploy troops on its border with Syria and then bring separatist/terrorist Kurds under its umbrella instead of working with Turkish armed forces. Obama knew what he was doing. Yet, in reality he was actually shooting the US on the foot in the long run.

In Osaka, it was time to clear tables. Obama's betrayal of his country for the sake of small political gains had to be brought to light. Call it inexperience, it was a colossal mistake none the less. First, Obama should have understood that Turkey did not have missile defense system and was determined to buy it from an adversary if the US did not permit the sale of Patriots. Two, Obama should have understood that for Turkey to have S-400s would have meant that half of Mediterranean Sea, all of Aegean and Black seas would be effectively in the hands of Turks who will no longer need US umbrella protection in the region. Finally, not selling F-35, the joint strike fighter, was not a punishment for Turkey. On the contrary, it was a gift. Turkey wanted to get out of the 2009 agreement it signed since 2016. The agreement was obligating Turkey to buy more than 100 of now these very expensive and after thirty-year development still problem-ridden technological wonders!

D. Compatible, capable and cunning Trump

Yes, Trump, like always, had understood long before most in the US, including the US senators who still do not notice the fact that not selling the F-35s is not a punishment for Turkey. Instead it is an effort to hurt long time US strategy, albeit a globalist thought and developed plan with lots of vulnerabilities. How naïve, could most of these US senators be and continue to remain?!

Single most important reason why the F-35 JSF project is created was to keep Turkey like countries under the US umbrella! The F-35, as a technological wonder, was supposed to be a US foreign policy instrument, controlled from the US mainland, at will. The data exchange system between each aircraft and the main base in the US was to allow control of the flight charts of these aircraft among other things. Along with that no US ally with F-35 would have the luxury to use these aircrafts as they wish but for, as its name sake, joint strike fighter or "force" purpose!

Did not these senators think one minute before enacting on a bill to stop the delivery of already paid off F-35s to Turkey, why Germany and France refrained from buying the F-35s from the start when they learned the real capabilities and purpose of these aircrafts?

Also, why does not anybody care when Erdogan says "if we Turkey is pushed out of the F-35 project, it will be the end of this project" what he actually means? It is not a threat or ultimatum or brinkmanship. It is a sample fact.

The irony for those who can understand in this day and age with all the cyber and space technologies in place, the secrets of the F-35 will be best kept when those who are part of the project have a stake to keep the secrets for the sake of their own investment. Simply put, if Turkey is pushed out of the project at this stage, after a full decade involvement in its development, where is the incentive for Turkey to protect what only it can protect? And that is not the only fact!!! Again, Trump knows them better, already!

III. Ending up with a different world

Losing Turkey is not an option because the world, as we know it, will change.

The new world order will not be a friendly or livable place anymore.

The F-35s and the Patriots missile batteries are platforms to keep Turkey on board.

Without such technology transfers, Turkey will look elsewhere to replace them.

That would mean, the Western Alliance will have to do without Turkey.

That in itself means Turkey joining the East and becoming an existential threat.

Consequently, that also means Middle East becoming a three-headed monster.

Imagine, nuclear Iran, Turkey and Saudi Arabia with agendas of their own.

On top of that, Africa to split into two halves between Christians and Muslims.

More avalanche of refugees coming home to Western Europe and North America.

Invasion of Europe becomes eminent.

What happens to the Western civilization then?

1. In the Middle East

Three more states become nuclear.

Some states disappear from map.

A. Iran goes nuclear

Turkey has Iran's back on the western front. Russia has Iran's back on the northern end. Iraq is no longer under Western hegemony in the south. There is Afghanistan with Taliban in the eastern front of Iran and Pakistan, over which, the US no longer has any influence.

Iran is isolated but also surrounded with states, regimes and militia that are in varying degree of good relationships with the country. None of them are Western powers.

Independent Turkey, becoming a working partner, is enough for Iran to ensure that it is isolated and protected from Western malice.

Civil war with a successful coup d'état or an out-right invasion are the only ways to prevent Iran from going nuclear.

B. Turkey goes nuclear

Turkey that is not in the Western alliance will become a nuclear power at the earliest opportunity. There is no alternative for Turkey to survive as an independent state without nuclear weapons when it is not allied with the West.

C. Saudi Arabia goes nuclear

Saudi Arabia will also go nuclear because nuclear Iran and Turkey do not leave any chance to survive in the region.

D. Smaller states disappear

Including Iraq, smaller states in the region will not be able to continue their independence. They will ally with one of the three nuclear powers.

2. In the West

The US will be on the defensive while the EU will face invasion.

A. North America at crosshair

The US will effectively lose its weight in the world without Turkey. But moreover, Muslims will target North America as a destination once they are done in Western Europe.

B. Invasion of Europe

Europe will be overran with Muslims. Instead of few millions of refugees, tens of millions of refugees will break through fences across Europe, literally and physically.

CHAPTER EIGHT

EAST VS WEST

In the West, at the turn of the 21st century, the globalist regimes were in power.

They arrived with the disintegration of the Soviet Union in the early 1990s.

Bill Clinton became the 42nd president of the US in 1992.

George W. Bush (43rd) took over in 2000 and continued with the same global policies.

Andrea Merkel became the chancellor of Germany in 2005.

By then, the decay of the West and the rise of the East was halfway through already. The election of Barack Obama (44th) in 2008 ensured the further demise of the West.

The globalists actually sped up the decay of the West, remaining in power twenty-four years.

Reportedly, the decline of the West was apparent at the beginning of the 20th century. But most everybody chose to ignore it. It was treated like a taboo.

As a result, the prospects for the West became lot worse than they could have been.

At the end of the 20th century, the Middle East was long lost.

The regression in Africa was almost complete.

In a sense, the election of a nationalist Donald J. Trump was no fluke.

A course correction was necessary after decades long globalist rule.

The globalists were not heeding the knock on the door from the East.

The rise of China and India to economic dominance in the world was one thing.

The emergence of a dozen Muslim countries into power and prominence was another.

But ignoring, Western alliance member Turkey moving away, was a fatal mistake.

Erdoğan of Turkey knocked on the doors of the 43rd and 44th presidents of the US.

No one was at home. Angela Merkel also did not listen.

By the time, Trump, the 45th president came to power, the boat had long left the port. Erdoğan no longer needed the US. He had options and leverages all around the world.

The East led by China, Russia, and India was waiting with open arms.

I. Changing times

In the last thirty years, the world has changed drastically.

The US and Western Europe declined.

Many countries from the East achieved rapid economic growth.

China, India, Indonesia and Turkey are projected as the top 4 performers of the future.

Economic growth also gave way to military prowess and brinkmanship.

Eastern power projection became global like it has been for the West in the past.

1. Decline of the West

In 2016, Donald J. Trump came to power to reverse the decline of the West.

The damage of the globalists was far reaching and on a point of no return.

Italy, Spain, Australia, Canada were on their way out of the top ten list.

Switzerland, Belgium, and Netherlands were not even considered in the top twenty.

Earlier in the 20th century, there were warning signs, but no one was willing to listen.

In 1918, Oswald Spengler published The Decline of the West. Today the word "decline" is taboo. Our politicians shun it in favor of "challenges," while our economists talk of "secular stagnation." The language changes, but the belief that western civilization is living on borrowed time (and money) is the same. Plus, the Islamic world contains 1.6 billion people, or 23% of the world's population.[73]

That was then, now the Islamic population is projected to become 35 percent, eclipsing Christianity at 34 percent.

2. Rise of the East

In the 21st, century, there are four countries to watch in the East.

---

[73]   https://www.theguardian.com/business/2015/nov/17/is-western-civilisation-in-terminal-decline

They are China, India, Indonesia, and Turkey.

They are projected to become first, second, fourth, and fifth economic powers, respectively.

The first two will soon have more than 1.5 billion population each.

Indonesia and Turkey, together, will have a direct say over half a billion people.

But Turkey alone will soon have influence over more than a billion Muslims.

Ethnic and religious factors will give Turkey a leadership role beyond its borders.

A. New economic realities

China, India, Russia, Brazil, and S. Africa are members of BRICS. In the Johannesburg meeting in 2018, they invited Turkey and Indonesia to become the newest members of their organization.

If Turkey and Indonesia were to join BRICS, ITBRICS will have about eighty trillion dollars economy by 2030. It will almost double the size of the leading Western economies in total, including the US.

This equation does not even consider, the next series of countries of the East, including six other Muslim majority like Pakistan and Nigeria. They will rank among the top twenty economies of the world.

a— Economic giants of the future

China and India will have by far the biggest GDPs in the world within a decade or so.

i— China

China emerges as the best and only possible candidate to fill the leadership void in the East. Yuan is suggested to act as a counterpart to dollar in the wake of eroding US power. Many countries view positively an increasing role for China and Yuan.

The Belt and Road initiative (BRI) is expected to solidify China's dominance in the world. It will be assuming similar role the US Navy and mighty Dollar assumed the same for the US in the 20th century.

ii— India

India, reportedly, soon to become the second biggest economy of the world, is sure to exert its power in the second half of the 21st century, like China is already doing it in the first half.

The effect of two major eastern powers striving for leadership role is something to watch but they may also choose to coexist for many reasons like they are currently doing it under BRICS and Shanghai Cooperation Organization (SCO).

b— Game-changers

In the past, the US economy was half of the world's economy. Plus, there was more than a dozen Western countries that made the top twenty economies of the world.

Times have changed. Now, Indonesia and Turkey are regarded as the two very important countries. They are projected to become fourth and fifth biggest economies in the world. Their appeal and influence over a vast demographics because of cultural, religious, historical and ethnic ties make them important. They are also two geo-strategic countries, controlling main shipping lanes and waterways. They are simply game changers.

If these countries were to join exclusively one side or the other between the East and the West, they will definitely shift the balance of power to the side they will join. Plus, they are likely to act together in the future as they are building formidable ventures together.

i— Turkey

Tukey has Turkic and Muslim heritage. It appeals to more than 150 million Turkic people directly and surely more than one billion Muslims because it has the capacity to reach them.

Africa alone is in the grasp of Turkey. The Turkish Airlines flies to fifty-five destinations in thirty-seven of the fifty-four countries in the dark continent on the last count. No other airline is able to match this feat. And that is before Turkey built the world's biggest airport by far in Istanbul. The Istanbul Airport is sure to ensure the dominance of the national airline for a long time to come.

Turkey has numerous other instruments to captivate Muslim populations around the world. The country became the biggest humanitarian donor country recently in Africa. TIKA has become another brand, solely focusing on Turkic and Islamic heritage recovery and refurbishing, carrying the flag further.

Turkey's varied economy is still miniscule compare to the US but nonetheless it is diversified and growing rapidly. Especially defense industry is making great strides. Turkey is already one of the top ten military powers in the world. It is also one of the top ten exporters of arms, armaments, and military platforms at every category from thanks, attack helicopters, missiles, drones, warships, submarines.

The country has something to offer to the Europeans, Middle Eastern countries, and Africans. But more importantly, it plays vitally important role for Chinese and Russian economies. Both countries depend on Turkey for their economic dominance and survivability, relatively speaking.

China and Russia are the two biggest client-states employing Turkey's geo-strategic location to ship massive amounts of goods to Europe. Russia supplies 30 percent of Europe's energy needs through Turkey. Of the six available routes, BRI prefers the one over Turkey to reach Europe, mainly because of the warmer weather compare to northern routes covered with snow half of the year. Highways and railroad networks are readily operational, exclusive contracts for trucks already operational between China and Turkey.

ii— Indonesia

Indonesia, by its sheer size and being the most populated Muslim country with soon to become fourth biggest economy in the world, is geo-strategically positioned to make a difference in the world in the 21st century.

Indonesia, an island in the Malay Archipelago, is located between south China Sea and the Indian Ocean. World's shipping lane goes through its straight.

President of the country Yudhoyono declared in 2011 "for Indonesia to be a great power between the years 2015 and 2025 must be evaluated for realistic attainment and implications since Indonesia is key to Southeast Asian Nations (ASEAN)'s strategic role in regional and world politics."

As a founding member of ASEAN and the largest country in Southeast Asia and its close ties to Turkey make them a powerful duo that play a great role in a balance of power between the East and the West. Indonesia like Turkey have always yearned to stay independent between the East and the West.

B. Rising military powers of the East

Parallel to economic growth, China and India are sure to settle permanently into the top four slots as military powers together with Russia. Turkey climbing to fifth slot, leaving only the US in the top five alone, representing the Christian West.

Military rise of Turkey is significant for two reasons. One, Turkey has made big strides with its ever-growing economy and concurrently with its expanding military reach. The military bases in Qatar, Somalia and Sudan are halfway to Indonesia.

The next leap forward are possibly more frequent port calls of one another, for the expanding and high sea navies of Turkey, Indonesia, Pakistan, and Bangladesh. With that the Muslim world will be all tied to one another more ways than one.

Two, Turkey has invested in its indigenous defense industry since 1970s. The US policy objectives were the single biggest reason for that along with the Western European approach to Turkey. When the West imposed embargos on transfer of technology, Turkey started to cultivate them on its own. A half a century later Turkey has leading indigenous technologies and very sophisticated and competitive products and platforms.

More importantly, Turkey shares its resources with other Muslim countries like Pakistan, Indonesia and Central Asian Republics. None of them were able to acquire much transfer of technology or sophisticated platforms from either the western or the eastern sources.

Another crucial development is the fact that the rising military powers of the East are replicating military powers of the West. They are sailing in the waters beyond their domains. They are also establishing overseas military bases to project their power even further, much like the West have done in the past century.

In the Mediterranean Sea, there was already joint Sino-Russian maritime exercise including live-fire drills, replenishment and escort operations in 2015.

In the 20th century, Turkey never ventured into the Indian Ocean with a maritime exercise like China is doing in the Mediterranean. It will be no surprise to see the Indian navy in faraway waters like Turkish navy, soon to be an ocean-going navy that has plans to visit waters beyond the Indian Ocean.

II. Changing prospects

In the last century, the West rebuilt Europe and "Asian Tigers" into economic powers.

They enjoyed peace and prosperity and exported their brands worldwide.

But modernity or security never visited much of the rest of the world.

Nowadays, the Middle East, Central Asia, Latin America, and Africa are on the rise.

But they are still in disarray and mainly export refugees to Europe and North America.

Walls are needed to be built all over the world to stem the ever-growing tide.

Meanwhile, the US or EU are on the defensive to protect their civilizations.

All the while, China is empowering the forgotten, albeit with much criticism.

Whereas, Turkey is acting as a pressure valve for the explosive Muslim masses.

None the less, the West mired with poor legacy still has to face one big problem.

Having new and powerful players in the field on top of that does not make it easy at all.

1. Poor legacy

The world is in grievance with the Western civilization.

It is in the belief that the West built its modernity at the expense of the East. They find it easier to put the blame on the West.

The West on the other hand maybe could do better to alleviate this notion!

The loss of Middle East and regression in Africa reflect the size of the problem.

That is without considering what the Asians and Latin American are thinking.

A. Loss of Middle East

In retrospect, the West lost Middle East when the US recognized Saudi Arabia, Israel and the shah regime in Iran in the first half of the 20th century.

Withdrawal of the West from Lebanon in the 1970s and from Iraq in 2014 followed the loss of Iran in 1979.

Continuing current quagmire in Syria also indicative of the West's enduring problems in the region. The fact that Turkey, Russia and Iran are in Syria shows of others are ready, willing and able to fill the vacuum the West is leaving behind.

Sadly, nowadays, the West is clinging to the Arabian Peninsula as the last refuge in the region. The irony of Israel and Saudi Arabia having close relationship with one another since the coming of the Trump administration clearly underlines the state of affairs in the Middle East for the West.

a. Turkey fills the vacuum together with China, Russia and Iran

In the meantime, Turkey became more independent and interactive worldwide and selectively started to fill the vacuum that the West left behind in the region. So much so that, over time, the West is sure to become ever more dependent on Turkey to be able to operate in the old Ottoman territories encompassing not only the Middle East but also in north Africa.

Simply put, in the absence of the US hegemony in the region, the West does not have much option in the Middle East anymore. Even though Saudi Arabia remains the sole safe haven for the moment, it is also surrounded with countries or bases with armed forces of rising eastern powers like China or Turkey. They are in Djibouti and Qatar, but also in Somalia, Sudan, Pakistan, and Sri Lanka, circumventing the region from east and south. All the while, Russia is to stay in Syria possibly for the next fifty years and Iran make inroads all over the region from Lebanon to Syria to Yemen uninterrupted.

b. Western attempts to regain foothold or to stay in control are in vain

In view of these dire circumstances, further attempts to try to split the region into camps create additional problems for the West and exacerbate other ongoing problems.

Qatar crisis in November 2017 is a case in point when Turkey provided economic and military aid to Qatar confronting easily the united front of S. Arabia, Bahrain, Egypt, and UAE with Western backing. Regime in Qatar not only survived but also became stronger with Turkey permanently settling there with a military base second only to the US.

Kurds attempting to go for a referendum to declare an independent state in Iraq was another Western disaster. Turkey easily brought Iran and Iraq on board and quelled the forty-year Western effort within days and for good.

Iran in the meanwhile continue to be pro-active against the US in the region. Yemen war on one end and attempt to acquire nuclear weapons on the other end cannot be ignored but also with no good alternatives for the West.

B. Regression in Africa

Losing Middle East has consequences. It makes regression in Africa to speed up for the West. There are clear signs to that effect. Turkey and China are very active in Africa. Neither had much presence in the dark continent throughout the 20th century. What they bring to the table is always better than what the decaying Western powers can offer these days.

On top of that, there is the issue of the Arab Spring. Some say it is devised by the West to take control of the eastern Mediterranean Sea where recently discovered natural gas resources will determine who will rule in the new world order. Some others point to the desperation of the West, resorting every which way to remain relevant.

a – China and Turkey replacing the West in Africa

China recently invested sixty billion dollars in Africa. Turkey has become the biggest humanitarian donor country there for the first time. Turkish Airlines flies to thirty-seven countries with fifty-five destinations, bringing the continent close to the rest of the world. No other airline in the world can meet the feat.

Nothing comes close in magnitude what two countries are doing in the continent. They are at least bringing a sense of modernity with a bridge, road, airport, or airline. In the meantime, the West displays totally opposing image. They are mainly visible at check points for example, in the desolate parts of Niger and Mali, trying to stem refugee migrations towards Europe.

In the meanwhile, debate can continue forever whether China is acting as the new version of a colonialist regime or not or for that matter whether Erdoğan's win-win approach has sinister plans behind it. Whether China is there with all the good intentions or not, or whether Turkey is there solely for the face value, one fact remains the same. They are both there with investments, the West is not.

One more thing. Like the late ABC news anchor Peter Jennings known to have said. "What is worse than being in the news with a bad story is not to be in the news at all." The West is not in the news in Africa. The leading guys in the news in the dark continent are China and Turkey. They are in the news. Optically, they are the ones saying: "Hope shall never die."

China's extraordinary outreach to Africa aside, regression in Africa will continue for the West in northern half of the continent as the Muslim population grows at a rate that would seem to split the continent into Muslim and Christian halves. Turkey on the other hand will surely benefit from demographic change, but it is also important that Turkey has a vision to capitalize on this opportunity since the turn of the Millenia when the West was bogged down in the Middle Eastern wars.

If there is one thing to learn from the misfortunes of the West is that, the West should have done the right thing for the region when it was the hegemon.

Turkey's role nowadays in Africa is to act as a "pressure valve" for the West. So long as Turkey's presence there would seem more a win-win, it will be win-win-win for the West when Turkey is able to stem the flow of the migrants. The best thing the West can do under these circumstances is to work with Turkey towards that end. All else will be a futile effort at his late hour when the opportunity is long lost, the West having already practically lost the Middle East.

As for the rumors swirling around the Arab Spring!

Muslim masses in Africa from Sudan to Libya to Tunisia look for Turkey and Erdogan as saviors. It is only a matter of time; their numbers and strength would turn tables around the usual suspects simply because too many factors side with Turkey from history to geography to religion to economy to military and to educational matters.

b – Grand Plan of the West or a natural phenomenon?

On that note, when examined little further it is clear how some believe Arab Spring was a newly designed grandiose Western plan to control eastern Mediterranean Sea natural resources. According to this theory, the West needed to control

Tunisia, Libya, and Egypt in order to lay claim significant portion of the eastern Mediterranean. First to go was Tunisia. President Zine El Abidine Ben Ali was forced to flee the country in January 2011 after twenty-three years in power. Next in line was Moammar Qaddafi of Libya. He was deposed a year later. Then came Tahrir Square demonstrations in Cairo, Egypt. That ended the rule of Hosni Mubarak.

After that, the goal was to replace these regimes with Western friendly rulers so that the life in the region can continue for another century. In other words, like in the 20th century, according to the plan, it was supposed to be business as usual with coup d'états and building new nations with autocratic rulers.

Others had naivety and they believed that the Arab Spring started in Tunisia in late 2010, when a self-immolation of a street vendor in a provincial town of Sidi Bouzid sparked mass anti-government protests or when people in Libya and Egypt no longer wanted to live with despots. They wanted modernity and prosperity or democracy.

Whatever the reasons were for the Arab Spring to flare up out of nothing, eastern Mediterranean Sea will be contested by all powers local and outsiders in the coming years. In 2019, this is a harsh reality. The other reality is no less important for the West. In the third decade of the 21st century, the West will be forced out of the northern half of Africa and will compete in the southern half with eastern giants like China and perhaps also with India. The north will be in total control of Muslims, led by the modern Republic of Turkey that would be known by then as the "New Turkey" by everyone.

2. One big and ever-growing problem

There are legitimate reasons why the future is bleak for the West.

The demographics will change soon in favor of Muslims.

Within two decades, the West will face the biggest problem it ever faced for a long time.

Muslims will rapidly grow in number in Africa and Asia and they will start to migrate.

They will come in hoards to Western Europe legally and illegally.

They will be the most disconsolate and despondent when they knock on the door.

A. Muslim explosion is swelling the world population

In the East, birth rate is high. It will double the world population within a century. At the beginning of the 20th century, there was 1.6 billion people on earth. At the end of the century it quadrupled to 6.1 billon and it is projected to double at the end of the 21st century to over eleven billion.

The number of Muslims will swell reportedly to 2.7 billion by 2050 when the world reaches 9.5 billon. Practically one out of three people on earth will be in Muslim faith. One out of three people in Asia too will be Muslim. So, will, half of Africa.

Seven of the top twenty economies will eventually be composed of Muslim countries simply because of the population explosion. But that will not be enough to stop refugee influx to Western Europe.

B. Refugees at the European gates

Refugees will head to Europe because they have nowhere else to go. Sixty percent of the world today lives in Asia. Africa is the second biggest with 16 percent. Plus, the biggest population explosions will take place in these already most populated continents. They will add another two billion to the world population in three decades.

If only 5 percent of them migrates that would mean tens of millions of people. Most of them travelling over Turkey to get there because that is the only country that connects Asia, Africa and Europe with a viable land-bridge.

3. New Roles

In the 21st century, China will be the engine of the world's economy.
The US will counter it as the only full-fledged, but also, benevolent superpower.
Turkey on the other hand will mainly regulate the flow of refugees to Europe.
Like Eisenhower said it best during the Korean war in the 20th century.
Turkey may end up saving the Western civilization again in the 21st century again.
This time from the millions of illegal refugee masses coming from Asia and Africa.
Basically, the world will depend on the refugee flow.
Turkey and the EU will be in the center of it all.
How they will play their multitude of roles will make the difference.

A. Turkey and Muslim refugees

More than half of, soon to be, three billion Muslims in the world are Sunnis. It is the biggest sect by far. Turkey has been the single most powerful ruler of the Sunni sect for six centuries when the Ottomans had the biggest empire the Middle East and beyond.

Modern Republic of Turkey inherited that empire a century ago when it was founded. Since the coming of the Erdoğan regime to power in 2002, the secular republic is being led by a political Islamist regime and have been positioning itself to assume a leadership role in the region and the world for this mass of humanity.

Turkey is projected to have the fifth biggest economy and military in the world in this century. Turkic heritage and Muslim faith make it a likely candidate to play an important role in the lives of many believers and help alleviate the world from mass migration problems that could spell disaster for the life on earth.

B. EU paradoxes

Western Europe is where the future of Christianity is at crossroads. But first, it has to deal with North America and Islam. It has to straddle both ends. America First is not the main problem of EU, Muslim emigration to Europe is.

The US has saved Europe twice from calamity during WWI and WWII. Turkey on the other hand was instrumental in resolving refugee crisis emanating from Syria, twice, in 2015 and 2018. Both the US and Turkey will come to Europe's help again, respectively. But what about Europe how will it pay back?

Add to that Russia, providing 30 percent of energy that the continent needs, has to ship its natural resources through pipelines over the Turkey, the land-bridge!

All the while, EU creates PESCO which simply becomes a competitor to NATO under the US leadership. To what end? To fight over Black sea and Mediterranean Sea riches? Against Russia? Turkey? The US? How will EU find its rightful place in the new world order?

C. New Russia with bigger role in Europe and Asia

Russia is no longer the second biggest economy in the world, but it is still the second most powerful military. On top of that, Turkey is its best partner in trade, tourism, technology transfer, and transshipment of its oil. Their successful role in Syria also give them an extra leverage when they immerse themselves exploring the riches of the eastern Mediterranean Sea.

Yet, that is only the start. Relationship with Turkey is sure to continue until 2023. There is no reason why it should not continue after that. Sooner or later, Turkey will become number five economy in the world while Russia will hold number six spot. Militarily, Turkey may still be, by then, few spots below Russia but they will have more in common than not. They will share more technologies and find new areas of cooperation.

Russia is building Turkey's first nuclear power plants in Akkuyu. It provided first set of S-400 batteries to Turkey outside Russia. Now there is even talk of Russia and Turkey may produce next generation batteries, S-500 that is, as a joint production. There is nothing to stop these two countries to work together on other military platforms or increase trade or tourism volume.

Russia is in harmony with Turkey, integrating economies further. They set a hundred billion-dollar total trade volume by 2023. When they reach it, they will be on another plateau. Russia, then, can easily take Europe hostage with its oil supplies. Southern stream goes exclusively over Turkey. Northern stream is to go exclusively over Germany. That makes more than half of the Europe's energy supply.

That is the worst-case scenario. Even worse than that is the fact that Russia in the East, are best friends with China and India. All three are working closely at BRICS and SCO. Pakistan and Central Asian Republics, S. Africa and Brazil are also part of these organizations, allowing them to work together, making Russia viable partner to many countries globally.

Yet, Russia too has its Achilles heals as well. One of the most important one is the fact that it has a soft belly. It has a large Muslim population and it is growing fast. Plus, the low birth rate among the rest of the Russians is a big problem. Good relationship with Turkey comes handy regarding the "pressure valve" role that Turkey will play like it did during the Chechen and Dagestan uprisings.

All the while, Russia has to achieve a delicate balance between the US, EU, China, and India to maintain its status among the elite of the world. It cannot take the ire of the US or the West overall, totally siding with the East. Simply put, it has to be a high-wire act.

D. Balance of power is vital between East and West

No matter how one slices it, there is a new East in the brewing in the end. China is growing so is India. Then there is a Muslim mass that is growing all around the world but also awakening. China and India are in one place. Muslims are spread everywhere except the Americas.

Could there be an alliance of China, India, and Muslims. Russia can also join this pact. If it does the West will become too small to counter even if Western Europe and Americas were all united.

Too farfetched?

Maybe. But there may be a real reason for Muslims to stay on an eastern coalition than joining a western block. A tide of discontent must be prevented. It can only be achieved with the right leadership.

Turkey is a viable candidate for that. In a larger sense, the US is the only viable economic and military power with larger capacity for global leadership. Together, they can achieve the goal and create the right balance of power across the world to make a stable environment for everybody.

Separately each has limitations, but the US has more to gain and more to lose in cooperating with Turkey in the face of inevitable rise of China to greatness.

III. Two to watch

There are two countries to watch out in the coming decades.

They are the only two countries that can play and are playing brinkmanship.

They have the resources, capacity, and political will.

They also have exclusive zones and share zones of influence to act together.

China plays brinkmanship in the south China Sea.

Turkey plays it in the eastern Mediterranean Sea.

They play it for the natural riches and strategic superiorities.

Turkey also plays additional brinkmanship against the US and Germany.

The goal is to continue to acquire transfer of technology.

China plays it for economic and military superiority against the US.

China's brinkmanship extends along the Belt and Road Initiative too.

India, Russia, and Turkey face brinkmanship from China along the way.

In Central Asia, Turkey, and China will test each other regularly.

Russia, the US, and India will determine the fate of the region when they take sides.

1. China

Lethal brinkmanship

China is on a path of no return from economic superiority.

Military prowess is not lagging much behind either.

Yet, China also resorts to brinkmanship on its quest to parity with the US.

And it does the same for superiority over others like Turkey, Russia and India.

A. South China Sea

Recently Rear Admiral Lou Yuan has told an audience in Shenzhen that the ongoing disputes over the ownership of the East and South China Seas could be resolved by sinking two US super carriers.

"They're the pride of the US fleet: enormous 100,000 tons, 333 meter-long nuclear-powered aircraft carriers. But Beijing thinks they're Washington's Achilles' heel."

His speech, delivered on December 20 to the 2018 Military Industry List summit, declared that China's new and highly capable anti-ship ballistic and cruise missiles were more than capable of hitting US carriers, despite them being at the center of a "bubble" of defensive escorts.

"What the United States fears the most is taking casualties," Admiral Lou declared.

He said the loss of one super carrier would cost the US the lives of 5,000 service men and women. Sinking two would double that toll.

"We'll see how frightened America is."

Admiral Lou, who holds an academic military rank—not a service role—said China should

"use its strength to attack the enemy's shortcomings.
Attack wherever the enemy is afraid of being hit.
Wherever the enemy is weak…"

In his speech, he said there were "five cornerstones of the United States" open to exploitation: their military, their money, their talent, their voting system—and their fear of adversaries.[74]

Is this a first salvo? Or is only war of words? Will the US continue to sail in the South China Sea at will and eventually force China to act first?

B. Bilateral trade

China is about to catch and surpass the US in economic sphere. If trade wars do not resolve the problem between two economic giants, military option may come into play. Then the question is still the same, who will pull the trigger first? Until then brinkmanship will continue.

Yet brinkmanship continues today between China and the US. Steel and aluminum trade, automobiles, and telecommunication companies are some of the lead-

---

[74] https://www.nzherald.co.nz/world/news/article.cfm?c_id=2&objectid=12184587

ing fields where Trump administration have taken actions against China. Huawei stands alone as the single biggest company where brinkmanship is most apparent.

Eric Harwit, an Asian-studies professor at the University of Hawaii at Manoa and the author of the book China's Telecommunications Revolution, argues that Huawei's fortunes have been damaged by Ren Zhengfei's inability to schmooze and sell. "You need a Jack Ma who can stand up with Trump and shake hands, and Trump can say you're a great guy," Harwit said, referring to the effusive founder of the Chinese e-commerce firm Alibaba. "They don't have a Jack Ma."

a— Huawei

It is widely believed that the rise of Huawei are the main reasons why Nortel of Canada and Ericsson of Sweden are no longer what they used to be. American companies, including Cisco Systems, have also accused Huawei of pilfering their intellectual property.

Reportedly, according to a story by Michael Schuman in the Atlantic magazine, "distrust of Huawei is spreading. New Zealand and Australia recently barred it from providing the equipment for cutting-edge 5G cellular networks. In Malaysia, Prime Minister Mahathir Mohamad recently halted high-profile infrastructure projects backed by Beijing while warning of a new 'colonialism.'"

Turkey have elected to counter Huawei in its own way. As recently as few years ago, Huawei was in control of 80 percent of the cellular networks in Turkey. When Turkey faced a cyber-attack on 31 March 2015 and forty-five cities across the country lost its electricity, the country woke up. Since then, Turkey is in the process of replacing Huawei completely with indigenous 5G ULAK base stations across the country. The country had embarked on the ULAK project in 2013 with three domestic companies in consortium.

The US prefers another way to deal with Huawei. As late as December 2018, the US raised the stakes against China. Huawei's chief financial officer, Meng Wanzhou, was arrested in Canada, accused by Washington of misleading financial institutions to break U.S. sanctions on Iran. Meng's arrest is the latest front in a multipronged standoff between Washington and Beijing, one that encompasses disputes over trade, intellectual property, naval lanes, and much else.

b— Trump doctrine

Huawei is only a latest and vivid example of how complicated and intensive the challenge is. But it also exemplifies how the Trump revolution is fighting to keep America great again.

Trump summarizes the issue with one statement.

"China is engaged in numerous unfair policies and practices relating to United States technology and intellectual property, such as forcing United States companies to transfer technology to Chinese counterparts."

That is the crux of the problem.

According to New York Times article, "the United States and China race one another to dominate the next generation of ultrafast wireless networks, known as 5G. The Trump administration has declared 5G mobile networks a key security and economic goal."

If Turkey with its domestic companies like Havelsan, Aselsan, Netas, and Argela can develop its own 5G technology indigenously, it is hard to imagine why would not the US should not be able to the same faster and better and remain leader in the world in this field.

Considering, Turkey is about a decade-removed from being top five economy in the world, able make great strides when the world's biggest economy relies on China. That explains how China is projected to become the world's biggest economy when the US is projected to regress to number three.

A simple arithmetic?!

C. Central Asia

This is another area where China will resort to brinkmanship regularly. The main competition will be Turkey. India, and Russia will determine their role over time. Sometimes, they will side with Turkey some other time they will remain neutral.

The US has to challenge China in the Central Asian republics. China will continue to make inroads and will be in fierce competition to ensure its path from Beijing to London functions effectively. For the West, the goal is not to prevent the railways and highways but rather to protect the independence of these republics so that they can continue to prosper and live in modernity.

When the US enters into fray, it will find Turkey as a fully committed ally so long as the independence of the Turkic republics are guaranteed not only from Chinese influence but also from Russian meddling.

2. Turkey

Nothing lethal but not always

Turkey on the other hand makes a living with brinkmanship, but not the lethal kind. Like Trump said, Erdoğan is a tough negotiator. Only another "Kasimpasali" can understand what a "Kasimpasali" says! Yet, when it comes to Turkic matters in the world at large, Turkish leaders are historically vicious warriors for the cause.

A. Non-lethal brinkmanship against the US

Turkey and Erdoğan play basically Catch-22 with the US and Germany when it comes to military technology. When it comes to nation-building, Turkey plays Zero-Sum game, nothing else.

a— Military technology

When the US did not want to sell Patriots missile batteries, Turkey bought S-400 batteries from Russia. The US countered it by putting a hold on the delivery of F-35 aircrafts to Turkey. Turkey countered it by starting development of indigenous 5th generation aircraft prototype to be readied by 2023. Turkey works with half a dozen countries on the project. Most of them are Western alliance partners.

b— Nation-building

Turkey also played brinkmanship against the nation-building attempts of the globalist US administrations. In northern Iraq, Kurds declared intention for independence. Turkey forced the West's hand. No one came to their help. Kurds lost their autonomy and territory they had gained since 1980s.

In Syria, too, before Trump announced to pull the US forces out from the country, Turkey made two incursions to northern Syria. The US found excuses not to interfere. Turkey then threatened to enter to the rest of Syria. Trump smartly turned the Turkish brashness into US advantage by joining forces with Turkey instead of countering it militarily.

B. Lethal brinkmanship against Russia

Turkey shot down a Russian aircraft. Russia responded first with an economic retaliation. Russia did not dare to go to war against Turkey. It knew it was going to be a Zero-Sum game if it did.

After a year, Russia and Turkey agreed to work again, and better than before. Russia needed Turkey more. Ukraine crisis had reached its peak and Russia had to shut down its pipeline and needed an alternative. Turkish land-bridge was perfect alternative.

At the end, it was win-win for both of them, instead of lose-lose.

C. Germany also faced brinkmanship from Turkey

Germany and Turkey have many contentious issues but like Erdoğan said recently, for the "sake of prosperity and the future of both countries." It is a relationship which matters to Angela Merkel, despite the conflicts.

But when it comes to brinkmanship, Turkey forced Germany's military to withdraw from Turkey's Incirlik airbase. Bundeswehr planes were instead sent to Jordan to be based. Germany simply had to pack and leave when Incirlik is the primary NATO base used by the US air force. The brinkmanship clearly showed the fact that Turkey now on its way to parity with Germany, which quickly turns the tables from Catch-22 to Chicken game.

D. In the Middle East, everything is Zero-Sum game for Turkey

In the Middle East everything is a Zero-Sum game for Turkey, yet it remains as a brinkmanship more often than not against the US.

When Saudi Arabia-Egypt-UAE threatened Qatar, Turkey countered with an airlift. The trio just pulled back. They could not match. They didn't have economic or diplomatic power whatsoever, not to mention military power. It was non-existent.

Few months after this bravado, Washington Post columnist Saudi journalist Jamal Khashoggi was brutally murdered in the Saudi Arabian consulate in Istanbul. Some say as a retaliation for Turkey's role in the Qatar crisis. Yet, Turkey countered this Saudi move as well, brazenly. Turkey kept the murder of Jamal Khashoggi in the news for a whole month, until Saudi Arabia confessed the murder, making it lose face and lot more in the international world.

In Iraq, brinkmanship was clear in 2003 when Turkey rejected invasion of Iraq from its territory. The US had to delay its Iraq campaign and assaulted from the Gulf instead.

In Syria, Turkey never invited the US to any meetings, instead joined forces with Iran and Russia to determine the country's fate. So much so that when for the first time Russia, France and Germany met on Syria in Istanbul, again Turkey elected not to include the US in this meeting. In 2019, this meeting will take place once again with same countries attending again, in Istanbul!

But Turkey's brinkmanship goes beyond diplomatic initiatives in Syria. Turkey, at the height of the ISIS problem refused to interfere in Kobani despite requests from the US.

Afterwards, Turkey organized first "Euphrates Shield" and then "Olive Branch" military operations, outmaneuvering the US diplomatically to free two enclaves from Kurdish armed groups it considers part of PKK terrorist organization like the rest of the world.

In the case of Israel, Turkey is most vocal against Israelis even when it sees the US acting favoring one side. For example, when the Trump administration recognized Jerusalem as the capital of the Jewish state, Turkey single handedly brought the issue to the United Nations and to the OIC and garnered overwhelming support only to undermine the US, the only superpower in the world today.

With that Turkey showed that nothing in the old Ottoman territories can be taken granted anymore. Libya was the latest example. UAE, Egypt, and Saudi Arabia sponsored, Israel and Western powers supported Khalifa Hafter led forces were not only rebuffed from taking Tripoli, but they also lost strategic Gharyan. After defeat when Hafter threatened Turkey and Turks in Libya and actually kidnapped six Turkish citizen immediately after losing the military battle, Turkey countered. Within hours Hafter had to give in to Turkey and release the hostages. Apparently, UAE, Egypt, and Saudi Arabia communicated to Hafter that Turkey was about to commit militarily to resolve the Hafter problem once and for all and bring peace to Libya like no one can other than Turkey.

E. Looking back–Turkish brinkmanship

Turkey in the past, too, had resorted to brinkmanship. And of all countries in the world, against the US. Turkey simply invaded Cyprus in 1975 and took one third of the island and few years later, it named it Turkish Republic of Northern Cyprus.

At the time, both the US and then the Union of Soviet Socialist Republics (USSR) were threatening Turkey to back off. They elected to make it a "chicken" game. Turkey turned it into a Zero-Sum game. Despite threats from both superpowers of the time, Turkey still invaded the island.

Eastern Mediterranean is the next sure bet for Turkey to play a Zero-Sum game because Turkey looks at the zone as its last line of existential defense whereas rest of the world look at it only as an economic competition and superiority. One would die for it, whereas for the others dying may be too big of a price to pay.

F. Looking ahead - The next Turkish brinkmanship

In any case, next brinkmanship will take place in the Eastern Mediterranean and it will involve multitude of powers beside the US and Russia. Western Europeans and Turkey will also play major roles. Others may join the grand game while Syria, Israel, Lebanon, Egypt, Cyprus, and Greece to remain as pawns.

Turkey has a claim over half of the Eastern Mediterranean via continental shelf. It has a geo-strategic advantage, a navy and a regime with capacity and will power. It is protective of its legal rights which is open to negotiation in certain cases. Yet Turkey has brute force and political authority. It has enough threat power for others to take sides. That includes the US and the Europeans.

Turkey has another major leverage. China comes in very handy. China has a similar claim in the south China sea, like Turkey in the eastern Mediterranean Sea. There, China seeks almost 90 percent of the region. In the eastern Mediterranean, Turkey is claiming about half of it. Whether the precedent is the same or not is not the issue, the balance of power between the East and the West is.

But Turkey has other cards to play in the Mediterranean Sea. Turkey and Russia are closely working in Syria, over pipelines and agree over how to share natural riches in the Black sea basin and can reach similar understanding in the eastern Mediterranean. Plus, they know if they work together it is win-win for them. Otherwise it is lose-lose.

The West on the other hand has to work with Turkey. In the Middle East, the US had hegemony. But now as President Harry Truman would have put it: "Buck stops with Turkey" more often than not. Moreover, time is not on the side of the West when the US can no longer depend on the declining power of the Western Europeans, not to mention the EU having another independent agenda.

EU with PESCO may go for a brinkmanship against NATO and the US over the riches of the Black Sea Basin or the Eastern Mediterranean continental shelves. But the US is not their only challenger. Russia and Turkey are more formidable whether they are together or alone. Plus, it is very likely that in a power game like that, Turkey would side with the US rather than a very vulnerable EU.

Nonetheless, it is a Zero-Sum game for Turkey and Russia against Western powers when the West can only afford to go into a "chicken" game when it does not side with the US 100 percent. Yet even then, China is lurking nearby ready to take the spoils of a confrontation, the brinkmanship should never lead to a Zero-Sum game in that region.

Thank god for President Donald J. Trump. He is the last president that would fall into this trap.

CHAPTER NINE

TRUMPCARD

Donald. J Trump came to power at the November 2016 presidential elections.

Only some, in the states and the world took his candidacy seriously since beginning.

Erbil Gunasti, author of this book and his life partner Daphne Barak were two of the few.

They came on board the day he came down the stairs with his wife Melania Trump.

Daphne Barak was with Kid Rock in Las Vegas, filming "The Kid from Detroit" doc.

As a "scooper" of "big gets" for the US network TVs Daphne is a global personality.

She conducts rating breaking exclusives for prime-time news shows in the US and worldwide.

Since 1990s, she had sit-downs with so many including "the Donald" and Ivanka Trump.

Since then she had stayed in touch with them and with their kids too.

So much so that Daphne was already part of the family when Trump announced.

But this was not unusual for Daphne, she has been with other US presidents too.

Her last friend among the presidential families is Mamma Sarah Obama.

She was with the grandma of Barack Obama in her home in Kogelo, Kenya twice.

Obamas also came to stay with Daphne at her home in California after his election.

But Daphne is also known for her close relationships with Bush-41 and Clinton.

Like Donald Trump, she was close to Clintons and supported Hillary's 2008 bid.

Daphne hosted at home a hundred fat cats from NY and some of her Hollywood friends once.

Hillary summed it up: **"Everybody has six degree of separation, Daphne has none."**

Yet today, not even Hillary can imagine how Daphne would be connected to Trump.

Like Hollywood stars, head-of-states, wealthy Americans, California politicians are.

Daphne surely has no separation with anybody in power, with money or global fame.

So long as they have it, they will be in her close circles, for a higher purpose.

Princess Diana, Mother Teresa, or Donald Trump were no exception since 1990s.

Ever loyal Daphne today always points out when he sees President Trump in play.

President Erdoğan is another leader of importance in the world Daphne is familiar with.

Her encounters with Erdoğan have always been memorable, personal, and frank.

Knowing Trump and Erdoğan up close and personnel is a unique opportunity for all.

As *GameChanger* makes the point how Turkey and the US must work together to confront China.

Daphne has an important role to play in the region.

Feeling connected to both presidents make a difference.

After all, if the Middle East goes, Africa is next.

Then there is no telling what would happen to the Western civilization.

I. A new beginning

Donald J. Trump is a new beginning for Daphne and this author.

Like he has become for the world at large, starting with the United States of America.

Trump is also a new beginning for Erdoğan regime and Turkey.

Like he has become for the Middle East and Western Europe immediately.

The rest of the world also want to see his impact, including Russia and China.

Don't forget the so-called rouge states or the fast-growing Muslim populations.

Donald J. Trump is a new beginning for everybody.

1. Realignment of the world begins with Trump

Donald J. Trump presidency is the renewed allignment of the world in the 21st century. Since the disintegration of the Soviet Union, the world went through lots of changes. Lately European Union is going through major changes with Brexit.

Rise of China and India are a reality for the West to reckon with.

Rearmament of Japan, and Germany with PESCO reflect what is to come.

2. Erdoğan and Turkey also view it as a new beginning with Trump

Erdoğan and Turkey also observe with interest the new role of the US with Trump. Erdoğan and Turkey are talking about a new century for Turks and Muslims as well. Trump would surely to play a role in it both directly and indirectly.

3. The Middle East, EU and NATO already know that it is

The Middle East, European Union and NATO already tasted its lasting effects. Jerusalem is recognized as the capital of Israel.

Trump recommended Emanuel Macron to leave the union like Brexit.

Whereas his predecessor Obama had practically threatened UK not to leave the union. It is for sure a 180 degree turn around.

NATO felt it too.

In the first two years, Trump pressed them to commit a hundred billion dollars they never did.

II. Common history

Trump has a long history with lots of countries and personalities worldwide.

Trump, Erdoğan, and Daphne Barak also have more than one thing in common.

Brutally murdered Jamal Khashoggi is one of the most recent.

Turkey, as a country, is another.

Jamal was a Saudi, Washington Post columnist but also a resident of Turkey with a Turkish fiancé.

His murder touched a dozen worldwide figures from Daphne's life.

President Erdoğan and President Trump aside, Khashoggi family was one.

Jamal's relatives Adnan and Lamia Khashoggi have always been close to Daphne.

Prince Talal and Crown Prince Salman too have long been part of this small circle.

Daphne knows both of them as much as she knows Trump and Erdoğan.

* * *

Like a prominent London editor said publicly: "Check if Daphne was there a week before!"

Yes, Daphne was there the moment when Jamal Khashoggi was murdered.

President Trump, too, one day may reveal where Daphne was when history was made.

That is when the world will learn even more about Trump presidency through Daphne.

Daphne first met, now President Erdoğan, long before he rose to power in Turkey.

Much like when, now President Trump, reached out to Daphne when he was a tycoon.

Both first time encounters have irie similarities.

Both non-presidents then, reached out to Daphne on their own, directly, for an interview.

* * *

Like the author of this book claims: Both presidents are from "Kasimpasa."

It is a neighborhood in the old Istanbul, much like east end of NY City in the old days.

Tough guys and gals come from there with attitude, including Daphne.

They all made it and now continue to contribute to the history in the making.

Daphne with her upcoming explosive book simultaneously to be announced with this book.

The presidents with their decisions in office.

1. Jamal Khashoggi murder

Daphne was there as usual when the crime was committed

The brutal murder of journalist Jamal Khashoggi, at the Saudi Consulate in Istanbul, on October 2, 2018, has shocked the world.

Whoever ordered to silence the vocal critic of Saudi Crown Prince Mohammad Bin Salman (nick named MBS) ended up with an explosive mess, threatening the future of the Saudi economy, its plans to get foreign investments towards a heavily promoted 2030 project and even public discussions questioning if MBS is fit to be the next ruler of the kingdom.

It also positioned Turkish President Erdoğan opposite his American counter-part, Trump. While Erdoğan has been keeping Khashoggi's assassination on Turkish soil, in the global headlines for months, calling for an international investigation and punishing ALL who were responsible for it, Trump has backed MBS, even after the CIA had reportedly connected him to the journalist's gruesome murder.

It seems like a horrific story, staged in a volatile region. It has also highlighted the recent rift between Saudi Arabia (backed by UAE, Egypt, Bahrain) and Qatar (backed by Turkey, and pushed in a way towards Iran). Trump chose to support Saudi Arabia.

Yet—many Americans, even if angered by the murder, view it as "a far-away topic."

Not many know, how close it is to home: To Fifth Avenue in New York, Trump Tower, Olympic Tower…

Jamal Khashoggi 's grandfather Muhammad, was a Turkish doctor, who married a Saudi women. He then started to treat King Abdul-Aziz Bin Saud, the founder of the Saudi kingdom. A position which gave him rare access to the royal family, and prestige.

One of his sons Adnan used his good fortune to build a fortune. When I conducted the first interview with him, following the "Iran Contra" scandal, during the Ronald Reagan latest years, Adnan was described as "The Richest Man in the World!"

He was also described as an "arms dealer"—a title he hated and fought against.

That was the era that very rich people loved to float their wealth. Adnan Khashoggi famously flew actresses Joan Collins and Brook Shields to his parties. I was with him, when he brought mega star Elisabeth Taylor to Turkey. He had homes in Saudi Arabia, Marbella in Spain, Paris, and New York, where he occupied the penthouse of the Olympic Tower on 5th Avenue. His home included a big pool on the roof.

A. World elite: they are only 'Usual Suspects' for Daphne

Five blocks from there, lived a new mega millionaire—Donald Trump. The two men had a lot in common: They both thought BIG. They were great promotors, and understood that floating their lavish lives, would attract investors and business leaders from around the globe, to try to associate with them. Naturally—they bonded.

Their wives then—Ivana Trump and Lamia Khashoggi—were known for their glamour. I have known both of them since I became an interviewer in my early 20th. I used to admire how they carried themselves and wished, I would grow up to look the same.

Both Ivana and Lamia are friends to this date. One of them sent me their photos together, having good time in a party in South France, this last summer.

That was the era of the TV show, "Life of the Rich & Famous." People loved to watch how the few fortunate others lived in their private jets, big yachts, opulent homes.

Until…until fame proved to be risky. Adnan Khashoggi and former First Lady of the Philippines, Imelda Marcos, were indicted by then New York's DA, Rudy Giuliani. Yes, President Donald Trump's outspoken attorney today. He accused the two famous international players for laundering money and other financial charges.

Khashoggi was jailed in Switzerland, and then—extradited to the US. I conducted the first interviews with Khashoggi and Marcos while they were awaiting their trials. I spent lots of time with them.

The legal costs were so heavy, that they burdened even such two wealthy people. Khashoggi then needed to liquidate some assets. He sold his yacht, named on his beloved daughter Nabila, too. Yes, to Donald Trump, who renamed it: "Ivana."

Few years later—Donald Trump would have financial problems. Then— he would sell the yacht to another wealthy Saudi—Prince Alwaleed Bin Talal. Ironically, history would connect these names decades later.

Adnan's brother, Ahmad, chose more low-key life. He married a woman, named Essaf and lived in Medina. One of their children was Jamal Khashoggi, who would become a famous journalist in Saudi Arabia, and tragically—world famous after his terrible murder.

Jamal who was close to members of the royal family, made a career move, which eventually cost him his life. After serving as columnist and even editor in Chief of Saudi newspapers, he joined forces with Prince Alwaleed Bin Talal, to launch a new Arab satellite channel. It was called "Al Arab News" and it was launched from Bahrain. Saudi Arabia's rulers did not like the idea of a critical channel out there. Baharan is close to the Saudi rulers. So, they pulled the plug eleven hours, after the channel launched.

B. Jamal Khashoggi

Khashoggi continued to be a commentator to Al Arabia and MBC TV channels, as well as Dubai TV. But the association with Bin Talal and its criticism of young Mohammad Bin Salman, already circled him as "a troublemaker."

On December 2016—the Independent newspaper quoted a report from the Middle East Eye, claiming that the Saudi authorities banned Jamal Khashoggi from expressing himself in video or print. The reason given: his criticism of US President elect, Donald Trump.

I seriously doubt if Trump is aware of the latter.

Reportedly— the Saudi king and his ambitious son had been focusing on building close relations with the new American President.

He in return chose Saudi Arabia as his first foreign official trip on May 2017. The three days of extra hospitality were a powerful show of this special relationship: Festivities combined with Saudi pledges for buying American weapon for the big dollars.

Khashoggi who could not tolerate being silenced and blocked from writing, relocated, in June 2017, to the US.

There he began his new life. He started to write columns to the Washington Post, and became a regular commentator in US and UK TV stations. His topics were usually about Saudi Arabia and the direction, its young ruler is pushing forward. What proved to be a much bigger problem, to some of the Saudi regime, who are not used to internal criticism.

C. NEOM

To complete the setting, one must bring up the months of such costly promotion of both NEOM, the ambitious 2030 city and the man behind it: Crown Prince Mohammad Bin Salman.

The Crown Prince visited UK, France, and the US, accompanied by huge entourage. He took two luxury hotels in New York, and two in Beverly Hills to accommodate the unprecedented big delegation. The message was that money is not an object.

It worked. Not many Americans understood then, that the Crown Prince was actually seeking for American (and overseas) investments. The whole 2030 grand project was initiated by the pro-active royal, because he realized smartly, that his country would run out of oil reserves—their main income traditionally.

Also, some prominent US tycoons, decided to multiple the oil drilling inside the US, in order to make America less depended on overseas oil production.

Wisely, MBS also promoted modern initiatives like giving women driving lessons. The heavy PR machine around him worked.

Even alerting events did not touch the well brushed image of the young royal.

The arrests of women rights activists went almost unnoticed by the world media.

The bizarre detaining of a head of state, Lebanese Prime Minister Hariri, even forcing him to state he was stepping down fueled some media. But after French President Emanuel macron intervened and the Lebanese leader was freed, the interest died.

Even the detaining of hundreds of Saudi wealthy businessmen at the posh Ritz hotel, where President Trump had been received few weeks earlier, made headlines for a while. Nothing more. Stories about torture and reportedly death of couple, would make disturbing headlines only months later. After October 2nd, 2018.

D. Daphne was there when Jamal was murdered

On October 1st— Erbil Gunasti and I found ourselves having drinks with Nadhmi Al Nasr— the CEO of NEOM. He came to see us at the Beverly Wiltshire hotel. After small talk, he told us why he was there. He was seeking a five hundred billion dollars investment from American, in his Crown Prince's dream city. He told us that, "any investment. With short return or long return of investment."

He talked with such passion about this, "Biggest project ever."

I asked to see some photos of the place. He opened his iPad.

We starred with disbelief: It was an image of an empty land. Nobody had expected questions like: "WHAT? WHERE?" The whole campaign had been about "WHO?" The progressive-modern image of the Crown Prince. That is the image which was put out there.

Al Nasr is a pleasant man. We took some photos together. Our smiling image would be probably one of the last times, the CEO of NEOM would be dispatched for pitches in the US. At least for now.

Few hours later in Istanbul, journalist Jamal Khashoggi would go into the Saudi Consulate to get his divorce papers, in order to start new life with his Turkish fiancée Hatice Cengiz. His life would be ended there in a horrific murder, which would send shock waves around the globe.

E. Erdoğan vs Trump: Airtime challenge

And here comes another key player—Turkish President Recep Tayyip Erdoğan.

Why the Saudis decided to murder Khashoggi in Erdoğan's territory?

Whoever made this fatal decision, threw the whole region into a "situation." It involved Turkey, US, Saudi Arabia, and even Israel, Qatar. and Iran.

The international community was divided following this murder: Europe, Australia, Qatar and others slammed the brutal act, and demanded an international credible investigation, which would point clearly to WHO ordered it.

a— Media wars

All led by Turkish President Erdoğan, who even penned an OP-ED for the Washington Post about how strong he felt about it.

On the other side was the strong denial of Saudi Arabia that MBS ordered it. It was echoed by its allies: Egypt, UAE, Bahrain, Kuwait. AND, it got two surprising backers.

One was Trump who described the murder and its cover up, in harsh words, but he refused to connect it to MBS. The other was the Israeli Prime Minister Benjamin (Bibi) Netanyahu. He surprised many. He condemned the gruesome murder, but then he rushed to highlight the importance of Saudi Arabia for the stability of the region, and its standing against Iran.

The comments of these two players might have been less surprising, to some who are in the know how. Donald Trump believes in personal relationships. That is how he built his empire. That is how he envisioned; he would conduct foreign policy. He may have a point! Personal chemistry between leaders has always helped. True, that there are other factors, other players who can complicate matters. Trump would learn it, but would continue to push for his gut feeling and personal one on one.

Both him and his son in law Jared Kushner have invested in personal relations with the Saudi Crown Prince. It included financial deals, and even involving MBS in Kushner's dream, to make peace in the Middle East. Too much investment just to wave it off.

b— Musical chairs

On the other hand, Bibi Netanyahu has been going through police investigations in Israel. The longtime leader might be indicted. First time in years a poll showed that former Chief of Staff Benny Guntz may win the next elections against Netanyahu.

Netanyahu is a savvy politician. He and his wife had been accused in corruption before. Beside yelling to his "base" that it is a "witch hunt," he likes to move the narrative to urgent security and foreign policy topics. His favorite one is the danger from Iran!

That danger units all three leaders: Netanyahu, Trump who had promised during his presidential campaign, that he would cancel the deal his predecessor Barack Obama signed with Iran, and MBS who's the de-facto leader of the country which view Iran as the biggest enemy of Saudi Arabia.

On April 2019, Bib Netanyahu would prove that he is a brilliant politician. His foreign policy strategy would win him the elections, for the fifth time.

Add to this boiling pot, Erdoğan's growing power and ambition to become the leader of the Muslim world. He has questioned why Saudi Arabia took the custody of the two holy cities—Mecca and Medina. He has been competing with Egypt's view that it is a natural leader. Erdoğan has created tense relations with Israel. Though the economic relationships between the two countries are still strong, the diplomatic relations have known more downs than ups.

Donald Trump inherited problematic relations with Turkey, from the Obama administration. In a conversation with me and Erbil, he asked Erbil, how to deal with Erdoğan. It was before the G20 in Argentina, end of 2018. He knew that the Khashoggi murder would be discussed there. Trump had any intention, to have a productive meeting with good results.

So, in this musical chair game, a horrific butchering of a man, pushed some big global players to challenging moments: should they change their seat or stick to their position even stronger?

That defined the bonding between Erdoğan and Qatar. Even with its neighbor Iran.

That pushed Egypt to take Saudi Arabia's position, followed by UAE, Bahrain, and Kuwait.

That pushed Trump to some delicate moments. Working on good relations with Turkey, while maintaining what he had built with Saudi Arabia, and still condemn a murder of a journalist. That is what brought Netanyahu to make these double-talking style comments.

c— More than a murder story, also international intrigue

Erdoğan went further… He entered into Jared Kushner's territory, brokering peace in the Middle East.

Turkish president hosted Arab Israelis for the first time in Istanbul. They are senior member of the Knesset, the Israeli parliament. He then declared that he would throw his weight behind their demand that Israel would leave the "occupied lands" and get back to the 1967 borders.

That is also going against Donald Trump moving the US embassy to Jerusalem in May 2008. In a way, most players considered how to go against their enemies, which resulted in even stronger bonding with their allies, hardening their positions.

It is no surprise Daphne would be part of this story and all the players mentioned. Her scoops have always had global interest because of her syndication in more than dozen countries throughout. They may include rise and fall of the world's biggest; Jamal Khashoggi encounter was no different than Princess Diana's Scotland yard report or Amy Winehouse, or Benazir Bhutto stories to name a few she made history.

2. Scooper of Big Gets

Daphne Barak is known among the US TV network news world as the "scooper."

Her "big-gets" always come with record breaking ratings for the US TV networks.

She has simply been scooping the biggest and the most important "un-gettable gets."

On December 2003, ABC 20/20 aired "Our Son: Michael Jackson" special.

Perhaps it made the biggest rating ever known in US Network TV history.

When all said and was done within forty-eight hours, it became the "greatest TV show."

It was widely reported that it aired in fifty-three countries and a billion viewers watched it. Daphne Barak and Elisabeth Murdoch were the producers.

It was simply another one of Daphne's so-called rating breaking scoops or "big-gets."

Daphne was not solely rating-breaking scooper for the US network TV news shows.

NBC "Dateline" and CBS "48 Hours," along with ABC "20/20," were not the only ones.

She was the leading scooper for all the world's leading media markets for two decades.

Turkey and Erdoğan also know her from the leading daily of the country since 1990s. So, does the Saudi Arabia and the Arab world from the Asharq Al-Awsat.

Italy, Germany, Croatia, Pakistan, S. Africa, Russia, UK, France are no different.

Each has their own "Michael Jackson" story to tell how they know Daphne.

President Trump is no different. He knows the world at large more so than most.

Most Americans due to isolated nature of the US don't indulge with the rest of the world.

But President Trump understands the impact of Daphne Barak exclusives worldwide.

President one day made a point to that effect in the presence of the First Lady Melania.

First Lady, being worldly, having a European background, lovingly concurred.

Scooper of Big Gets no doubt was honorably pleased for the recognition.

Yet, she did not expect no less from brethren Yankees, the New Yorkers.

Knowing all too well how important to represent the US to the world at its best.

She never wavered to be the best example of the "American Exceptionalism" overseas.

From presidents Zuma of S. Africa to Musharraf of Pakistan many acknowledged it.

President Erdoğan of Turkey was no different and at the height of his power in 2006.

A. Daphne's encounters with Recep Tayyip Erdoğan

Daphne's encounters with the Turkish leader Recep Tayyip Erdoğan were monumental in their own right. They were reminiscent of her encounters with, then business tycoon, Donald J. Trump. Initial encounters, in both case, took place early on, long before they jumped into political frays as national or presidential candidates in their respective countries.

What is remarkable is that both President Trump and President Erdoğan, then started the conversation with Daphne with the same premise: 'Would you interview me?' or their variation of it like 'Why don't you interview me?' or 'It is my turn to be interviewed…'

No other president or celebrity, more than hundred Daphne interviewed over time, was as frank, except perhaps when Al Pacino muttered something in the similar scale, bringing up the fact that Daphne had already interviewed Oliver Stone and now it was his turn. It was a genuine approach that was very meaningful and charming.

Others were mostly more diplomatic. None was as headlong as either one of these two presidents. President Trump's, then, first ever phone call to Daphne and President Recep Tayyip Erdoğan's outreach to Daphne in 2000 and in 2006, respectively, were very meaningful and to the point. Now with history in the making, they are even more significant first impressions with greater value.

a— *Take One*

Recep Tayyip Erdoğan was like Donald J. Trump before he became president. He was direct, relentless and sure of himself.

Here is how Daphne summarized it.

i— 'Would you interview me?'

'I first heard about Recep Tayyip Erdoğan when I went to Turkey in 2000 to interview Tansu Ciller, the only woman prime minister of Turkey.

Since I have been syndicated in Turkey through one of leading newspapers Hurriyet, my visit was what some like to call: 'High Profile'. While my interviews with leaders and Hollywood A-Lister appeared in Turkey on Hurriyet's front pages, and then picked up by other Turkish media afterwards, it was flattering to Ciller to be included in my pick of interviews.

But, then, I had a surprise. While I was preparing to go to Ciller's beautiful home, or 'villa' at the Bosporus in Istanbul, I was approached by several guys, who told me, 'our leader sent us to your hotel, to bring you over. It would be his honor to meet with you…'

Since my TV crew was waiting to take me to Ciller, I said: 'Oh, Mrs. Ciller sent you over? How nice! I am coming with my crew.'

The guys who spoke very little English looked confused. The manager of the hotel came to my help. After a brief talk with them, he clarified it for me. 'No, they have nothing to do with Ciller. They are sent by a new, up and coming conservative Muslim leader. His name is Recep Tayyip Erdoğan.'

I asked the hotel manager to apologize and explain them that I was in Turkey for the interview with Tansu Ciller and was now getting late to my visit with her because of this episode. The guys looked very unhappy, as I left.'

ii— 'I will be the leader of Turkey'

Later that day— I was with the pretty Mrs. Ciller at her lavish villa. She showed me her art collection. She took me to her balcony, and described how, **'the fish ended up by her home when the water on the Bosporus was wavy…'**

It was a big scoop in Turkey and other markets in the world.

When I came back to my hotel, I was invited to celebrate my journey in Istanbul with Mustafa Koc, then, one of the wealthiest and most influential men in Turkey. But, on my way to his car, I was served with an envelope by the hotel's helpful manager. I opened it, and found a personal letter, typed in broken English. It was from Recep Tayyip Erdoğan. He said, it was a shame that **'the most famous American interviewer in Turkey will not meet the future prime minister of Turkey.'**

His confidence and the 'out of the box' tactics compelled me to ask my editors in Hurriyet about him. They found the interactions funny. Then, they could never imagined him, climbing that high, the ladder of political power in a country so secular, so pro-Western. Yet, they were also amused how he would have to deal with an American, dressed in a revealing summer dress as myself. To that end, they continued with the flow and added couple of my photos, dancing in Istanbul, to the next piece, just as a private joke, for Erdoğan to see.

For some reason, this encounter and the intricate elements of the story stayed in my mind. No, not as a joke, rather as a testimony of a man, who had planned to lead his country from early on. A man who was smart to be pushy, yet, charming. A politician who said from day one: **'I will be the leader of Turkey.'**

b— Take two

Six years later, Recep Tayyip Erdoğan was indeed the prime minister of Turkey. Yet, he was the same old same old. Nothing has changed with his demeanor or character, solid as ever, like President Trump repeatedly pointed out: **'He is a though man.'**

i— 'Would you interview me?'

'The next episode that comes to my mind was on December 2006, at the United Nations Headquarter in New York City.

I had just returned from London, with musician Yusuf Islam, formerly Cat Stevens, who had converted to Islam. It was Islam's first flight to the US, since George W. Bush diverted his plane famously, since he was…Yes, Muslim. He was a bit nervous, but it all went well this time around.

Islam and I walked into a high-end reception at the United Nations in New York. It was such a big ball, celebrating 'Alliance of the Civilizations' with two prime ministers, representing Catholicism and Islam, together with the an outgoing and incoming secretary of generals in presence. The event was taking place at the gargantuan lobby of the Headquarters, the only place where most people can have the biggest of all parties in the city.

The hosts were then Prime Minister of Spain Jose Luis Rodriguez Zapatero, his counterpart, then Prime Minister of Turkey Recep Tayyip Erdoğan, then outgoing Secretary General of the United Nations Kofi Annan and his incoming counterpart Ban Ki Moon. Plus, lots of media, few hundreds at best, within and outside the ropes. It was a spectacle to say the least.

Erbil Gunasti, the author of this book, then was press officer in charge for the prime minister of Turkey, came forward and greeted me and Yusuf Islam. He led us to Erdoğan and his wife, Emine [hanim]. She wore a head scarf and had an interpreter next to her. Erdoğan was so happy to see both Islam and me. He paid compliments to Islam, and said, he loved his music.

Then Erdoğan turned to his Spanish counterpart: 'Daphne is more famous in my country than I am…' Zapatero surprised me and answered: 'She is also famous in my country…' I guess it was the power of ongoing syndication and landing big interviews for years.

Then— Erdoğan asked me: 'Why won't you conduct an interview with me?'

It was soon after my famous interview, and first ever, with then President of Pakistan Pervez Musharraf and his wife Sehba Musharraf at the presidential residence in Islamabad, Pakistan.

I answered: 'Why not! Let us do it with you and your wife…'

ii— Women solidarity

'Emine [hanim] reached out to my hand. She liked what I said.

Erdoğan said: 'No, no. With me. I am the Prime Minister.'

I argued back: 'And she is your other half. People have heard from you. Never, from you together. It would reveal another side of you. And she is your life partner.'

His wife was now holding my arm firmly and lovingly. We two bonded in front of his eyes. The media was trying to understand what was going on from their positions behind the ropes.

By then, it had already become a power match.

Erdoğan was stuck to his position, while I stuck to mine.

The next day, Erbil and I had lunch with an editor in chief of a rival newspaper to Hurriyet. He was close to Erdoğan. It looked like he was trying to serve as a peace maker. He suddenly said: 'The Prime Minister said: 'Daphne has strong will. But I like her mini dress better. Great legs...'

Oops... Big mistake, to say such a sexist thing in the US. Even then! With 'Me Too' generation today, no telling...

The next day— I saw Prime Minister Erdoğan at a gathering. I made sure. I was wearing long jeans. We greeted each other warmly, without re-visiting our little argument.'

III. Trump Card

Machismo, bravado, and ultimatum aside, there is an underlying regime with Trump.

Erdoğan with similar character and personality is a great match for him.

At this crucial juncture in history, Trump card comes into play with greater importance.

Turkey will complement US policies so long as it is treated on equal footing.

Meanwhile, policies towards Israel, Saudi Arabia and Iran will be consequential.

The US must make radical changes in all three, not to lose Turkey and the world.

Turkey will be a loyal partner for the US until middle of the 21st century.

With Turkish support, the US will be able to focus on the rising Chinese power.

For that to materialize, President Trump must be in concert with President Erdoğan.

Yet, the rest of the American regime must also be in-sink with realities.

Ignorance and arrogance in the international arena will have consequences.

In the 21st century, the US too must replace its 20th century methods and stands.

Trump Card will be the best way to rearrange them.

Especially when President Trump is in the company of like-minded nationalists.

1. Are Trump and Erdoğan friends or foes?

Erdoğan always loudly reacted to Trump's policies in his domain and beyond.

He questioned Trump on the US policies towards Israel.

He then questioned Trump's statements regarding Saudi crown prince.

Lastly, they have been exchanging public messages on Syria withdrawal.

Behind the public spats though there is another private regime in place.

It started right after Thanksgiving and reached its first milestone in December 2018.

Next milestone was an agreement in principle to increase trade volume to $100 billion.

The US-Turkey trade at $16 billion was nowhere near Russia-Turkey at $26 billion.

Friends or foes is not the question after a century of trial and tribulations between two.

Friendly and never-enemies will continue to be the motto between Turkey and the US.

But before opening a new page under Erdoğan-Trump era, old ones had to be closed.

Israel and Saudi Arabia, two of the 'Bermuda Triangle' pieces still consume attention.

And they still need to be dealt with in public, but also at private meetings.

Not until then, the region will remain as a soft belly of the only superpower in the world.

A. Israel and Saudi Arabia spats were first

In the first two years in office, Trump and Erdoğan did not have a good beginning. After 8 years of acrimonious relationship with Obama, Erdoğan was expecting something for the better.

Trump's decision to move the US embassy from Tel Aviv to Jerusalem was the breaking point. The rhetoric between two leaders started late 2017. Then came the brutal murder of the Saudi journalist Jamal Khashoggi in Istanbul by Saudi agents linked to the crown prince of the Saudi regime.

On both cases, the spats lasted for months. On the movement of the US embassy, Turkey went so far as bringing the issue to the United Nations and passing a decision against the US by a big margin. On the Jamal Khashoggi murder, Turkey kept the issue alive in the global news for many months until a voluminous outcry against the crown prince of Saudi Arabia became a universal call.

In either case, Erdoğan appeared to have won the public opinion, but Trump continued with its domestic and international agenda unaffected. The US embassy is in Jerusalem and the world did not come to an end. Crown prince Muhammed Bin Selman is still expected to rule the Saudi regime when his father abdicates, and the Saudis continue to buy hundreds of billions of dollars of US arms. The Mueller Report is out and there is 'no collusion with Russia!'

Bottomline is both Erdoğan and Trump came out winners. In public, they may seem averse to one another. Privately, they are on the same page. They have bigger plans. Their target is China and the road there is through Syria. After that comes the rest like the Mediterranean Sea continental shelves, Central Asia and Africa. And Erdoğan and Trump will have to tackle all of them together.

B. The notion of withdrawal from Syria brought a new series of spats

In 2019, Erdoğan and Trump continue their public salvos on Syria, as if they are not the ones that were dueling publicly on Israel and Saudi Arabia since 2017. Since Trump suddenly announced in December 2018 that he will withdraw the US troops from Syria, Erdoğan and Trump are exchanging new series of salvos. One would think that they are the worst of enemies and they will fight on any international issues that arise in the region. But when the between lines of Erdoğan and follow-up tweets of Trump are examined, two crafty, shrewd and cunning leaders emerge.

a— Erdoğan, between lines, as late as January 2019

'Trump's recent initiative, especially in the Syrian context, has failed the plans of those who undermine Turkish-American relations.'

Did Erdoğan mean to say there is a deep state in the US? No. Not necessarily. He is referring to the policy differences.

'Our relations have overcome many difficulties due to occasional disagreements. We want to look ahead to our bilateral relations and focus on the positive agenda. President Trump share the same conviction with me.'

Some specific policies and executive decisions of the US executives since 1960s harmed the relationship between two longtime allies. JFK's betrayal of Turkey with Jupiter missiles during Cuban missile crisis, Lyndon Johnson's ill-advised letter to then president Inonu during Cyprus crisis, arms embargo that Carter did not lift for three years, and failure of Obama to act with Turkey in Syria in 2012 are historical facts. President Trump is very aware of them and their ill-effects on the loss of confidence.

> 'Turkey is ready to take over responsibility in Syria were the US to withdraw. We will eliminated DEASH altogether from the region. We will destroy them. World witnessed, how we already neutralized 3,000 DEASH militants in El Bab.'

Since 2011, the US is in a downward spiral in Syria. Trump could not stop the bleeding since 2016 but he understood that it will even get worse over time unless he had a 180 degree change of course. Secular Turkey with Erdoğan regime is a willing and able ally.

> 'Continuing your efforts with the militia groups will cause you further problems. It is not right for our strategic partner US to work with a terrorist organization. YPG-PYD is an extension of the PKK organization recognized worldwide. The ill-effects of working with them will come back and hunt US in future.'

9/11 is vivid in the minds of many people in the world not just the Americans. The terrorists/freedom fighters fighting against the Soviet regime in Afghanistan came back to take vengeance from the US with Osama Bin Laden. Militant Kurds, maybe only few thousand in numbers but nonetheless they don't represent more than 20 million Kurds that live, spread in four countries. They will always be disgruntled so long as they are in the status they are in in the mountains of the region, plus armed and lawless.

> 'From Jarablus to Afrin, people with varying belief and religion now live in peace.
> This only became possible under Turkish rule in these areas.
> During Kobani crisis, 300 thousand people emigrated to Turkey.
> Turkey welcomed these people from Kobani and provided them refuge.
> Turkey has always done the same for the refugees in history.
> History taught us this, our civilization taught us that.
> Refugees become our brothers and sisters.
> They receive health, education, security guarantees.
> They are able to involve in trade and agricultural production.'

Turkey received nearly 4 million Syrian refugees since 2011. Most are incorporated more ways than one into Turkish society having lived there nearly a decade. For some they may be 'container Ville', but they are better than shantytown, considering the numbers of refugee influx in the millions. 4 million, that is!

> 'Our agreement with Mr. Trump's 30-32 km plan means something.

The zone covers terrorist infested border region for us.

We are obligated to take all measures against any attack emanating from here.

We are determined to fight against all terrorist organizations in this region.

They may be threatening our country or the world, it does not matter.

that threaten our country, our region and the world.'

Turkey primarily cares about a terrorist free zone along its 911-mile-long border with Syria. That will ensure a security buffer to stop infiltration of terrorists but also a protective area where significant number of Syrian refugees can be resettled.

'I think the US also shares the same conviction.

Turkey is fighting against DEASH.

Yet some are trying to portray it as if Turkey is not.

Meanwhile, Turkey is also fighting against the PKK-PYD-YPG.

That does not mean that Turkey is going after Kurds.

Today in my cabinet I have four Kurds and they are my friends.'

DEASH organized many attacks in Turkey, resulting hundreds of deaths and injured. PKK led terrorists in the name of Kurdish causes also organized many violent acts since 1970s. Most PKK led terrorism were committed against Kurds living in the eastern and southeastern provinces of Turkey. PKK terrorists are based in Iraq, Iran and Syria benefited from US-Mexico type border conditions that existed in the 20th century. No wall, no barbed wire, and not as many border patrols compare to nowadays.

'Turks cannot differ Kurds form Turks or others for that matter.

Islam does not permit discrimination. No race has superiority over other.

Since Trump made his decision, unfortunately, smear campaigns increased.

Turkey never had deep rooted problems with Kurds in Iraq or Syria.

Turkey has always been protective of Kurds.'

In Islam, ummah is one. In other words, Muslims view themselves as members of the same nation. Like a 'Red Sox Nation,' for example. In other words, nationalism is in a sense a contradiction for a Muslim when it is looked from religious lenses. Erdoğan refers to the Islamic notion of 'Islamic ummah is one' when he speaks. Those who are against Erdoğan can easily interpret this as if he is preaching for the unification of all Muslims as one nation. Others who are zealots, they believe Erdoğan really means the way it is meant. Here Erdoğan simply means that a Muslim Kurd cannot be discriminated against by a Turkish regime or leader that is Muslim in the first place. Among Muslim ummah everybody is equal, no matter what they call themselves to identify their race, origin, tribe, region or any other categorization. They are all same.

'In this period, there were Kurds and Yazidis who took refuge in our country.

As per our civil responsibility, we opened doors to these refugees.

Kurds running away from PKK-YPG and DAES, find refuge only in Turkey.

The US intelligence reports confirmed that the PYD-YPG is a branch of the PKK. This bloody terrorist organization even armed children and sent them front.

It is an insult to Kurds to tie the local Kurds with the terrorist organization.'

No one in the Middle East would refer to Kurds and PKK-PYD-YPG as one. In the West, especially among the government officials, putting Kurds in one basket is a great insult. Kurds are proud with their varying culture and linguistic differences in a vast region they live in, composed of four countries. They are Kurds and Muslim but only less than 1 percent of the more than 20 million is designated as terrorists. PKK-PYD-YPG make up most of it. And more than half of it are composed of abducted and/or deceived kids that cannot get out of the grip of the terrorist organization.

'It is not possible to understand the reasoning behind supporting killer herds. Why would anybody support and provide heavy arms to the PKK-YPG-PYD? In recent years, they received 23 thousand truckloads of arms and armaments. As a result, we are catching them with American arms in our territory.

What would it take for some in the US to accept them as a terrorist organization?'

PKK is a terrorist organization, formally designated by the US and EU. YPG and PYD is also acknowledged by Western institutions and leaders and US secret service agencies that they are extension of PKK. Turkey rightly is posing a legitimate question as to how the US administration can still continue to justify association with an extension of a formally accepted terrorist organization, irrespective of the fact that the sole purpose of the terrorist organization at this time is an armed struggle against the very and staunch ally of the US in the NATO.

'Friend tells the truth and truth hurts.

I would like to ask our American friends to explain these facts to the US public.

During Obama regime, I repeatedly brought up the importance of safe zones. Obama said that I am right with you. Let's do it. But he never did.

Now I notice President Trump is bringing up the safe zones in his conversations. Let's take these steps. They will be a right decision we make.

Let's open doors to refugees. Let's create container cities in these safe zones. We can even built cities there. It will be the right humanitarian approach.'

Erdoğan urged the US on the necessity to create safe zones in northern Syria in 2012. But Obama administration missed the boat by not acting on it. Now that there is a new administration in the US, it is important to communicate about past mistakes and act to ameliorate the problems instead of exacerbating them further.

'Instead of all these weapons, let's create these opportunities for these refugees. Whoever wants to support this cause have already stated their commitments. Angele Merkel of Germany mentioned about big numbers that she would commit.

She said: 'Instead of taking care of these refugees at home, let's do it there. Saudi Arabia crown prince told me the same, but nothing came out of it so far.

European Union did not keep its promise either.'

Yet, the regime that caused the problems to get out of hand is still in charge, providing weapons to militia that is one of the roots of the problems in the region. Instead, the world community at this stage should be investing in creating safe-zones and then turn them into new cities for millions of refugees.

'1 billion 750 million euros came from the EU. None of it ended in our coffers. We also did not receive a response to our offer to resolve refugee problem. We are now building schools in Afrin and El Bab. We are building hospitals. We are also speeding up development of social projects for kids.'

The influx of nearly 4 million Syrian refugees cost Turkey approximately 35 billion dollars and their integration to Turkish society is still ongoing. They live in 'container ville' communities on the Turkish side of the border. In the meantime, two Turkish military incursions into Syria created safe zones with liberated cities that need to be rebuilt. There, Turkey alone is building schools and hospitals, allowing hundreds of thousands of the refugees to return back to their homeland. More needs to be done but EU has to put up its share not a symbolic billion euro through aids organizations that do patchwork when war thorn cities need to be rebuilt.

'In the meanwhile, the leader of the terrorist organization lives in Pennsylvania. His being there free, causes pains to those that got hurt and lost loved ones. We are waiting US authorities to take steps sooner than later. We are NATO allies and strategic partners.'

All the while, Erdoğan regime insists that Fettullah Gulen who lives in Pennsylvania be turned over to Turkish authorities so that the charges against him be pressed. Gulen is accused of perpetrating 15 July 2016 coup d'état against Erdoğan.

b— Trump on Turkey

Two years into power, President Trump sent out a tweet on December 24, 2018.
He announced that the US forces will pull out of Syria.

Then he sent out another tweet a month later further clarifying the US policy in Syria.

He was firm to bring to US troops back home but not indifferent to Syria either.

i— December 2018

After December 14 phone call, President Trump declared a policy change in Syria.

'President @RT_Erdoğan of Turkey has very strongly informed me that he will eradicate whatever is left of ISIS in Syria...

and he is a man who can do it plus, Turkey is right 'next door.'

Our troops are coming home!

96.8K 8:54 PM— Dec 23, 2018

Reportedly Erdoğan responded to Trump, saying:

'In fact, as your friend, I give you my word in this.'

Trump wrote on Twitter, regarding the remaining ISIS forces, that

'When I became President, ISIS was going wild.

Now ISIS is largely defeated and other local countries, including Turkey, should be able to easily take care of whatever remains. We're coming home!'

Trump's tweets on Syria withdrawal came after a phone call on Dec. 14, 2018 with Erdoğan, following their meeting at G-20 in Argentina after Thanksgiving. What Erdoğan and Trump talked was not a new topic. For Erdoğan, it was a long road. He was basically snubbed by Obama since 2012.

For Turkey, Barack Obama was no different than JFK, Lyndon Johnson and Jimmy Carter administrations. They all treated a staunch NATO ally in a way that after few decades, the ally no longer trusted the US administrations as before.

It was not fair for the Trump administration, but he had inherited the legacy of previous Democrat presidents. And the legacy had holes in it. Yet, the Trump administration also had its own difficulties because of the domestic antagonism. Leaks, never-Trumpers and globalist influenced ideologues simply caused further confusion in Turkey as to what the US policy was and will be in the future in the region.

Not until the trip to Argentina, the message to Turkey from the Trump administration was never clear.

ii— January 2019

President Trump summarized Syrian policy, pointing at the weak state of ISIS in the region and Turkey to remain benevolent against Kurds while creating an agreed safe zone by the Turkish border.

**'Starting the long overdue pullout from Syria
while hitting the little remaining ISIS territorial caliphate hard,
and from many directions.
Will attack again from existing nearby base if it reforms.
Will devastate Turkey economically if they hit Kurds.
Create 20-mile safe zone…'**
120K 2:53 PM— Jan 13, 2019

In a tweet directed at President Trump, spokesperson for President Erdoğan countered.

**'Terrorists cannot be your partners and allies.
Turkey expects the US to honor our strategic partnership,
and doesn't want it to be shadowed by terrorist propaganda.
'It is a fatal mistake to equate Syrian Kurds with the PKK,
which is on the US terrorists list, and its Syria branch PYD/YPG.
Turkey fights against terrorists, not Kurds.
We will protect Kurds and other Syrians against all terrorist threats.'**

Soon after, President Erdoğan publicly lashed out at US national security adviser John Bolton for saying the US withdrawal was contingent upon Turkey's pledge not to attack US-backed Kurdish fighters in Syria once troops leave.

**'Bolton made a serious mistake. If he thinks that way,
he is in a big mistake. We will not compromise.'**

President Trump tweet further clarified Syrian policy by addressing parties beyond Turkey in the country.

**'…Likewise, do not want the Kurds to provoke Turkey.
Russia, Iran and Syria have been the biggest beneficiaries
of the long-term U.S. policy of destroying ISIS in Syria— natural enemies.
We also benefit but it is now time to bring our troops back home.
Stop the ENDLESS WARS!'**
91.7K 3:02 PM— Jan 13, 2019

Simply put, President Trump would like to see Turkey create a safe zone along its Syrian border. All the while he also pointed out to the fact that the US military might will still play a role as necessary to counter the terrorists and the powers like Russia, Iran and Syrian regime that are at odds with the US policies in the country. In Turkey, on the other hand, President Erdoğan made it clear that he will only deal with President Trump, the US overall, having lost all credibility because of the Obama administration policies and inactions in Syria.

C. Eventually Trump and Erdogan figured to make better use of G-20s.

Having had rough start on complicated matters involving Saudi Arabia, Israel and Syria, by 2019, Trump and Erdogan were on the same page. They agreed to deal with a major issue at a time between two countries every time there was a G-20 meeting.

Syria was the first in Buenos Aires. S-400s became the focal point in the ensuing Osaka meeting. Will delivery of F-35s be the topic of the next meeting in Riyadh or by then it will already be resolved so they can focus on something else?

None the less, November 21-22 meeting in 2020 will be momentous because it will take place after the November 3rd, 2020 presidential elections in the US. This meeting in Riyadh will not only allow Trump to make a presidential decision of consequence but it will also set the tone for the next G-20 meetings to come between two allies.

Considering every encounter with Turkey is becoming more important than before for the US, as Turkey is rapidly climbing the steps towards a bigger economy and much more powerful military, what Trump has established so far with Erdogan sets a great precedent in order not to lose Turkey.

2. Where do Trump and Erdoğan go beyond the Middle East together?

Until 2020 November, where could Trump and Erdogan go beyond the Middle East together? Beyond the Middle East because, the question how to resolve all the problems accumulated and exacerbated in the Middle East since the breakup of the Ottoman Empire and during the Western hegemony in the 20th century cannot be unraveled within one term of a US president.

Trump needs a second term in office to make a real difference in the Middle East. In the meantime, until the 2020 presidential elections in the US, Trump and Erdoğan have no choice but to cooperate in the eastern Mediterranean Sea. There, the US and EU interests soon to clash over the riches of the continental shelves.

As a superpower, the US must keep EU intact in the Western alliance.

With PESCO in the horizon, NATO in the back burner is not the way to go forward.

The Pentagon and the US leadership must be at the helm as a superpower.

And that issue must be resolved before confronting rising China in Central Asia.

Turkey and Erdogan sure to play a big role as the dominant regional power.

Trump, with these two G-20s under his belt with accomplishments is in a good place.

They have become like the confidence building measures between two allies.

Now they can focus on eastern Mediterranean Sea, Central Asia and Africa promptly.

A. Eastern Mediterranean Sea

Turkey is with Russia in the eastern Mediterranean. Turkey and Russia need one another to counter mainly Western European interest over the riches of the eastern Mediterranean and Black Sea basins. Henceforth, they are to cooperate on both seas.

But they also have to deal with the only superpower the US that is sure to play a role in the overall balance of power in the region and the world.

From the US perspective it is no brainer. Western Europe is still the most formidable economic giant, until China really takes over and becomes the world's biggest economy within a decade.

It is all up to two leaders to put all of this in order. When Trump and Erdoğan agree what to do, EU and Russia will surely join.

B. Central Asia

In the meantime, the US cannot allow itself to be stagnated with the Western European power plays in the Mediterranean and Black seas. Not to mention, petty problems that arise from Saudi Arabia or Israel or Syria. There is a fast-growing problem in Central Asian Republics with China making great strides there.

Turkey is the only viable partner that would be a formidable force to confront China so that the playing fields will be equitable in the region. After all, the premise of coordinating policies with Turkey or acting on equal footing with Turkey in the Middle East and Eastern Mediterranean Sea is to use the leverage of Turkey against Iran and Afghanistan regimes, so that the projection of the US power over Central Asia can be possible.

The Middle East and Western Europe acting as Achilles heels for the US, China will have a free hand not only in Central Asia and the rest of Asia but also in Africa.

C. Africa

In fact, as of 2019, the US has already embarked on a policy to be counter active against Chinese intrusion to the dark continent. Turning over the Syrian mess for Erdoğan to finish it off, simply allows for Trump to focus on Western Europe and Africa and the Chinese expansion to the latter and to prevent the former becoming a sore thorn.

For the West, having lost the Middle East means losing Africa is next. If Chinese were to control Africa soon, what is to save Western Europe next, never mind irresponsible EU goals to confront the US for the riches of the inner seas where Turkey has the biggest share.

All the while, it is a simple reality that Turkey is the best partner the US can have in Africa against China. Turkey is the second country with the biggest presence in all African countries. Plus, Turkey has a win-win strategy that is welcomed by all African countries, unlike where Chinese and Western countries have to worry about Africans coming after them with a vengeance.

At present, in Africa Turkey is looked upon as a benevolent power that comes with humanitarian help and win-win strategies whereas Chinese and the West, including the US is looked upon as colonialists even though the US has never been a colonialist. Nonetheless, loss of face in the Middle East, surely hurt the image of the US in the dark continent as well.

All things considered, why does not the US take advantage of Gamechanger duo Turkey & Erdogan?

CHAPTER TEN

GAME CHANGER

GameChanger is written with an American audience in mind.

It is to explain the relevance of the modern Republic of Turkey mainly for the US. A longtime staunch ally of the Western Alliance that is left in the backburner. The sole Muslim in the alliance not only snubbed but also pushed away by the rest.

GameChanger focuses on presidents of Turkey and the United States of America. They have irie similarities in belief, character, personality and action. They will overcome their domestic and international obstacles and perform. They will deliver for masses of humanity not just to their own citizens. Dire conditions across the world in the third decade of the 21st century beg answers. The West needs leaders that can deliver and lead the planet. Their counterparts on the East are well aware and acting with ferocious measures. Unless the West wakes up it will be to their detriment for a long time to come. *GameChanger* puts everything into perspective, explaining what Turkey is. Next it points at where two presidents stand today and how they are making progress. They weave throughout the international environment one step at a time. Even though they are subjected to never ending intrigues, plots and take downs. Here in this last chapter, *GameChanger* asks the most pertinent question of all. What does the "Gamechanger" mean for everyday Americans seeking a better destiny?

GameChanger answers this promptly but also reminds us that there is also divine revelation.

After all, how often two leaders that can address masses of humanity with capacity and good-will, can appear at the same time in history, complementing one another's efforts?

What does the "Gamechanger" mean for everyday Americans?

It is a warning and guide for a better life, prosperity and happiness.

Gamechanger presents the best and worst alternatives for Americans.

The choices must be made after learning the realities at hand.

Gamechanger points at life as we know it that must go through transformation.

Realistically, it means pocketbook issues will go through big changes overtime.

In worst case scenario, it will be the end of Western civilization in Europe and more.

The calamity can be prevented with change of course in methods and strategies.

Donald J. Trump presidency represents the milestone for that change to take place.

What started with John D. Rockefellers of the world in the 1970s came to an end.

21st century is not the 20th century, even less the 19th century, the West has to wake up.

21st century may be the payback time, but it does not need to be tit for tat.

The West can live with the East, the Muslims in particular, and still enjoy the good life.

It means that the destiny of the West is in its own hands and the warning must be heeded.

It also means that the West must start 21st century with new methods and strategies.

It finally means that there is to be a better path for more prosperity and good life.

1. Gamechanger means that the destiny of the West is in its own hands and the warning must be heed.

Transformation that started with the Trump Administration must continue. Trump must be reelected for a second term. Congress must work with the Administration to pass necessary bills to make America great again domestically and internationally.

Pocketbook issues from jobs to wages and from health care to opioid type narcotic crisis must be put in order. In the long term, they will be the reason why the chaos and anarchy will take over across the continental USA like it was in the 1960s and 70s in Western Europe. This time they may even be worse considering how violent the events may take their turn.

Migration coupled with peace and security issues worldwide must also be prioritized. They are the core problems exacerbating domestic problems to get out of control.

Jobs, wages, health care, opioid, narcotics, they are tied all tied to one single issue.

Mass, legal and illegal migration.

If Migration is not resolved which is a natural phenomenon that can never be reversed or stopped or terminated, it will become one with domestic problems and engulf the Western Civilization into something different and foreign. Migration can only be regulated, and it can be accomplished in concert with other countries, Turkey in the lead.

Hence, when Trump Administration sets forward the controversial issue of "building a wall" on the southern borders of the United States. It is stating the least of all the necessary steps towards regulation of Migration, it is not the end of all steps. It starts from there, but it has to have other layers and the US Congress must contribute its own share so that the cooperation of the international community can be incorporated promptly. There must be harmonious relationship worldwide.

2. Gamechanger also means that the West must start the third decade of the 21st century with new methods and strategies and Trump is a God-sent for the job.

Nation building and methods like coup d'états must come to an end. Like some who would argue it is nowadays the end of fossil fuel era, it is also the end of certain methods and strategies of the old widely employed in the past century. Yet, as the transformation from old methods and strategies have to go through a period of transformation, what started with Trump revolution must evolve smoothly.

Reportedly, of the 193 countries registered at the United Nations today, more than 128 have experienced a coup d'état, an abrupt regime changes or an attempt to replace the regime altogether.

United States of America, United Kingdom, Sweden, Switzerland, Spain, Poland, Norway, Netherlands, Japan, Italy, Germany, France are also included among those that faced the wrath of coup d'état or as Donald J. Trump stated explicitly since the Mueller Report came down, "no other US president should face anything like that" he faced. He simply called his experience at the hand of his opponents as a "take-down."

Modern Republic of Turkey also faced its share of coup d'états and the likes, including its current president Recep Tayyip Erdogan as late as 15 July 2016. Erdogan regime in place today continues to face other barrage of attacks, mostly economic.

Unless Donald J. Trump, the leader of the sole superpower in the world takes the lead with regional leaders like Recep Tayyip Erdogan that can lead masses of humanity like the Muslims of the world to join forces, the number and frequency of these coup d'états will never subside. With that the world will continue to change ferociously that no human would like to see, the least of all, the Westerners.

3. Gamechanger finally means that there is a be a better path for more prosperity and good life unlike what Trump's predecessors could not offer past 24 years!

Alliance of civilizations instead of clash of civilizations is a good place to start like any other. Turkey and Spain had taken an initiative and celebrated once at the United Nations when, then Prime Minister Recep Tayyip Erdogan of Turkey and Prime Minister José Luis Rodríguez Zapatero of Spain had come together in the mid-2000s.

Such an alliance between Muslims and Christians, nowadays must be led by presidents Erdogan and Trump respectively. The capacity of the US and modern Republic of Turkey a decade later under the same Recep Tayyip Erdogan leadership will elevate the reach of such unity and cooperation to another higher level. Considering the world soon to be in parity between Muslims and Christians for the first time ever each at about 33 percent of the world, it is high time for an alliance of civilizations instead of clash.

Grandson David D. Rockefeller who passed at age 101, in 2017, once had noted how the world was ran by the rich and powerful like his family since 1870s. He had simply listed how many coup d'états were employed to date and how much vicious and inhumane experiment were done over the poor and huddled masses of the world. He had said it then and there: "in order to give prosperity to "one billion of the world, five billion had to be enslaved."

If that was the method that ruled in the past century and a half, the trend today indicates that this thinking has to change otherwise "Gamechanger" will at the end be annotated as the "messenger of the worse-case scenario" for the billion living the good life today!

Thank you to my partner Daphne Barak.
This book could not have been done without your help.

Also special thanks to Dovey, Miri, and Ehud for being part of our family.